Leadership Behaviour and Teacher Morale

LEADERSHIP BEHAVIOUR AND TEACHER MORALE

By

Dr. Noorjehan N. Ganihar
Dr. B.M. Hurakadli

DISCOVERY PUBLISHING HOUSE
NEW DELHI

First Published–2005

ISBN: 81-7141-973-9

Published by:

DISCOVERY PUBLISHING HOUSE

4831/24, Prahlad Street, Ansari Road, Darya Ganj
New Delhi–110 002 (India)
Phone: 23279245, • Fax: 91-11-23253475
e-mail: dphtemp@indiatimes.com

Printed at:
Amit Enterprises, Delhi

PREFACE

Decision-making is an indispensable component of management process and manager's life is filled with making decisions after decisions. Managers see decision making as their central job because they constantly choose what is to be done, who is to do, when to do, where to do, and how to do.

Decision-making, though permeates all managerial functions, is at the core of planning because it is the planning where major decisions are made which set the organisational tone. It is the stage at which major decisions regarding setting of organizational objectives, formulating major plans, laying down of policies, procedures, rules, etc. are made. Collectively, the decisions of managers give form and direction to organisational functions.

Saying that he should be a dynamic leader can sum up the role of the Head of the school in modern schools. The modern Head of the school should be a leader and not a director. As a leader it is his responsibility to see that the objectives of education are being effectively realised through co-operation, planning, decision-making and execution. Effective decision-making is an ability that most Head of the schools need to develop. General weaknesses in the decision making process are uncertainty as to who is responsible for making what decision and lack of adequate information for making decisions.

To be an effective educational leader the Head of the school must first of all be adept in decision-making ability and be able to consider himself expendable in his position.

He must derive highest satisfaction not from his official title, but from what it may enable him to contribute to the vital, educational and cultural processes in which the organization is engaged. The Head is the king pin of the school. It is said that as is the Head, so is the school. The Planning, Organising, Staffing, Directing, Co-ordinating, Reporting and Budgeting (POSDCORB) functions of the Head of the school are dependent on his decision-making style. The quality and style of decision-making influences the rank and file of the school towards quality, excellence and productivity. The style of decision-making makes or mars the quality of the school system. The style of decision-making brings in change-proneness and a climate for experimenting innovations and bringing positive ripple effects in the school. The style of decision-making is dependent on various factors operating within and outside the school system.

Various variables such as school climate, change-proneness, school organisation health, teacher morale, teacher involvement, teachers value system, teacher commitment, leadership behaviour of Heads of the schools shape the decision-making style of the Heads of the schools. In Indian context research studies relating these variables are very few. Hence, the present study attempts to fill this gap.

Contents

1
The Problem

Introduction

The Head of the school is the chief executive and acts as the link between the management and the routine administration of the high schools. In a private high school the Head of the school is usually a member of the governing council. But the precise scope of his rights and duties vis-à-vis the governing council may vary a great from society to society and within the same society from time to time depending on the degree of confidence of the governing council he enjoys.

Other high school officials such as the Vice Head of the school and the Heads of the departments both academic and non-academic too form part of the administration.

The different management functions are sponsoring a high school, staffing it, making policy decision, controlling finances, etc. The management literature distinguishes between six major management functions, which are present in a high school. They are planning, organising, staffing, directing, controlling and communicating.

'Planning' involves the formulation of objectives and goals. In order to achieve objectives strategies have to be worked out, policies formulated, programmes to be arranged and procedures developed. Planning includes, of course, decision-making. The following statement strengthens the view that high school administration in general is in doldrums. The administration of school education is not founded on sound principals but on the idiosyncrasies of the administrators.

If the high school is to measure up to the tremendous tasks before it, the right type of person must man it. The Head of the school happens to be the catalytic agent in shaping, supporting, operating and controlling the educational programmes.

Educational administration by its very nature is generally tradition based, for one of the important functions of education is preservation of tradition. As a result high schools manifest themselves prominently into what is popularly called 'maintenance administration' which believes in keeping the routine going. This pattern worked satisfactorily when educational systems were rather static in character and limited in size. But now the very size and viability of educational establishments bring forth demands for a sound educational management as a necessary ingredient of the legitimacy of the prevailing arrangement. While education has become a vast undertaking, administrative bodies and methods remain as they were in the beginning of the century.

Now the range of education has been extended, but the administrative structures have not been reorganised correspondingly. The existing system of high school administration handed down from the political past, is essentially concerned with controlling, its purpose being to make certain that everything slow, lethargic, uninspiring and time-consuming. So if the plans of educational development are to be implemented successfully the traditional administrative set-up must be thoroughly overhauled. For this the Head of the school must be aware of the innovative techniques of educational administration.

Moreover, as a result of the development of the organisation theory and the science of operations research the traditional concept of educational administration has been undergoing a change. A comprehensive research is needed in the area of educational administration. Above all the new administrative and budgetary technique collectively known as 'modern management techniques' embody the spirit of effective planning and implementation. They provide powerful tools in comparison with more traditional techniques, which can help administration to be more efficient.

Mathematical techniques and systems analysis have been successfully applied to complex scientific, economic and industrial problems. The executive has a very powerful and versatile tool in his hand as a provider of information for effective decision-making, planning and control. One of the planning techniques which has received wide acceptance and has demonstrated its effectiveness in terms of savings on cost and time is PERT (Programme Evaluation Review Technique)- and CPM (Critical Path Method). Similarly, O and M (Organisation and Management), simplifying office procedures, reducing waste and promoting organisational efficiency is universally recognised.

Management Science has made rapid advances in recent years and these techniques are playing significant roles in business and industry and they prove to be fruitful to a large extent. So the occasion demands that these techniques have to be implemented and the educationists should find out to what extent the modern management techniques can be adopted in educational administration. Taking this into consideration, the study was undertaken.

But before any of these can be utilised for educational administration, their relevance, suitability and practicability have to be ascertained in the light of specific objectives and targets of educational efforts.

But owing to non-availability of trained personnel, educational administration is carried on by persons who learn by their own experience the hard way.

In educational administration the problems are more future-oriented and more human-oriented than in business management. Educational administration involves long-range objectives.

From the foregoing consideration, it is clear that there is a need for systematic research to assess the applicability of these techniques to educational administration.

In short, democratic pressures, rising expectation and need for equality of educational opportunity, student unrest, demand for student participation in Head of the school's administration, political interference in education demand a systematic study in educational management.

School education having rapid horizontal and vertical growth in recent years and labour intensive activities rapidly expanding, there is a strong and inevitable need for scientific development of educational administration. In the words of Coombs (1969) "unless educational systems are well equipped with appropriately trained modern managers who in turn are well equipped with good information flows, modern tools of analysis, research and evaluation and are supported by well trained teams of specialists, the transition of education from its semi handicraft state to a modern condition is not likely to happen." Instead educational crisis will grow steadily from bad to worse. In seeking to modernise its management system, education can find many useful clauses in the practices –including the concepts and the methodologies of system analysis and of integrated long range planning.

In educational administration, management skills and educational experience interlock at every point. A high school administrator who has no insight of education is likely to prove a poor administrator, however accomplished he may be in terms of management skills.

So the secret of good administration lies not in the administrator's vast and exact knowledge but in his skill at navigating in areas of ignorance. Administration is an uncodified art. Therefore the only sure way to learn administration is to administer.

So, if it all any advancement is to be made in the field of higher education, it is necessary that such administrative practices be evolved that were suitable for the growth of these new programmes and projects. In the lines of 'green revolution' and 'white revolution' an administrative revolution is also imperative.

Blocker et al. (1965) opine that "Administration is creative; it provides both structure and functions necessary for the systematic operation of an organisation. Furthermore, it maintains equilibrium and stability within the organisation, hopefully without stultifying the creativity of individuals and the necessary trend towards gradual change and improvement".

Administration should be effervescent enough to stimulate organisational change and modification and adaptation to changing needs. So, if any innovations and modifications are to be done in any organisation, the concept of decisions making should be decision-making in the process of educational administration. Griffith (1969) states as follows, "Central function of administration is directing and controlling the decision-making process." McCamy (1947) lends support to this idea when he remarks, "the making of decisions is at the very center of administration".

Since the decision-making is at the very core of the process of administration, it becomes the pivotal task of any Head of the school. Livingston (1953) emphasizes the place of decision-making in educational administration... "This is a continuing dynamic process rather than an occasional event; then decisioning means something quite different and becomes the basis of all managerial action".

Concept of Decision-making

Decision-making is an indispensable component of management process and manager's life is filled with making decisions after decisions. Managers see decision-making as their central job, because they constantly choose what is to be done, who is to do, when to do, where to do, and how to do. Looking at the role of decision-making in management, William Moore (1978) has equated it with management when he says "management means decision-making". Decision-making, though permeates all managerial functions, is at the core of planning because it is the planning where major decisions are made which set the organisational tone. It is the stage at which major decisions regarding setting of organisational objectives, formulating major plans, laying down of policies, procedures, rules, etc. are made. Collectively, the decisions of managers give form and direction to organisational functions.

Decision-making is both managerial function and organisational process. It is managerial function because it is a fundamental responsibility of every manger. It is organisational process because many decisions transcend the individual managers and become the product of groups, teams, committees, etc. In fact, more important decisions are made by group of managers rather by managers individually. Therefore, managers should develop decision-making skills and acquaint themselves with the dynamics of decision-making because of the following reasons:

(i) Managers spend a great deal of their time in making decisions. In order to develop their decision-making skills, it is necessary that they know how to make effective decisions;

(ii) Managers are evaluated on the basis of quality of their decision-making. To improve the quality of decisions, they should know how quality of decision-making could be improved.

Before we go through the various aspects of decision-making, it is essential to go through the concept of decision-making. The word decision has been derived from the Latin word 'decider', which means a 'cutting away or a cutting off in a practical sense.' Thus, a decision involves a cut of alternatives between those that are desirable and those that are not desirable. The decision is a kind of choice of a desirable alternative. Lopez (1977) has defined a decision as follows:

"A decision represents a judgment, a final resolution of a conflict of needs, means or goals, and a commitment to action made in face of uncertainty, complexity and even irrationally".

Decision-making is a process to arrive at a decision, the process by which an individual or organisation selects one position or action from several alternatives. Shull et al (1980) have defined decision-making as follows:

"Decision-making is a conscious human process involving both individual and social phenomenon based upon factual and value premises which concludes with a choice of one behavioural activity from among one or more alternatives with the intention of moving towards some desired state of affairs".

Decision-making, thus, is an act of projecting one's own mind upon an opinion or a course of action. In decision-making, three aspects of human behaviour are involved: (1) cognition—activities of mind associated with knowledge; (2) conation—the action of the mind implied by such words as willing, desire, and aversion; and (3) affectation—the aspect of mind associated with emotion, feeling, mood, and temperament. Based on the above concepts of decision-making, its features can be derived as follows:

(i) Decision-making implies that there are various alternatives and the most desirable alternative is chosen to solve the problem or to arrive at expected results. A problem situation, which does not have alternatives, is not really a problem requiring solution though the problem may be quite injurious.

(ii) Existence of alternatives suggests that the decision-maker has freedom to choose an alternative of his liking through which his purpose is served.

(iii) Decision-making may not be completely rational but may be judgmental and emotional in which personal

preferences and values of the decision-maker play significant role.

(iv) Decision-making, like any other management process, is goal-directed. It implies that the decision-maker attempts to achieve some results through decision-making.

Today's managers face a whole new era of challenges. Government, labour unions, consumers, stockholders, suppliers and a host of other groups are all of concern to today's managers. Many different demands are placed on the modern manager in satisfying these groups.

Today's manager must thus play the role of an innovator, a negotiator, a fireman, a motivator and a resource allocator in the decision-making process. The innovator role demands that the manager lead the organisation into new products, new fields and new technologies. As a negotiator, the manager must bargain, compromise and harmonize various groups and factions. As a fireman, the modern manager must be alert to small disturbances and be decisive in eliminating them. Today's manager must be able to motivate others to action. The successful manager is decisive in allocating resources to competing projects and effective in setting timely priorities.

Thus, today's manager must supplement experience and intuition with more powerful tools and processes. Organised and systematic processes are necessary in order to cope with the demands of this new era. The structured decision process and its associated techniques and methods can be a potent tool, especially when combined with seasoned judgment.

Structured Decision Process

The structured decision process is a logical systematic procedure for selecting actions that will achieve one's objective. It consists of the following seven steps.

(i) Problem definition.

(ii) Specification of the goals to be achieved and their relative importance.

(*iii*) Enumeration of the decision alternatives.

(*iv*) Evaluation of each alternative.

(*v*) Selection of the optimum alternative or alternatives.

(*vi*) Post-optimal analyses.

(*vii*) Controlled implementation.

Problem definition involves becoming fully aware of the existence of the problem and its larger context.

The specification of the goals and their relative importance establishes the desired state of affairs.

The enumeration of the decision alternatives establishes the various ways of achieving some or all of the goals.

The evaluation of the alternatives determines their relative benefits, regrets and costs.

In the post-optimal analysis, the optimum decision is tested to determine whether or not it is the best choice under a wide range of possible circumstances.

In the controlled implementation step the decision is carried out in such a way as to prevent any inadvertent consequences.

In practice, the application of the structured decision process is usually a very dynamic and heuristic experience. It may involve a substantial amount of human interaction. The seven steps often overlap and they may not be performed in sequences. The decision-maker may return to an earlier step at several points in the process. There may be considerable recycling through all the seven steps before arriving at a final decision. Or, there may be some oscillation back and forth between the steps for some period of time. This does not mean that the structured decision process is not working. Rather, this is simply the nature of management decision problems and settings.

Management decision problems are usually so complex that they often don't become fully visible or understood until quite late in the structured decision process.

There are few situations in which all the alternatives are known, and in which their effectiveness can be unequivocally determined. In the face of these uncertainties, some decision-makers may be reluctant to make any decisions at all. Still others may be psychologically challenged to take the responsibilities for high-risk decisiveness.

Thus, the structured decision process must be thought of as a prescriptive guide. It cannot be rigidly applied to most management problems. And it certainly cannot be expected to make decisions for us. But it can be used to guide us through the often complex maze of real world of decision-making. It is a systematic process that forces us to consider all the aspects in their proper order. It aids in sharpening decision-making skills and analyses. It can point out otherwise hidden aspects and enlarge our awareness of the total decision system.

Elements of Decision-making

Though decision processes usually differ with the nature of the problem, the situation and the individual decision-maker, Figure 1.1 presents a general picture of decision processes. This model depicts decisions as being precipitated by the recognition of problems or opportunities. If the problem or opportunity is perceived as routine, the decision-maker may go immediately to the selection of the best alternative solution. If the problem or opportunity is familiar, little time may be devoted to its definition. If the problem or opportunity is well defined, the search for alternative solutions or ways to take advantage of the opportunity may be brief. If the relative effectiveness of the alternatives is known, very little time may be spent in analyzing and evaluating the alternatives and deliberating about the best one.

In terms of the Figure 1.1, the nature of the problem may influence whether or not the decision-maker moves

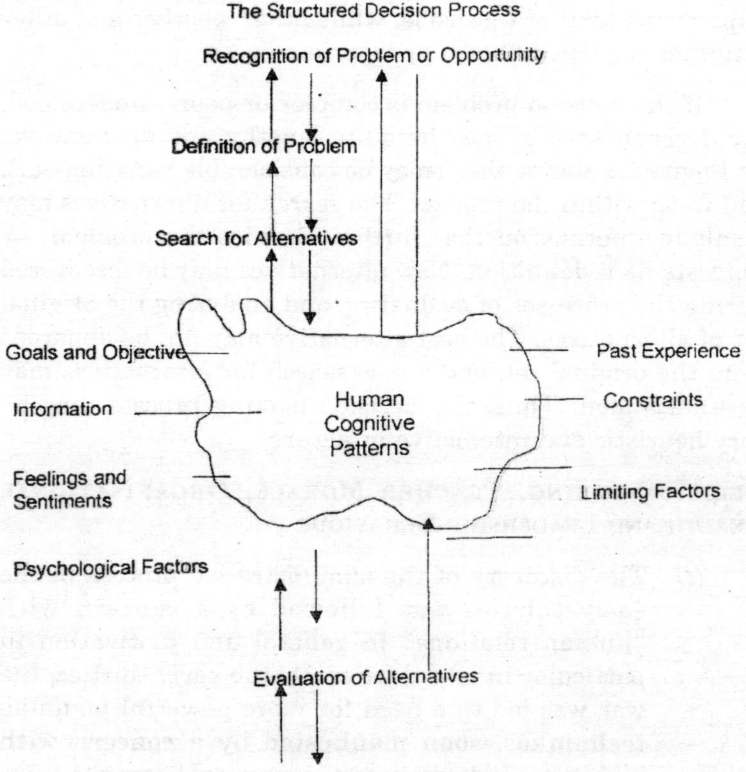

Fig. 1.1 Elements of a decision-making process

through the process slowly or quickly. If the problem is a routine one that is solved by habit, the decision-maker may jump from problem recognition to the selection of the best alternative solution. If the decision is one that has been pre-programmed, the decision-maker may skip the problem definition and the search for alternatives. In a pre-programmed decision there are a finite number of alternatives with known effectiveness, and the decision-maker must match up the appropriate alternative with the problem stimulus. An example is deciding what clothes to wear in the morning. The problem stimuli include the weather and the planned daily activities. Sunny, warm weather and recreational activities require one kind of wardrobe, while other weather and other activities require different appropriate dress.

If the decision problem is complex or poorly understood, the decision process may be quite lengthy and deliberative. As Figure 1.1 shows, there may be considerable recycling back and forth within the process. The search for alternatives may result in information that further clarifies the problems or suggests its redefinition. New alternatives may be discovered during the processes of evaluating and analyzing the original set of alternatives. The best alternative may not be apparent from the original set, and a new search for alternatives may be undertaken. Thus, the decision-making process may be very heuristic and interactive in nature.

Decision-making, Teacher Morale, Organisational Health and Leadership Behaviour

(i) The discovery of the administrative process in the early thirties was followed by a concern with "human relations" in general and motivation in particular in late thirties. By the early thirties, the war was led to a need for more powerful planning techniques, soon manifested by a concern with budgeting and programme planning. Later the focus of the management problem shifted to leadership. Some of this concern led to an interest in communication techniques. Another fragment of this belief that the key to more effective administration could be found in leadership came to rest in decision-making. Thus the current interest in decision-making is not incidental but rather the result of an unfolding progression of professional judgment.

(ii) Decision-making is basically the process of choosing among alternatives. In most situations there exist two or more alternatives and a Head of the school must decide which alternative to pursue. Before making a decision he must thoroughly understand

the problem and develop alternatives. Then he must assess the merits and demerits of each alternative and the probabilities of success in each case.

(iii) Effective decision-making is an ability that most Heads of the schools need to develop. General weaknesses in the decision-making process are uncertainty as to who is responsible for making what decisions and lack of adequate information for making decisions.

(iv) Decision-making is a process wherein an awareness of a problematic state of system influenced by information and values is reduced to completing alternatives among which a choice is made based on perceived outcome states of the system (Lipham and Hoeh 1974).

(v) All Heads of the schools make decisions about how to handle their staff, their students and public. The Heads of the schools request allotments of funds and decide how to spend the funds assigned to them. They prepare the budgets and budget the time of their personnel and themselves. Beyond such decisions, which are common to virtually all Heads of the schools, there are various decisions needed to fulfil specialized job responsibilities. There is an urgent need for humanistic consideration.

Since decision-making ability of the Head of the school is a pivotal factor in his function and his decisions pervade the entire organisational set up, there is an urgent need to explore the decision-making style and its relationship.

Relationship Between Decision-making and Teacher Morale

Gore (1966) while emphasizing the importance of decision-making argues "much of the current interest in decision-making stems from the quietly emerging conviction that choice is a potent cause in determining the efficiency of organisational process."

The Head of the school's decisions touch every aspect of high school structure. Since the faculty is considered to be one of the pillars of the high school, it is assumed that there is a terrific impact of the Head of the school's decisions on the faculty morale. A number of studies on both industry and education have revealed that the style of administration has profound influence on productivity and morale.

The following statement of Basu (1979) delineates the existing relationship between the faculty and the administrator: "The relationship now obtaining between the teacher and the administrator is not one which the administrator caters to the needs of academicians, it is very much a case of administrators issuing directives to the faculty in academic as well as other matters. They enjoy this topsy-turvy arrangement as much as the faculty resents receiving orders from less qualified people. Resentment leading to conflict between administrators and the faculty is common." From the existing state of affairs it can be summarized that the style of administration, especially Head of the school's decisions, certainly influence the morale of the faculty.

Altbach (1977) emphasizes the impact of the decision style of the Head of the school on the faculty as follows: "The Head of the school has considerable impact on the high school teacher. The day to day working conditions are determined to a significant extent by the atmosphere created by the management as are the physical facilities and amenities. Teachers have no role in policy-making and only a limited voice in determining their own teaching schedules. Nonetheless, there is basically no involvement of the rank and file of the teaching community in any of the key decisions, affecting their working conditions or environment in the majority of the high schools." To emphasize his view further— "... working conditions in the high schools also directly affect morale, orientation and professional standards of teaching community".

Theoretically a high school Head is confronted with several phases of administrative tasks. Even though others share the tasks in the administrative machinery the Head of the school being the Head holds sole responsibility for taking decisions in trivial as well as crucial issues. His decisions influence the teaching staff, students and community in general. So the decisions of Head of the school cover the entire personnel involved in higher education. It follows that the decision-making style of Heads of the school are the pivotal aspect in the process of high school administration. Hoy and Miskel (1978) emphasize, "Decision-making is a major responsibility of all administrators."

Simon (1968) while highlighting the place of decision-making says, "The task of deciding pervades the entire administrative organisation.... A general theory of administration must include Heads of the schools of organisations that will insure correct decision-making just as it must include Heads of the schools that will insure effective action."

It is all a question of whether the faculty displays a sense of pride in the school, enjoys the assigned work, exhibits a sense of loyalty to the high school, accepts the educational philosophy underlying the curriculum of the school, and respects the sentiments of the Head of the school.

The answers to these questions depend upon the decision-making style of Heads of schools. Hence the focus in this study on the decision-making style of the Heads of schools, the exclusion of other administrative process.

"Einstein did not convince the world of his genius the merely claiming that he was a genius. His public image was created by what he did, not by what he said he did" he says Killan (1979). The public image of a high school is what it does and not what it says it does. The levels and dimensions of morale are determined by the decision-making style of the Heads of schools.

Relationship Between Decision-making and Organisational Health

Another approach in the description of organisational climate derives from literature on organisational health

(Miles, 1969) and the schools as a social system. The notion of organisation health maintains that organisations not only survive in their environment but also continuously develop and extend their surviving and coping capabilities. Such surviving and coping are the working out of Parson's (1951) imperative functions. Indeed all social systems must solve four basic problems if they are to endure and prosper. These four needs, according to Parson, are Adaptation, Goal attainment, Integration and Latency. It means the organisations must solve the following:

(i) The problem of acquiring sufficient resources and accommodating to their environment;

(ii) The problem of setting and implementing;

(iii) The problem of maintaining solidarity within the system; and

(iv) The problem of creating and perusing a distinctive value system, Parson has identified three levels of authority over these three basic functions, viz., Technical, Managerial and Institutional.

The technical level of the school is concerned with teaching-learning process.

The managerial level controls the internal administrative function of the organisation. Heads of the schools are the administrative officers of the schools. They allocate resources and coordinate the work. They motivate teachers and influence their own supervisors. They mediate between the members of the organisation.

The Institutional level links the schools with its environment. Every school needs acceptance and legitimacy in the community. Both administrators and teachers need the support of the community if they are to perform their respective functions in a harmonious fashion without pressure from sources outside the schools.

Specifically, a healthy school is one in which the technical, managerial and institutional levels are in harmony, and the schools needs its imperative needs as it successfully copes with disruptive external forces and directs its energy towards the attainment of goals.

The research studies on organisational health have proved that organisational health and decision-making are related.

In other words the level of organisational health will help the Heads of the schools to take right type of decisions, which will lead to effective functioning, and performance of the schools concerned. The studies of this kind are very few in India. Hence a study on the relationship between decision-making style and organisational health is very much needed.

Relationship Between Decision-making and Leadership Behaviour

The word 'leadership' refers to showing the way and guiding the organisation in taking definite directions and decision.

The two major dimensions of leadership behaviour are 'consideration' and 'initiating structure'.

Consideration: 'Consideration' refers to the extent to which leader is considerate towards subordinates and concerned about the quality of his or her relationship with subordinates. Leader behaviour included in the consideration dimension is friendliness, consultation with subordinates, recognition of subordinates, open communication with subordinates, supportiveness and representative of subordinates interests.

Consideration refers to behaviour indicative of friendship, mutual trust, respect and warmth in the relationship between the leader and the members of his staff.

Initiating Structure: Initiating structure refers to the extent to which a leader is task-oriented and concerned with utilising resources and personnel effectively in order to accomplish group goals. Specific types of leader behaviour included in the initiating structure dimension include planning, coordinating, directing, problem solving, classifying subordinate roles, criticising poor work and pressurising subordinates to perform more effectively.

Coming to the role of leadership in organisations, it is that quality of behaviour of an individual, where he or she guides people and other activities like planning, communication and decision-making into an organised effort. The success or failure of an organisation to a large extent depends upon the quality of leadership. Hence, an inquiry into the leadership behaviour in relation with decision-making is of great significance to determine how leadership can become effective.

SIGNIFICANCE OF THE STUDY

Saying that he should be a dynamic leader can sum up the role of the Head of the school in modern schools. The modern Head of the school should be a leader and not a director, as a leader it is his responsibility to see that the objectives of education are being effectively realized through co-operation, planning, decision-making and execution. Effective decision-making is an ability that most Head of the schools need to develop. General weaknesses in the decision-making process are uncertainty as to who is responsible for making what decision and lack of adequate information for making decisions.

Decisions must be based on factual information. When factual information is not available the validity of the decision must depend on the judgment and experience of the Head of the school making decision. Many decisions that successful Heads of the schools make appear to be snap judgments because there has not been time to gather and evaluate the facts.

To be an effective educational leader the Head of the school must first of all be adept in decision-making ability and be able to consider himself expendable in his position. He must derive highest satisfaction not from his official title, but from what it may enable him to contribute to the vital, educational and cultural processes in which the organisation is engaged.

So there is an urgent need for such humanistic, effective and educational leadership with decision-making ability to facilitate the continuing renewal of the schools.

The Heads of the schools realise these objectives taking the right type of decisions at the appropriate time. Since realisation of objectives depends upon the climate of the organisation, researches need to be undertaken to find out the relationship between decision-making and organisational variables such as climate, health and morale.

The discovery of the administrative process in the early thirties was followed by a concern with "human relations" in general and motivation in particular in late thirties. By the early thirties, the war was led to a need for more powerful planning techniques, soon manifested by a concern with budgeting and programme planning. Later the focus of the management problem shifted to leadership. Some of this concern led to an interest in communication techniques. Another fragment of this belief that the key to more effective administration could be found in leadership came to rest in decision-making. Thus the current interest in decision-making is not incidental but rather the result of an unfolding progression of professional judgment.

Decision-making is basically the process of choosing among alternatives. In most situations there exist two or more alternatives and a Head of the school must decide which alternative to pursue. Before making a decision he must thoroughly understand the problem and develop alternatives. Then he must assess the merits and demerits of each alternative and the probabilities of success in each case.

Effective decision-making is an ability that most Heads of the schools need to develop. General weaknesses in the decision-making process are uncertainty as to who is responsible for making what decisions and lack of adequate information for making decisions.

Decision-making is a process wherein an awareness of a problematic state of system influenced by information and values is reduced to competing alternatives among which a choice is made based on perceived outcome states of the system (Lipham and Hoeh 1974).

The Problem

The Head is the king-pin of the school. It is said that as is the Head, so is the school. The Planning, Organising, Staffing, Directing, Coordinating, Reporting and Budgeting (POSDCORB) functions of the Head of the school are dependent on his decision-making style. The quality and style of decision-making influences the rank and file of the school towards quality, excellence and productivity. The style of decision-making makes or mars the quality of the school system. The style of decision-making brings in change-proneness and a climate for experimenting innovations and bringing positive ripple effects in the school. The style of decision-making is dependent on various factors operating within and outside the school system.

Various variables such as school climate, change-proneness, school organisation health, teacher morale, teacher involvement, teachers value system, teacher commitment, leadership behaviour of Heads of the schools shape the decision-making style of the Heads of the schools. In Indian context research studies relating these variables are very few. Hence, the present study attempts to fill this gap.

The present study is entitled as *"A Study of Decision-making Style and Leadership Behaviour of Heads of Schools in Relation to Teacher Morale and Organisational Health in Secondary Schools"*.

Objectives of the Study

1. To study the relationship between schools under Heads with different decision-making style (Routine, Compromise and Heuristic) and organisational health as a whole.

2. To study the relationship between schools under Heads with different decision-making style (Routine, Compromise and Heuristic) and the following dimensions of organisational health.

    (i) Integrity

    (ii) Consideration

    (iii) Initiating Structure

    (iv) Resource Support

    (v) Principal Influence

    (vi) Morale

    (vii) Academic Emphasis

3. To study the relationship between schools under Heads with different leadership styles (Initiating Structure and Consideration) and organisational health as a whole.

4. To study the relationship between schools under Heads with different leadership styles and the following dimensions of organisational health.

    (i) Integrity

    (ii) Consideration

    (iii) Initiating Structure

    (iv) Resource Support

    (v) Principal Influence

    (vi) Morale

    (vii) Academic Emphasis

5. To study the relationship between schools under male and female Heads and organisational health as a whole.

6. To study the relationship between schools under male and female Heads and the following dimensions of organisational health.

(i) Integrity

(ii) Consideration

(iii) Initiating Structure

(iv) Resource Support

(v) Principal Influence

(vi) Morale

(vii) Academic Emphasis

7. To study the relationship between schools under Heads with varying experience (Below 15,15-25, Above 25) and organisational health as a whole.

8. To study the relationship between schools under Heads with varying experience (Below 15,15-25, Above 25) and the following dimensions of organisational health.

   (i) Integrity

   (ii) Consideration

   (iii) Initiating Structure

   (iv) Resource Support

   (v) Principal Influence

   (vi) Morale

   (vii) Academic Emphasis

9. To study the relationship between schools under Heads with different decision-making styles (Routine, Compromise and Heuristic) and teacher morale as a whole.

10. To study the relationship between schools under Heads with different decision-making styles (Routine, Compromise and Heuristic) and the following components of teacher morale.

(i) Individual characteristics

(ii) Behavioural characteristics

(iii) Group spirit

(iv) Attitude towards the job

(v) Community involvement

11. To study the relationship between schools under Heads with different leadership styles (Initiating Structure, Consideration) and teacher morale as a whole.

12. To study the relationship between schools under Heads with different leadership styles (Initiating Structure, Consideration) and the following components of teacher morale.

    (i) Individual characteristics

    (ii) Behavioural characteristics

    (ii) Group spirit

    (iv) Attitude towards the job

    (v) Community involvement

13. To study the relationship between schools under male and female Heads and teacher morale as a whole.

14. To study the relationship between schools under male and female Heads and the following components of teacher morale.

    (i) Individual characteristics

    (ii) Behavioural characteristics

    (iii) Group spirit

    (iv) Attitude towards the job

    (v) Community Involvement

15. To study the relationship between schools under Heads with varying experience (Below 15, 15-25, Above 25) and teacher morale as a whole.

16. To study the relationship between schools under Heads with varying experience (Below 15,15-25, Above 25) and the following components of teacher morale.

    (i) Individual characteristics

    (ii) Behavioural characteristics

    (iii) Group spirit

    (iv) Attitude towards the job

    (v) Community involvement

17. To study the association between decision-making style (Routine, Compromise, Heuristic) and leadership style (Initiating Structure, Consideration) of Heads of Schools.

18. To study the association between decision-making style (Routine, Compromise, Heuristic) and sex (Male and Female) of Heads of Schools.

19. To study the association between decision-making style (Routine, Compromise, Heuristic) and experience (Below 15,15-25, Above 25) of Heads of Schools.

20. To study the association between decision-making style (Routine, Compromise, Heuristic) of Heads of Schools and type of management (Government, Aided, Un-aided)

21. To study the association between leadership style (Initiating Structure, Consideration) and sex (Male and Female) of Heads of Schools.

22. To study the association between leadership style (Initiating Structure, Consideration) and experience (Below 15, 15-25, Above 25) of Heads of Schools.

23. To study the association between leadership style (Initiating Structure, Consideration) of Heads of Schools and type of management (Government, Aided, Un-aided)

24. To study the relationship between organisational health and teacher morale.

25. To study the relationship between dimensions of organisational health and components of teacher morale.

26. To study the relationship between dimensions of organisational health.

27. To study the relationship between components of teacher morale.

28. To study the significant influence of leadership styles (Initiating Structure and Consideration), decision-making styles (Routine, Compromise, Heuristic), teacher morale, sex, experience and type of management on organisational health.

29. To study the significant influence of leadership styles (Initiating Structure and Consideration), decision-making styles (Routine, Compromise, Heuristic), organisational health, sex, experience, and type of management on teacher morale.

30. To study the interactive effect of Heads of schools decision-making style (Routine, Compromise, Heuristic) and leadership style (Initiating Structure and Consideration) on organisational health.

31. To study the interactive effect of Heads of schools decision-making style (Routine, Compromise, Heuristic) and leadership style (Initiating Structure and Consideration) on teacher morale.

LIMITATIONS OF THE STUDY

(i) The present study is limited to Dharwad Taluka.

(ii) The study is restricted to Heads of schools and assistant teachers of secondary schools of Dharwad Taluka.

2

Theoretical Background

Concept of Decision-making

A Head of the school chooses to close down the high school in the event of students strike and asks the students to vacate the campus. The students take out a procession and three students are shot dead in the encounter with police outside the campus. The public complains that the Head of the school's faculty decision costs lives of three students this incident eventually costs the Head of the school his career.

Much of the current interest in decision-making stems from the quietly emerging conviction that choice is the potent cause in determining the efficacy of organisational process. Even an academically sound Head of the school cannot succeed unless he has a well-engineered management system.

The discovery of the administrative process in the early thirties was followed by a concern with "human relations" in general and motivation in particular in late thirties. By the early thirties the war had led to a need for more powerful planning techniques, soon manifested by a concern with budgeting and programme planning. Later the focus of the management problem shifted to leadership. Some of this concerns led to an interest in communication techniques. Another fragment of this belief that the key to more effective administration could be found in leadership came to rest in decision-making. Thus the current interest in decision-making is not incidental but rather the result of an unfolding progression of professional judgment.

The term 'decision' may refer to the choice of selecting a solution for a petty problem or it may just as well refer to a momentous and unprecedented sensational act (Head of the school's decision to close down the high school forever). The gulf between these terminals of continuum of decisions is too large to traverse with the use of only a single term.

Generally, decision refers to the consideration of the consequences of some act before undertaking it.

Primarily a pattern for making a decision is a collective device for responding to a situation that requires action or at least concern.

Perrone (1972) defines decision as "the appropriate response of an intelligent being to a situation, which demands action." Decision-making is the process through which administrators prescribe particular actions in view of the unique demands of a given situation.

Nickerson (1978) defines decision-making as the rational selection of a course of action from among two or more alternatives. Halpin (1969) defines it as "a settling or terminating, as of a controversy by giving judgement on the matter also a conclusion arrived at after consideration."

To Killian (1979) decision-making "is the critical test of management—the ability and the courage to reach the right conclusions and take the right course of actions, skill in persuading others to co-operate with total commitment and then follow through to successful results."

Gorton (1976) defines it simply as "the process of choosing among alternatives." Oxenfeldt (1979) gives an entirely different explanation: "Decision-making is a mental process which reflects and depends on the working of the brain."

Duncan (1965) says "a decision is the appropriate response of an intelligent being to a situation which demands action".

Many management scientists consider decision function so important as to accept it as the central activity of management. A few would deny that the process occupies a major portion of the Head of the school's time. The Head of the school engages in decision perhaps more often than in any other process; it is the single most important process in high school administration. Halpin (1969) emphasizes the above view when he says that "central function of administration is directing and controlling decision-making process."

Decision-making is basically the process of choosing among alternatives. In most situations there exist two or more alternatives and a Head of the school must decide which alternative to pursue. Before making a decision he must thoroughly understand the problem and develop alternatives. Then he must assess the merits and demerits of each alternative and the probabilities of success in each case. So, decision-making is not a smooth flowing process dispensing choices when and where they are required. Rather it is a twisted, unshapely, halting flow of interactions between people, interactions that shift constantly from a rational to a heuristic mode and back again.

The Nature of Decision-making

Most decisions are repetitive and fortunately the store of information a Head of the school gathers for making the previous decisions may be carried forward and applied to the decisions coming up.

There are many decisions, which though repetitive are each little different from previous decision. Appointing part-time teachers or promoting staff are examples of repetitive but different decisions. Decisions may also be classified as the degree of importance of the outcomes. If the future existence of the high school hinges on the outcome of the decision, this decision will receive a different degree of consideration.

Placing the decision in perspective is extremely important. Taking a broad point of view—how important is the decision?; Is it worthy of the effort being devoted to its resolution?

There is another important characteristic of decision-making. A Head of the school may make an incorrect decision and make it correct, or he can make a correct decision for all the wrong reasons. He may decide incorrectly and arbitrarily not to promote Mr. X who then moves on to a better job and he may replace him with a man who is not qualified, but who turns out to be outstanding. A well-made and well-researched decision may turn out to be incorrect.

Frequently a decision is an instant reaction, which is more an impulse or an instinctive action than a conscious decision

Decision is the end process preceded by deliberation and reasoning. Rationality is another characteristics of decision-making. The human brains with its ability to learn to remember and to relate many complex factors makes this rationality possible.

Decision is the choice of the best course among alternatives. It may be negative and just may be decision not to decide.

There is also the concept of commitment in every decision. The Head of the school is committed to decision for two reasons:—firstly, it leads to the stability of the concern, and secondly, every decision taken becomes part of the expectations of the people involved in high school organisation. Decisions are so much interrelated to the organisational life of a concern. Hence the Head of the school is committed to decisions not only from the time that he decides but till such time that they are successfully implemented.

The characteristics of evaluation exist in decision-making in two ways—firstly the Head of the school must evaluate the alternatives, and secondly, he should evaluate the results of the decisions taken by him.

The Process of Decision-making

Effective decision-making is an ability that most Heads of the schools need to develop. General weaknesses in the decision-making process are uncertainty as to who is responsible for making what decisions and lack of information for making decisions.

Decisions must be based on factual information, when factual information is not available the validity of the decision must depend on the judgement and experience of the Head of the school making decision. Many decisions successful Heads of the schools make, appear to be snap judgements, because there has not been time to gather and evaluate the facts.

In general Heads of the schools go in either for negative or positive choices. Certain Heads of the schools do nothing. They may let the problem solve itself, allow someone else to decide, appoint a committee, or delay. The positive approach is to accept the responsibility to recognize the needs, to make the decision without undue delay or to see it implemented successfully.

In obtaining a better understanding of the Head of the school's decision-making role, attention must first be directed to the substantive content of the role. The specific tasks of high school administration can be catalogued in a number of ways. In general high school Heads are concerned with and are responsible for (a) curriculum and instruction (b) physical facilities (c) finance (d) student personnel (e) supervision (f) recruitment and retention of staff (g) public relations. The decision-making process encompasses all these above tasks.

Tawney (1976) says that the administrator cannot straightaway decide issues. In the event of making decisions, the available information influences the decision-maker and other side the values of the problem come in the way of decision-making and other angle existing options may touch the choice behaviour of the administrator. Ultimately he chooses the alternative, which results in educational improvement.

When a Head of the school is confronted with a problem, in order to understand the problem he gathers information,

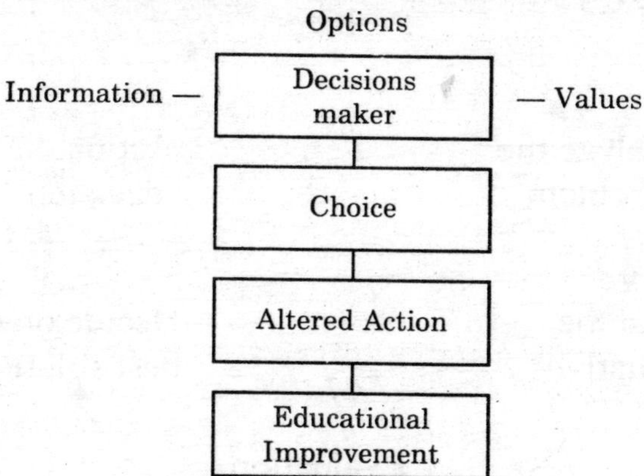

Fig. 2.1 The Process of Decision-making

decides further course of action and sees that his decision is put into action. This can be expressed in the following simple diagram.

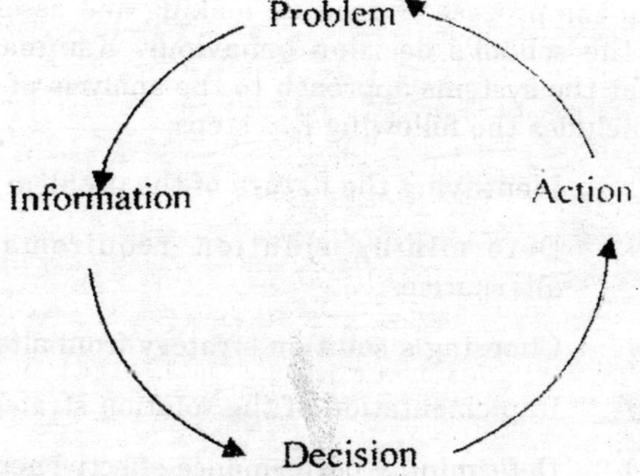

Fig. 2.2 Simple decision loop

When a problem arises the solution to the problem is not got on the spur of the moment. The Head of the school has to analyse the problem, has to find alternative, evaluate alternatives and only then can he decide the best alternative. His problem is not solved until his decision is implemented. This is represented in the following diagram.

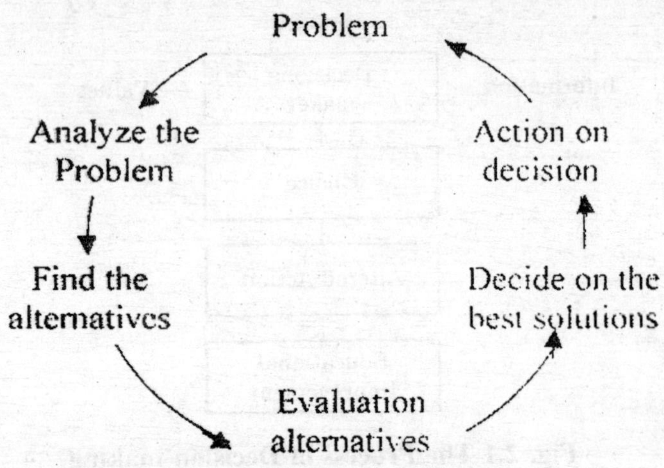

Fig. 2.3 Complex decision loop

The systems approach to administration is particularly relevant for the analysis of decision-making, in terms of both describing the process of decision-making and assessing the Head of the school's decision behaviour. Kaufman (1970) writes that the systems approach to the analysis of decision-making includes the following five steps.

(i) Identifying the nature of the problem

(ii) Determining solution requirements and alternatives

(iii) Choosing a solution strategy from alternatives

(iv) Implementation of the solution strategy

(v) Determining performance effectiveness

Lipham and Hoeh (1974) state that systems approach has fostered the use of several viable management tools and techniques—needs assessment, management by objectives (MBO), Input-output analysis, programme evaluation and review technique/critical part method (PERT/CPM). All these can serve to sharpen considerably the decision-making skills of the Head of the school.

"Decision-making is a process wherein an awareness of a problematic state of a system, influenced by information and values, is reduced to competing alternatives among which a choice is made based on perceived outcome states of the system"—Lipham and Hoeh (1974). This definition contains a number of key concepts and the first of these is that of process itself.

Process implies action, a particular set of continuing activities, steps, stages or operations. Process is always inferred, usually sequential and sometimes cyclical. Since Process is inferred, it is only an abstraction for the analysis of decision-making behaviour. As Halpin (1957) remarks, an outside observer can never observe 'Process' qua 'Process'; he can observe only a sequence of behaviour. Thus in analysing the decision-making process it is necessary to obtain data from the decision-maker himself, as well as from observers of the behaviour.

Awareness of a Problematic State

Awareness of a problematic state of a system constitutes the first step in the decision-making process. Barnard (1938) was the first to consider the significance of this aspect. He states, "The fine art of executive decision consists in not deciding questions that are now pertinent, in not deciding prematurely, in not making decisions that cannot be made effective and in not making decisions that others should make."

Information serves the basis for decision-making, yet three points are worthy of consideration—amount, form and flow of information.

Values serve as a perceptual screen for the decision-maker, affecting both his awareness of the problematic state of a system and his screening of information relative to the problem. Secondly values condition the screening of possible alternatives. Many factors in addition to values constitute the perceptual screen of the decision-maker, including such personalistic variables as intelligence, creativity, need disposition abilities and even biological states of the decision-maker.

The perceptual screen surrounds the decision-maker in a sense and affects all elements of the decision process, including problem awareness, information processing value estimates, formulating and weighing alternatives and making the decision choice.

Competing alternatives represent actions that might be taken or things that might be done to solve the problematic state of a system.

The act of selecting a solution strategy from among the decision alternatives is termed the *decision choice.*

Lipham and Hoeh (1974) fit the above aspects in a model (and present it as in Fig. 2.4.

Types of Decisions

In addition to analysing the decision-making process it becomes inevitable to identify different types of decisions. According to Katz(1955) Headmasters in general make decisions only in three areas viz., technical, and human and conceptual. Even though all the decisions those Headmasters make, fall either of the above area, their types of decisions differ. It is so because different types of situations and managements require different decision-making styles. Management scientists have christened different nomenclature for the different decision-making styles. For instance McFarland (1964) classified decisions as under:

(i) Organisational and personal decisions

(ii) Basic and routine decisions

(iii) Programmed and non-programmed decisions.

Griffiths (1957) classified decisions into intermediary decisions, appellate decisions and creative decisions. According to him intermediary decision means the decision coming from top management downwards, appellate decision means the

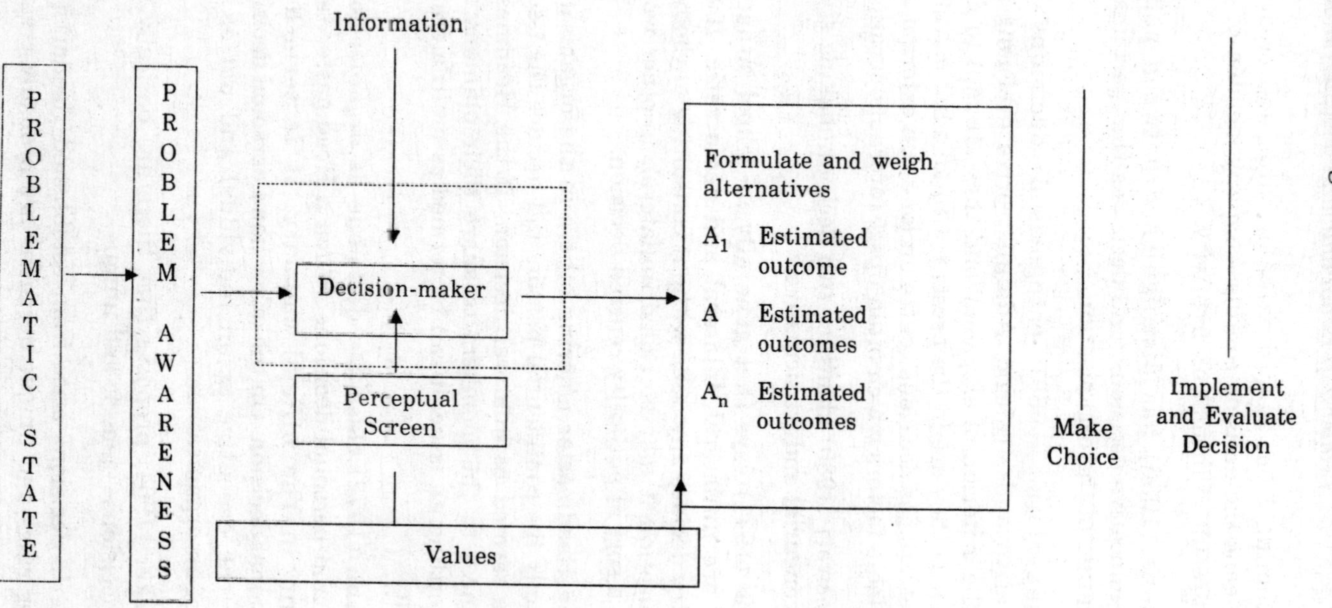

Source: Lipham, J.M. (1974)

Fig. 2.4 Model of a Decision-making Process

decision coming from subordinates upwards and creative decision means the decision coming from any member of the group as a result of insight or creativity.

Parsons (1956) has distinguished between policy decisions, allocative decisions, and decisions that pertains to the integration of the organisation.

Chamberlain (1968) categorised decisions as administrative and strategic. Administrative decisions are ruled by the criterion of efficiency and they attempt to deal with things as they are in the present. Unlike administrative decisions strategies decisions centre on long run external and uncontrollable factors which often upset internal operations.

Maheswari (1980) identifies two decision-making styles as entrepreneurial and participative.

Jarvis (1971) says that generally in school situation decisions are unilateral, bilateral and democratic. If the Headmaster decides any issue without consulting anybody in the organisation it may be called unilateral, in other words it may be a sort of authority centred decision.

If the Headmaster ignoring others in the organisation consults only his confidential person and decides the issues, it may be termed as bilateral decision. If the Headmaster gives chances to the members to share their opinions and ideas in settling an issue, it can be termed as multilateral or democratic.

Saxena (1972) classifies decisions as organisational decisions and personal decisions. When a Headmaster takes a decision in the official capacity, it is termed as organisational decision. On the other hand personal decisions relate to the executive as an individual and not as the member of an organisation.

Drucker (1964) proposes that there are basically two kinds of decisions—generic and unique.

Generic decisions arise from established Headmasters, policies or rules and unique decisions are probably creative decisions, in fact they go beyond established procedures for a solution. They may require modification of the organisational structure.

Lipham and Hoeh (1974) have given a sound classification of decision-making style, which envelops the ingredients of all the aforesaid classifications. Their typology has concern for the structure of the relationship between individuals, the behaviour required to facilitate decision-making, the manner of proceeding in decision-making and the social as emotional tone of the inter-personal relationships. This typology includes routine decision, compromise decision and heuristic decision-making.

Routine decisions are taken to keep the institution going. In the words of Lipham and Hoeh (1974), "in routine decision-making the situation is usually structured hierarchically, the role behaviour is characterised by specialised yet co-operated effort, the processes utilised are largely formal and the relationships themselves are likely to be somewhat stressful." In short, it is programmed type of decision.

Ideas clash occasionally under a competent Headmaster. The Headmaster must be capable of arriving at a compromising formula without offending either party. The Headmaster must be a human relations facilitator and see that occasional ill feelings and feelings of animosity and jealousy among the faculty as a result of such clashes are adequately diagnosed and analysed and remediation taken. In short, it is negotiated type of decision.

In heuristic decision-making there is a lack of emphasis on hierarchical structure, role behaviour is characterized by freedom for each individual to explore all ideas. The emotional and social tone is relatively relaxed; openness, originality and seeking of consensus are the essentials of heuristic decision-making. In a nutshell it is a creative type of decision.

Even though these different decision-making styles are in vogue, unless the Headmaster has certain decision-making skill he cannot prove to be a successful decision-maker. Abbot (1974) identified five decision-making skills such as skill in differentiating among types of decisions, skill in determining the amount and type of information needed to reach a decision, skill in determining the extent of involvement of other people in reaching decisions, skill in establishing priorities for action and skill in anticipating both intended and unintended consequences of decisions. To sum up, decision-making was viewed as central to all states of administrative processes. It was defined as a process wherein an awareness of a problematic state of a system, influenced by information and values, is reduced to competing alternatives among which a choice is made based on estimated outcome states of the system. Besides the process, the different decision-making styles mentioned by management scientists were cited including those of routine, compromise and heuristic mentioned by Lipham and Hoeh (1974). This section concluded by stressing certain competencies required for effective decision-making on the part of the Headmaster.

Concept of Organisational Health

The New Concept: Organisations, like people exist within a fluctuating state of wellness. Organisational health or well being is dependent on the interaction of the collective internal and external forces that intervene the fulfilment of the purpose of the organisation. Organisational health refers to the organisational ability to identify and adjust to the requirement for change influenced by internal as well as external determinants.

Miles (1973) gave a clearer concept of organisational health as a set of fairly durable and secondary system properties, which tend to transcend short-term effectiveness. A healthy organisation in this sense not only survives in its environment but also continues to cope adequately with time and continuously develops and extends its surviving and coping abilities. Short-run operations on any particular day may be effective or ineffective but continued survival adequate coping and growth are taking place.

Miles has described ten dimensions of organisational health in a book titled "Organisations and Human Behaviours; Focus on schools", edited by Carver and Sergiovanni (1969). These dimensions are:

- *(i)* Goal Focus,
- *(ii)* Communication Adequacy,
- *(iii)* Optimal Power Equalisation,
- *(iv)* Resource Utilisation,
- *(v)* Cohesiveness,
- *(vi)* Morale,
- *(vii)* Innovativeness,
- *(viii)* Autonomy,
- *(ix)* Adaptation, and
- *(x)* Problem-solving Adequacy.

The explanation of each dimension is as under:

(i) Goal Focus

In a healthy organisation the goals of the system would be reasonably clear to the staff members and reasonably well accepted by them. Goals must be achievable with available resources and be appropriate, that is, more of less congruent with the demands of the environment. Elsewhere, Miles (1967) calls for instruments and work methods in schools for specifying areas of vagueness about goals and for increasing understanding of goals through discussion. Instruments are needed to help teachers assess precisely what the short-run consequences of their work have been.

(ii) Communication Adequacy

The organisations are not simultaneous face-to-face systems like small groups. The movement of information, within them, therefore, becomes crucial. This involves distortion free communication vertically, horizontally and across the boundary of the system to and from surrounding environment. That is, information travels reasonably well just as a healthy person knows himself with a minimum level of regression, distortion, etc. In a healthy organisation there is a good and prompt sensing of internal strains, there are enough data about problems of the system to ensure that a good diagnosis of system difficulties can be made. People have the information they need and have forgotten it without exerting undue efforts. As a corollary, education system has such indicators as adequacy of communication between teachers and administrators and between teachers and children.

(iii) Optimal Power Equalisation

In a healthy organisation the distribution of influence is relatively equitable. Subordinates (if there is a formal authority chart) can influence upward and even more important as Likert has demonstrated, they perceive that their boss can do likewise with his boss. In such an organisation, inter-group struggles for power would not be bitter, though inter-group conflict (as in every human system known to man) would undoubtedly be present. The basic stance of persons in such an organisation, as they took up, sideways and down, is that of collaboration rather than explicit coercion. The units of the organisation (persons in roles, work groups, etc.) would stand in an interdependent relationship to each other, with rather less emphasis on the ability of the 'master' to control the entire operation. The exertion or influence in a healthy organisation presumably rests on the competence of the influence vis-á-vis the issue at hand, master's stake in the outcome, and the amount of his knowledge or data rather than on his organisational position, personal charisma, or the factors with little direct relevance to the problem at hand.

The first three dimensions are related to the tasks, organisational goals, the transmission of message and the way in which the decisions are made.

(iv) Resource Utilisation

We say a healthy person, such as second grader, that he is 'working' up to his potential. To put this in another way, the classroom system is evoking a contribution from him at an appropriate and goal-directed level of tension. At the organisational level 'health' would imply that system's inputs, particularly the personal, are used effectively. The overall co-ordination is such that people are neither over loaded not idling, and there is a close correspondence between their personal characteristics and demands of the system. In the healthy organisation, people may be working very hard indeed, but they feel that they are not working against themselves or against the organisation. The fit between people's own dispositions and the role demands of the system is good. Beyond this, people feel reasonably 'self-actualised'. They not only 'feel good' in their jobs, but they also have a genuine sense of learning, growing and developing as persons in the process of making their organisational contribution.

(v) Cohesiveness

We think of healthy person as the one who has a clear sense of identity. He knows who he is underneath all the specific goals he sets for himself. Beyond this, he likes himself; his stance towards life does not require self-derogation, even where there are aspects of his behaviour, which are unlively or ineffective. By analogy at the organisational level system health would empty the organisation knows 'who it is'. Its members feel attracted to membership. They want to stay with the organisation, be influenced by it and have an influence on it.

(vi) Morale

The implied notion is one of well-being or satisfaction. Satisfaction of course is not enough for health. A person may report feelings of well-being and satisfaction in his life, while successfully denying deep-lying hostilities, anxieties and conflicts. Yet it still seems useful to evoke at the organisational level, the idea morale, summated set of individuals sentiments, centering around feelings of well-being, satisfaction and pleasure, as opposed to feelings of discomfort, unwished for strain and dissatisfaction. In an unhealthy system, life might be perceived easily as 'good' or as unabashedly bad. In a healthy organisation it is hard to entertain the idea that the dominant personal response of organisation members would be anything else than of well-being.

A second group of three dimension deals essentially with the internal state of the system, and its inhabitants' maintenance needs. These dimensions are resource utilisation, cohesiveness and morale.

A healthy organisation would tend to invent new procedures, more towards new goals, produce new kinds of products, diversify itself and become more rather than less differential over time. In a sense, such a system could be said to grow, develop and change, rather than remain routinized and unchanged (Miles 1964). School systems with these properties could be expected to institutionalise innovation to devote space, time and money for personal career and organisational development and renewal programmes They can also set up change generating and experimental units with research and development functions, provide rewards for innovators, instil 'environmental scanning' mechanisms whereby new developments in neighbouring schools, in community agencies and in ministerial policy making can be applied to schools itself.

(vii) Autonomy

A healthy person acts outward from his own centre. Such a person in a training or therapy group appears nearly free of the need to submit dependently to authority figures, and from the need to rebel and destroy symbolic features of any kind. A healthy organisation is independent from the environment in the sense that it does neither respond passively to demands from without, nor destructively or rebelliously to perceived demands. Like a healthy individual in his transactions with others, the school system would not treat its responses to the community as determining its own behaviour.

(viii) Adaptation

The notions of autonomy and innovations are both connected with the idea that a healthy person, group or organisation is in realistic and effective contact with his surroundings. When environmental demands and organisational resources do not match, a problem solving, restructuring approach evolves in which both the environment and the organisation become different in some respects. Continued coping of the organisation, as a result of change in the local system, the relevant portions of the environment, or more usually both undergo a change. Such a system has a sufficient stability and stress tolerance to manage the difficulties, which occur during the adaptation process. Perhaps inherent in this notion is that the system's ability to bring about corrective change in itself is faster than the change cycle in the surrounding environment.

(ix) Problem-solving Adequacy

Finally, any healthy organisation theoretically impervious to fallibility, as a computer, always has problems, strains, difficulties, and instances of ineffective coping. The issue is not the presence or absence of problems, but the manner in which the person, group or organisation copes with them. Miles (1964) has suggested that in an effective system, problems are solved with minimal energy, they stay solved, and the problem-solving mechanisms used are not weakened but maintained or strengthened. A healthy organisation then has well developed structures and procedures for sensing the existence of problems for inventing possible solutions, for deciding on the solutions, for implementing them and for evaluating their effectiveness. Such an organisation would conceive of its own operations (whether directed outward to goal achievement, inward to maintenance or inward-outward to problems of adaptation) as been controllable. We should see acting as coping with problems, rather than passive withdrawing, compulsive responses, or denial.

The last fcur dimensions of organisational health deal with growth and change, the notions of innovativeness, autonomy, adaptations vis-á-vis the environment, and problem-solving adequacy. All the ten dimensions are mutually inclusive, which gives the total picture of the organisational health of the institution. If any of the ten dimensions of the organisational health is weak, the health of the institution is found to be deteriorating.

Concept of Teacher Morale

The concept of morale, another variable in the study should be discussed in detail.

Morale is intangible. It cannot be seen or isolated. But it is possible to determine the quality of morale by careful observation of the way the faculty behaves. Gentleness, cheerfulness, promptness, enthusiasm, dependability and co-operation are indicators of morale.

'Morale' is one to which various meanings have been given. To some it means zeal of enthusiasm with which an individual performs his duties. Others insist that morale is the willingness of a group to work towards a collective purpose. The investigator would like to define faculty morale as the way a faculty feels, acts and believes. The kind of feelings, actions or beliefs determine whether there is high or low morale. Group morale depends upon the feelings, actions and beliefs of all persons concerned. In other words faculty morale means the collective feelings and the attitude of the faculty as a whole towards their profession and colleagues in the institution.

The concept of 'morale' has been perceived in varied ways. Persistence, job price, punctuality, loyalty, co-operativeness, spirit and dependability are frequently listed as component parts of morale.

Drever (1973) defines morale as a term employed by "an individual or of a group, signifying the condition with respect to self-control, self-confidence and disciplined action."

Guba (1957) suggested when an individual becomes a member of some organisation such as a high school he must conform to certain norms and expectation if he or she and the high school are to maintain harmonious relationship, to function effectively, but at the same time he/she has the opportunity to fulfil to some degree his/her unique personality needs.

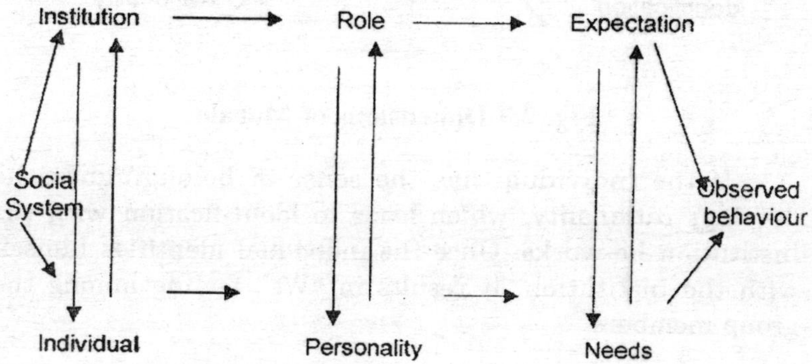

Fig. 2.5 Dimensions of a Social System

When the needs of the individual and the goals of the system are congruent, there is a feeling of identification with the system. When the needs of the individual and the expectation of the role-set are congruent, there is a feeling of rationality regarding the system.

Getzels and Guba (1971) represent the above description in the following manner.

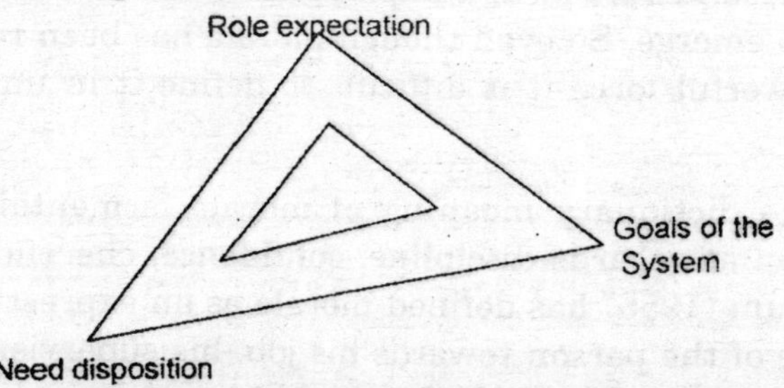

Fig. 2.6 Relationship between Role Expectation, Need Disposition and Goals of the System

Dimensions of morale can be pictorially represented as follows:

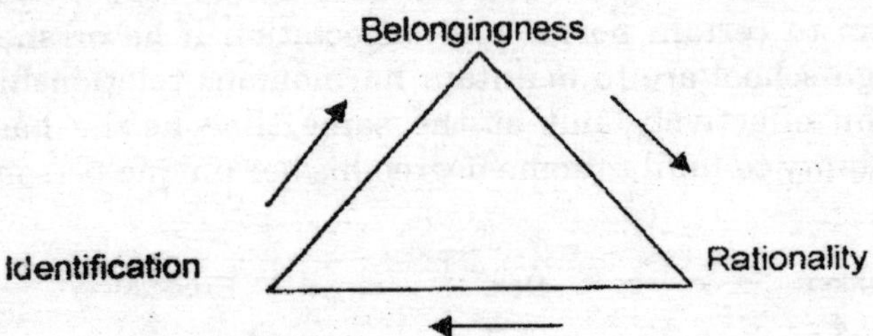

Fig. 2.7 Dimensions of Morale

If the individual has the sense of belongingness he develops rationality, which leads to identification with the institution he works. Once the individual identifies himself with the institution, it results in "We" feeling among the group members.

Stodgill conceives morale as the degree of freedom from restraint exhibited by a group in working towards a goal objective. Morale is seen as being related to motivation.

If freedom is given to act, the level of morale may be highly related to the strength of motivation. Thus morale may be viewed as evidence of the motivation exhibited in overt action towards a goal.

Morale is a phenomenon that is discussed at great length but little understood. A comprehensive definition of morale is yet to emerge. So even though morale has been recognized as a powerful force it is difficult to define it in unequivocal terms.

The dictionary meaning of morale is mental state or condition as regards discipline, confidence, cheerfulness and zeal. Blum (1956) has defined morale as an expression of the attitude of the person towards his job, his supervision. If the attitude of the faculty is favourable towards institution, it shows high morale. On the other hand, if the faculty has unfavourable attitudes towards institution it shows low morale. Harrell (1958) defines morale as the combination of attitudes towards job, company and supervision.

Guion (1958) states that morale is the extent to which the individual needs are satisfied and the extent to which he perceives that satisfaction as stemming from his total job satisfaction.

According to Henemen et. al. (1958) morale is sometimes used to describe the degree of frustration felt by a group of persons.

In the opinion of Burtt (1959) morale is a tendency to work enthusiastically for common purpose,.

To Kay and Palmer (1961) morale is the general enthusiasm of a group—its *esprit de corps*.

Yoder (1950) in this book *Personnel Management and Industrial Relation* has defined morale as an overall 'tone' or 'climate' vaguely sensed among members of a group or association.

Atkins and Lasswell (1957) have defined morale as the collective will, which it builds into groups by securing a subordination of the individual to the group and willingness to be disciplined in terms of group purpose.

The American Association of School Administration states morale is a disposition on the part of persons engaged in an enterprise to behave in ways, which contribute to the purpose for which the enterprise exists. When this disposition is strong morale is said to be high. It manifests itself in a tendency to subordinate personal considerations to the purpose of the enterprise to work as a member of a team for the accomplishment of common goals and to derive satisfaction from achievements of the organisation when the disposition towards the achievement of common purpose is weak, morale is said to be low.

Most of the definitions of morale describe it as a mental condition and cite various factors affecting it. Two points in particular should be mentioned about the concept of morale. First, whatever it is, it is not an un-dimensional concept. It has more than a single component and each component can be defined best only in respect to the operations by which it is measured.

It will be appropriate to quote Wilson Robert (1968): morale is a configuration of many component parts, all of which are important. Most important of all, morale is not a thing apart from the life of the individual.

Two things should be noticed of group morale. Morale may be low or high. High and low morale is not a constant phenomenon, nor is it the same for all the members of the faculty. Morale differs from individual to individual, group to group, institution to institution, Morale can be measured.

Concept of Leadership Behaviour

Leadership is of utmost importance in the development of any significant, ongoing movement, designed to improve social, economic, political and educational conditions in our society. Since the ultimate solutions to educational problems will be discovered according to the vision and skill of educational leaders, the abilities and competencies of the professional personnel must be developed to the fullest degree possible.

We are living in the most exciting and challenging period of time in the whole history of the world. The challenge of this revolutionary period extends into all aspects of life. Education can no more remain complacent to the needs that such a challenge than the need can resist the effect of the sun and rain at springtime. Our educational structure, programme, and practices must change. The rapidity and degree to which this change will occur are dependents upon the educational leaders at all levels of administration.

Importance of Educational Leadership

Leadership is a basic element of education. A great leader can inspire entire communities; his influence radiates, and he exemplifies in his own life and ideas of education. For the successful implementation of the educational programme the classroom teacher, the Headmaster, the supervisor and the administrator should assume leadership. In a period of crisis and transition the position of the educational leader is more significant than at any other time. We look to education to solve the perplexing problems of our time. The task of the educational leader is to become aware of the opportunities. His function is to create love where antagonism prevails; to spread the flame of knowledge where ignorance exists; and to create real when so many are smug and self-righteous. He must not only communicate ideas, but then must be a representative of a creative way of life, a symbol of peace and serenity.

The Leader and the Led

The leadership role is determined by the perceptions held by the leader and the led. A person assigned to a position of leadership is said to be a status leader, he may or may not be the real leader if he is more than the status leader. He will meet most of the expectations of leadership held by those affected by his actions. But in the normal situations where leadership is involved, the followers are likely to hold many differing kinds of expectation from their leader. When the leader finds it impossible to conform to many different kinds of expectations, role conflict is said to exist. To strengthen the leader-led relationship the former must keep upper-most in his mind the need-dispositions of workers-followers, such as the search for meaning, self-fulfilment, and self-realisation.

In order to be an effective administrative leader to build and maintain effective relationship with his subordinates three factors are essential:

(i) Small face-to-face groups are necessary in planning and communicating.

(ii) Decentralisation of authority and encouraging staff participation in decision-making are

acknowledgement of one fundamental aspiration of the led.

(iii) The leader should be a person oriented to engender supportive relationships and he in turn should be supportive of his followers motivation.

Leadership Styles

Leadership have been classified into six types,

(i) Institutional or Positional: who leads by virtue of the authority or prestige of his position.

(ii) Intellectual: who gains followers through his recognized ability in specialised functional fields.

(iii) Democratic: who obtains the loyalty of his followers by associating them with the decision-making process to the maximum extent possible.

(iv) Autocratic: who leads through domination and drive.

(v) Persuasive: who has a likeable personality and prefaces his decisions with explanations as to why they are necessary.

(vi) Creative: who inspires others with ideas, and stimulates them to emulation.

Leadership may also be classified into impelling and compelling types. Compelling leadership relies on authority and power, rules and regulations, reward and punishment to secure obedience. The motive power comes from outside the followers or employees.

The compelling leader firmly believes that he is there to do all the thinking for his department. Most executives use compelling methods for getting things done. Little do they realize that compelling produces only half-hearted obedience at best and often arouses lasting opposition or apathy. In the ultimate analysis, the force of leadership depends on the followers' will to follow and not on the good sense or loudness of the leader's command.

The basic idea of impelling leadership is that people follow their own decisions beat; they may obey an order meekly if they have to, but they follow it enthusiastically when they are led to believe that it is their own decision. The technique of impelling leadership, therefore, consists in leading people to decide for themselves. Telling people what they should do seldom makes them want to do it. But they decide it for themselves when they feel impelled to do it. It is said, "Almost every man can do twice as much if he wants to do it."

The strategy of impelling leadership has three main planks. In the first place widest possible areas of activity should be earmarked for workers who have a more or less free hand to decide things for themselves and use their initiative and inventiveness. Targets and goals should be set and standards of performance laid down, but the workers should be allowed to work out the detailed procedure and evolve their own systems of efficiency by process of experimentation. This requires maximum delegation of powers and functions. Within these areas of delegated authority the boss should neither interfere nor give unsolicited advice. He will judge performance by the results produced without worrying about the actual means.

The second part of the strategy of impelling leadership is to restrict as much as possible the areas in which decisions have to be taken by the loss without consultation with the workers. Matters of policy, large financial commitments, plans for expansion are decided upon with the help of appropriate advisers but without reference to those who will be required to implement them. But these reserved subjects should be strictly limited to those, which, on account of their confidential nature or for other reasons, do not lend themselves to the consultative method.

Between these two extremes there are vast areas, which are particularly suited for the application of impelling methods. Within these areas a process of consultation best arrives at important decisions between the boss and his assistants. Such consultations means pooling of knowledge and experience, it promotes the birth of new ideas through contract of mind with mind; it enables the workers to adopt the decision as their own creation if not wholly at least in part.

The impelling type of leader treats people as seedbeds for ideas. He sows ideas in his subordinates minds. For this purpose, he shares problems with them; he inspires them to think until they come to sponsor the same idea as he has in mind.

Impelling leadership requires patience, foresight, self-restraint and self-denial. Another requirement of impelling leadership is that the leader should keep himself in the background. He should not express his own views; much less force them on the assistance. Impelling leadership requires much more humility, patience and spirit of self-denial. An impelling leader has to be big enough to let others have the praise, which truly belongs to him.

Lippit and White (1939) have classified leaders into three main types, namely;

(i) autocratic or authoritarian,

(ii) democratic, and

(iii) laissez-faire or free reign.

An autocratic leader is a one-man bank. He is fully convinced that he alone can run the organisation and that his subordinates are there merely to help him by doing what they are told. They should not, therefore, be permitted to act without his specific approval. In consequence, the special characteristics of such leaders are: -

(i) Retention of maximum power in his own hands,

(ii) Use of commands or direct emphatic orders covering minute details, and

(iii) Maintenance of close supervision.

The democratic leader realizes that his followers are indispensable for his success, so he wants to carry the group with him. His techniques of direction are calculated to evoke co-operation rather than mere obedience from the group. In making plans, in giving orders, in involving policies he wants to keep the group in the picture as far as possible. He regards himself as one member of the group and not as a superior entirely apart.

The laissez-faire type of leader is hardly a leader. He does not try to make his presence felt. He lets the group function more or less on its own. He does not administer, but leaves all responsibility and most of the work to his subordinates. He is a mere figurehead. At higher levels, if competent assistant is available, such a manager may be useful as an ornamental head. At lower levels, a laissez faire type of leader cannot be very successful. As he hardly gives any guidance and does not exercise any control over his subordinates, the subordinates just muddle on, virtually leaderless. In consequence, under free-rein management discipline is lax and efficiency at low ebb.

Thus, in autocracy the seat of responsibility is the leader, in democracy responsibility resides in the group and under laissez-faire management it is distributed among the members as individuals.

Stogdill (1948) studied leadership behaviour in numerous types of groups and situations by using Leadership Behaviour Description Questionnaire and two dimensions of leadership emerged—'consideration' and initiating structure'.

Consideration reflects friendship, warmth, mutual trust, respect in the group members. Consideration for ideas and feelings of subordinates is also there. Initiating Structure reflects the extent to which individuals are likely to refine and structure their roles and those of their subordinates towards goal attainment. He tries to establish well-defined patterns of organisation, channels of communication and methods of procedure.

3

Review of Related Literature

Introduction

A wide survey has been made in the area of Decision-making Styles of Heads of Schools, Organisational Health, Teacher Morale, and Leadership Behaviour of Heads of Schools. They are presented in the form of abstracts below.

Previous Studies

Studies on Decision-making

Casello, (2001) undertook "A Study of Site-based Decision-making Based on the Perspectives of the Participants".

One of the more favourable and popular strategies to emerge from the educational reform movement of the 1990's was the decentralisation of decision-making authority from the school district central office to individual school sites. Site-based Decision-making for control to be shared with central office personnel and the individual school site to give stakeholders, such as principals, teachers, teacher aides, parents, students and community members, more put into the decision-making process. Since specific school personnel are closest to the action, and most familiar to the day-to-day issues of the school, they are in a better position in many situations, to make a more productive, and effective decision, than a central office administrator.

The framework for this study was based on the identification of common characteristics found in the research that depict successful site-based decision-making elements, which help to affect behaviour in a productive way. The notion that shared decision-making among a professional faculty and staff, and its community can increase their level of commitment to work together to ultimately raise students' achievement. This study focused on the collaborative efforts that occurred in each Site Council, the steps and procedures the committees used to make decisions, and the perceptions of the participants as they saw themselves in the shared decision-making process. The purpose of this study was to examine the key elements, phases and products that resulted in a collaborative, shared decision-making environment that was introduced and implemented in two elementary schools by the schools' principal, the author of this study. The data collected was reported based on the perspectives of the individuals who participated in the shared decision-making committees from both schools. Data was collected through the use of surveys, interview/discussions with focus groups, and observations documented in a journal.

This study demonstrated the powerful impact site-based decision-making has on a group's behaviour. When teachers, administrators, parents and community members regularly work together to improve the learning environment for the children of their school, a desire to purpose excellence in education prevails. What is critical to the success of site-based decision-making is the level of communication that is necessary between the school, the principal and the central office, and when all parties possess a strong desire to communicate and relate to one another.

Site-based decision-making can be a powerful tool for a building level administrator. This research is presented and offered to all principals and other administrators who aspire to initiate a shared decision-making culture in their schools of district.

Dolan (2000) studied "Decisions of the Commissioner of Education of New York State on Residency".

The purpose of this study was to analyse all of the Commissioner of Education's decisions on residency rendered in the last forty years, with an eye on developing a better understanding of how these decisions are made and to codify the rules that they establish. In addition, this study examined the observable impact that these decisions have on school districts and on parents/guardians and students.

The study relied on a reading of every residency decision rendered, interviews with some of the major parties involved in making them, a review of pertinent regulations and laws that control this area of the law, an examination of the historical factors that account for the Commissioner's powers in New York State and further analysis of litigation in the courts that have challenged these rulings. Based on this research certain established policies can be identified. The result has been the discovery that these decisions contain an internal logic that consistently supports the interest of the state, with some notable exceptions in determinations dealing with homeless students and foster children. The courts on the state and federal level have supported the Commissioner's judgment.

Kiefer (2000) studied "Visible control: The art of district decision-making".

This study analysed district policy, curriculum and fiscal decision-making processes to ascertain whether factors present in schools that were successfully restructuring were evident in district level decisions. Successfully restructuring schools were characterised by strong principal leaders who involved the schools staff and community in ongoing decision-making processes focused on improving student performance. Utilising the site-based management literature base, the traits evident in successfully restructuring schools were used as a lens to observe district decision-making to understand the nature, patterns, and factors, which influence district decision-making. No attempt was made to evaluate the effectiveness of the district decisions.

Since successfully restructuring schools had a characteristic of wide participation, a high performing district that espoused broad involvement was studied using the conceptual model for successful school-based management by Wohlstetter, Kirk, Robertson, and Mohrman (1997). A descriptive qualitative case study of three district level decisions was conducted in a small suburban school district with one high school, one middle school and two elementary schools in the mid-west during the 1998-1999 school year. The scope of the study was limited to a selected set of policy, curriculum and fiscal district decisions. The study included thirty-three interviews, twenty-one meeting observations, and supporting documents.

District leaders in each decision had a clear idea of an acceptable decision outcome before the process began, shared the process carefully, and played a key influence role in shaping the decision during the deliberation process. While the level of involvement was strong for the majority of participants, the groups never fully integrated into a cohesive unit. The lack of group connectedness resulted in decisions, which refined, but did not alter the status quo. In the absence of fully functioning groups, influence exerted by the leader on the decision process can be used to achieve the leader's desired decision outcome.

Kildow (2000) undertook "A Case study of decision made by a school management team in the initial phase of Whole School Reform".

The purpose of this study was to identify the nature of the decisions made by a school management team in the early phases of whole school reform, and how these decisions impacted the reform process. There is a current mandate by the State of New Jersey to institute. Whole School Reform in an effort to overcome the disadvantages experienced by children in New Jersey's poorest urban school districts. A major component of Whole School Reform is the restructuring of the decision-making process as it relates to the local School Management Team. The nature of these decisions and their impact on the reform process is the basis for this single case study. This study determined what effect decision-making at the school level had on a school management team as it attempted to implement changes through whole school reform.

Qualitative interviews were conducted to collect data. A descriptive case study was conducted in which responses were coded according to recurring themes and patterns. These themes and patterns were observed and extracted so that generalisations regarding the decision-making process were able to emerge. Areas of importance included the governance structure of the school, the power relations and/or hidden agendas of participants, and leadership roles as they pertained to administration, staff, and parent/community members of the team. In the particular case studied here, the findings indicate that the team made decisions, which they felt, would be most beneficial to their specific circumstance. The decisions in which they felt most comfortable were those issues in which they had the most knowledge. Other issues arose that were consistent with the findings of other site-based management studies. Although the added responsibilities were at times overwhelming, the team worked towards resolving issues centered around team building, consensus and the new governance system.

O'Prey (1999): The purpose of the study is to compare middle school teachers perceptions, middle school assistant principals' perceptions, and middle school principals' perceptions of the assistant principal as an instructional leader. Assistant principals may not be venturing into instructional leadership because they see the principal as wanting them to fill a more traditional role.

A qualitative study design was used to describe how the perceptions of middle school teachers, middle school assistant principals, and middle school principals compare regarding the role those assistant principals should play regarding instructional leadership. A multiple case study approach focusing on ten middle schools was used to provide insight into perceptions of the assistant principal's role at each school. The schools were analysed individually, before the researcher compared for patterns across the schools.

The target population for this study were middle school teachers, assistant principals, and principals from ten schools in Regional Educational Service Centre in a Southwestern Metropolitan area. The sample drawn from the target population represents urban and suburban school districts.

A survey questionnaire of assistant principal's role/ functions was completed by the faculty assistant principal, and principal of each school. The assistant principal completed a time log, with associated codes, over a two-week period of school time. Structured interviews were carried out with both the principals and assistant principals, and observations made at the school site. Time logs and on-site observations allowed for triangulation of the interview data.

The findings showed that assistant principals are still spending the vast majority of their time on non-instructional tasks. Most of the principals and assistant principals surveyed wanted assistant principals to spend more time on instructional supervision and curriculum development.

There are a few instances where the school and districts have recognized the value of the assistant principal as an instructional leader. The types of skills that principals have in regard to the total school setting are not the same as what is reflected in many assistant principals daily "on the job" duties.

Ellen (1999): Site-based decision-making in Fort Worth, Texas—Analysis of variability within a single district.

Throughout our country, today, educators, policy makers, legislators, and researchers are all working with one goal in mind: the restructuring of schools to improve the education of our children. One of the most popular strategies currently used to pursue that goal is site-based decision-making (SBDM). The Council of Great City Schools reported in 1992 that 85 per cent of member school districts, including the largest school districts in the nations, have implemented some form of SBDM. Others have noted that SBDM has been adopted and implemented by school systems in every corner of the nation. Accompanying this tremendous investment is a significant variation in how SBDM is being designed and implemented. Variability arises from the empowering of different actors and the stressing of different components and strategies to varying degrees.

The purpose of this dissertation is to show that not only do these variations exist between different states and school districts, but even within a single school district. Furthermore, this work explores possible relationship between the decision-making style of schools and other school characteristics, namely student achievement, school size/age of the students the school serves, racial demographics of students and relative wealth of the students population.

At this time, significant research is being conducted to assess the relative impact and success of SBDM without acknowledgement of how it is structured, implemented or carried out on an individual basis. Ignoring the underlying SBDM structure, researchers have developed a body of work fraught with inconclusive and conflicting findings. Furthermore, understanding the variability within district is all the more important considering districts are usually the standard unit of measurement for analyses and unstated assumptions are made suggesting commonality throughout the district. This analysis of SBDM in Fort Worth expands upon current literature by extending the until of analysis to the individual school. It is through this level of detail that we will be able to more accurately assess SBDM.

Peters (1999) studied "Site-based decision-making: The Perceptions of Teachers and Administrators in Oakland County."

Site-based decision-making is a joint planning and problem solving process that seeks to improve the quality of work and the delivery of education in the school. Site-based decision-making is a process through which those individuals who are responsible for the implementation of a decision at the building level are actively and legitimately involved in making this decision. As such, it represents an approach to problems and issues. Specific programmes and policies are the outcomes of the site-based decision-making process. The process of site-based decision-making permits and even encourages change. This research attempted to determine, the perceptions of teachers and administrators toward site-based decision-making.

A non-experimental, descriptive research design was used to examine the perceptions of educators, including building principals, assistant principals, teachers, counsellors, librarians, and other staff members who were certified teachers; in eight Oakland Country school districts on shared decision-making as a primary factor in restructuring in their schools. These educators completed an original survey that measured two independent sub scales, knowledge of site-based management and authority, to determine perceptions of site-based management. In addition, a short demographic survey was included to provide a profile of the respondents.

Educators in Oakland Country schools were positive in regard to their perceptions of their knowledge of and authority associated with site-based management. Building-level administrators need to support the use of site-based management, allowing teachers and profession support staff to provide input into the decision-making process. While all groups were positive about the use of site-based management, principals had the highest mean scores indicating a more positive perception of this component of restructuring.

For restructuring efforts to be effective, all the staff members must be included, with these staff members willing to accept both the responsibility and authority associated with decision-making. Pervious research has supported the need for principals and teachers to work together collaboratively to promote effective learning and teaching in their schools. Sharing decisions regarding curriculum and instruction can promote a team concept that could lead to better student outcomes and relations with parents and community members.

Hopkin (1999) studied "Group decision support systems: An investigation of communication technology applied to the team planning process for technology integration in a private Saudi Arabian school."

This field study explores the effects of computer mediated Group Decision Support System (GDSS) on a decision-making process within the men and women's division of a sexually segregated private high school in Dhahran, Saudi Arabia. At the time of the study, the school is developing a three-year school wide plan for integrating advanced technologies into the schools existing curriculum.

Group deliberations are conducted, and decisions made using the GDSS software, CO-Motion, on purpose-build computer tables. Since legal and cultural prohibitions prevent men and women from coming into face-to-face contact, the networked tables are installed in two segregate conference rooms connected by Group Decision Support Systems, creating networked electronic communication environment. The GDSS software structures group participation (electronic and verbal conversations) around a group generated organising question dealing with technology integration plans. Team members, using their networked computers, identify goals or targets, as well as facilitating and inhibiting factors affecting those targets. The group members may anonymously add definitions, comments, and clarification, and finally vote on the identified issues.

The question that this study proposes to examine is: How does a computer mediated Group Decision Support System affect: (1) group participation levels? (2) The quality of communication? (3) Members' implementation of technology in decision-making practices?

Data collection is generated through GDSS group interaction and group dialogue. The verbalisations in the GDSS meetings are recorded on audio and videotape.

Retzlaff(1998) studied "The Perceptions of Leadership in Shared Decision-making Schools."

Shared decision-making in schools has been a focus of educational reform in the 1990s. Orginating in the 1960s, shared decision-making has continued its momentum as educators look at alternatives to the top-down, bureaucratic system of schooling. The 1960s and 1970s versions of shared decision-making were adopted to give political power to local communities, increase administrative efficiency, or offset state authority. In the 1980s and 1990s, the focus for shared decision-making sought to reform educational practice, to empower school staff, to create conditions in schools that facilitate improvement, innovation and continuous professional growth.

The potential for creating more effective learning environments for children emerges as the focus in the shared decision-making definitions. Transferring decision-making authority from state and district offices to individual schools provides principals, teachers, students, and parents greater control over the education process by giving them the responsibility for decisions about budget, personnel, and curriculum.

The principal plays a critical role in establishing and maintaining shared decision-making. The principal's new role in the shared decision-making process has shifted from the traditional authoritarian role, to the democratic leader, to the principal as facilitator. This facilitator role encompasses a leadership style that fosters empowered stakeholders, risk takers, team builders and ultimately collaborators for student achievement. Identifying the leadership skills and behaviours of principals in shared decision-making schools is a means of understanding the leaders in these school. How principal's skills and behaviours are two view points that can lead to further cognition of the shared decision-making principal's profile.

The research provides an analysis of the skills and behaviours of principals in shared decision-making schools as perceived by the principals and the principals' teaching staff. A relationship of perceptions is analyzed, along with an analysis of the significance of the demographic variables to the perceived principals' skills and behaviours.

The study survey represented 11 St. Louis Country elementary schools implementing shared decision-making. With over 50% participation, the respondents represents 187 teachers and 11 principals. The research reports that principals' and teachers' perceptions of the principals' skills and behaviours had no positive relation to the demographic variables, and there was no positive relationships of perceptions of the skills and behaivours that principals implementing shared decision-making possess.

A discouraging aspect of this research study was the very small listing of skills and behaviours exhibited by principals in shared decision-making schools, 6 out of 36, in the compared data of principals and teachers.

Geraghty (1997) studied "Site-based Decision-making in the Realm of Middle School Reform."

The purpose of this study was to identify the current level of implementation of site-based decision-making (SBDM) in middle schools in a large South-western urban school district. These middle schools were in the process of establishing elements of the middle school concept as defined by the district. Implementation of site-based decision-making had brought the responsibilities of daily decision-making and problem solving as well as the challenge of making decisions about middle school philosophy much closer to the classroom.

Implementation of SBDM in these middle schools had also brought an increase in the amount of teacher involvement in the deliberations that affected their lives in school. The primary purpose of SBDM may not be to improve student achievement but to improve the quality of life for the various staff that is responsible for improving student achievement. The instrument employed in this study measured the degrees to which teachers and staff perceived their actual and desired levels of participation in SBDM. It is necessary to measure growth and progress of SBDM for administrators to create a focus for future planning. The survey information indicated key areas of importance to school staff and served as a determinant of the climate in the district's exemplary middle schools. Administrators must delegate leadership roles and trust pedagogical expertise to teachers. The change in paradigms to transformational leadership allows for this empowerment of teachers and the possibility of SBDM to emerge. SBDM gives the decision-making community a sense of the ownership of innovation. Leadership practices potentially contribute to the outcomes to which schools aspire for students.

Teachers' actual and desired levels of participation in SBDM differed substantially on almost every item in each sub-scale of the survey instrument. Desire for more participation was indicated in the area of curriculum, instruction, goal setting, standards, staff development, and staffing. Less interest in participation was exhibited in budget management, evaluation, and making decision about staff development. Respondents did not consider their sites to be strong examples of the district's middle school concept.

Ganapathy (1982) "A Study of Decision-making Process in relation to Innovation and Change in Schools."

The objectives of the study were: (i) to find out decision-making process used by the headmasters of progressive schools in Coimbatore district, (ii) to find out the components of decision-making process, (iii) to find out communication patterns followed by decision-makers, (iv) to find out decision-making styles followed by decision-makers, and (v) to find out constraints for decision-making.

The sample consisted of thirty school headmasters and three teachers selected from each of the schools selected for the study. Using a list of innovations, a decision-making process questionnaire, a checklist of constraints for decision-making, an interview schedule and a decision-making style checklist collected data. The collected data were analysed by chi-square and t-test.

The major findings of the study were: (i) the headmasters followed a process while arriving at a decision. The decisions were not based on subjective judgment, (ii) The decision-making process took place at two levels. The first level was the individual level and the second level came into operation when the headmaster communicated his ideas of innovation and tried to get his ideas translated into action through the teachers, (iii) Very rarely an innovation was introduced for the sake of prestige, (iv) The headmaster sometimes consulted all teachers and other headmasters while analysing the felt need, (v) The headmasters clearly understood the disequilibrium and cause for it, (vi) The source of innovation was the headmaster's own thinking, (vii) The headmaster tentatively decided to introduce the innovation, if the evaluation was favourable, (viii) The headmaster followed three methods for evaluating the innovation these were observation, evaluation of consequences in meeting and informal enquiry, (ix) Fear of failure preconceived notions, disinterested staff were some of the constraints in implementing innovations.

Newton (1972) studied "The Relationship among Teachers' perceptions, of their Participation in Decision-making, Openness of Organisational Climate, and Organisational output in a sample of non-secondary Public Schools."

Public school teachers, like many other professionals, may face a conflict between their professional orientation and the bureaucratic structure of the organisations within which they work. One possible way of lessening this conflict is to involve teachers in the decision-making process within the school organisation. This study investigated the relationships among teachers' perceptions of their participation in decision-making, their perceptions of organisational climate, and their perceptions of organisational output. These relationships were investigated with respect to the perceptions of individual teachers within a school and with respect to the mean perceptions of 12 school faculties. Specifically the following six null hypotheses were tested:

(i) Within each school there is no correlation between individual teacher's perceptions of their participation in decision-making and their perceptions of the openness of the organisational climate.

(ii) Within each school there is no correlation between individual teacher's perceptions of their participation in decision-making and their perceptions of organisational output.

(iii) Within each school there is no correlation between individual teacher's perceptions of the openness of the organisational climate and their perceptions of organisational output.

(iv) There is no correlation between mean teacher perceptions of teacher participation in decision-making and mean teacher perceptions of the openness of organisational climate of the schools in the study.

(v) There is no correlation between mean teacher perceptions of teacher participation in decision-making and mean teacher perceptions of organisational output of the schools in the study.

(vi) There is no correlation between mean teacher perceptions of the openness of the organisational climate and the mean teacher perceptions of organisational output of each of the schools in the study.

Twelve school districts were chosen at random from the nine-county. Genesee Valley region of western New York State. A non-secondary school was randomly chosen in each of the districts. A non-secondary school was defined as a school whose students are in grade eight or below. The teachers in each of the 12 schools responded to three questionnaires: The Decision-making Questionnaire, the

Organisational Climate Description Questionnaire, and the Organisational Output Questionnaire. Scores from these questionnaires were used to test the six null hypotheses.

The chi-square test of combined probabilities was applied to test null hypotheses one, two, and three. These three hypotheses were rejected at less than the 0.001 level of significance. This indicated that within a given school there are significant relationships among individual teacher's perceptions of their participation in decision-making, their perceptions of organisational climate, and their perceptions of organisational output.

Null hypotheses four, five, and six could not be rejected at less than the .05 level of significance. This indicated that mean faculty perceptions of participation in decision-making, organisational climate, and organisational output were not significantly correlated, but it should be noted that computing mean perceptions appeared to mask the wide differences in perceptions found within each of the schools.

Further examination of the data indicated that three variables investigated in the study were related to a number of other organisational variables studied. The three variables were: the Disengagement subtest of the Organisational Climate Description Questionnaire, the Organisational health dimension of the Organisational Output Questionnaire, and the per cent of building-level decisions perceived as being made by teachers.

The results of the study also indicated that the Organisational Output Questionnaire provides a theoretically based conceptualisation of organisational output and a useful instrument for measuring perceptions of organisational output in non-secondary public schools.

Robert (1971) undertook "A Study of Relationships among faculty Morale, Philosophies of Human Nature of High School Principals, and Teachers' Perceived Participation in Educational Decision-making."

The major purpose of this study was to examine relationship among teachers' morale, principals' general beliefs about people, and teachers' perceived participation in educational decision-making, specifically, and the concerns of this study were to determine what relationships exist between:

(i) Teachers' perceived participation in decision-making and teacher morale;

(ii) Teachers' perceived participation in decision-making in the task areas of (a) curriculum, (b) pupil personnel, (c) business management, (d) staff personnel, and (e) school community relations and teacher morale;

(iii) The teachers' perceived participation in decision-making and general beliefs about human nature held by the high school principals of the particular schools to which those teachers are assigned;

(iv) Teachers morale and general beliefs about human nature held by the high school principals of the particular schools to which those teachers are assigned;

(v) Teachers' agreement/disagreement in their decision-making role and morale;

(vi) Teachers' perceived participation in decision-making and (a) age, (b) degree status, and (c) the size of the faculty in which they work.

Instrumentation and Procedure

Three instruments were used in data collection. The Philosophy of Human Nature Scale was used to assess principals' general beliefs about people. The Purdue Teacher Opinionative was administered to teachers to measure morale. Perceived and desired participation in educational decisions was measured from teacher responses secured by the Decision Point Analysis.

The sample consisted of a 50 per cent random sample of teachers and all of the principals from twenty-two high schools in one school district. The instruments, cover letter, and answer sheets were sent to assisting teachers in each of the twenty-two high schools. These teachers distributed, collected, and returned the research materials. 381 teachers completed the instruments, or 84.3 per cent of those sampled. All twenty-two principals responded to the Philosophy of Human Nature Scale. Raw data from the returned materials were punched into individual IBM cards for analysis by machine. The variables were dichotomised at the median scores in order to determine cell membership. Phi-coefficients were used for those hypotheses requiring a test of correlation between variables. Phi-coefficients were converted to chi-squares and significance was tested by reference to a chi-square table with one degree of freedom at the .05 confidence level.

In the minor hypotheses t-tests were used to determine if significant differences existed between means of different samples.

Conclusions

The evidence derived from analysis of the data supports the following conclusions that positive relationship exists between:

(i) Teachers' perceived participation in educational decision-making and teacher morale.

(ii) Teachers' perceived participation in curriculum decisions and teacher morale.

(iii) Teachers' perceived participation in business management decisions and teacher morale.

(iv) Teachers' perceived participation in staff personnel decisions and teacher morale.

(v) Teachers' perceived participation in school-community relations decisions and teacher morale.

Further analysis of the data indicates that no significant relationship exists between:

(i) Teachers' perceived participation in pupil personnel decisions and teacher morale.

(ii) Teaching staff's perceived participation in educational decision-making and principal's beliefs about human nature.

(iii) Teacher agreement with their perceived and desired decision-making roles and teacher morale

(iv) Principal's beliefs about human nature and the teaching staff's morale.

Analysis of the data related to the minor hypotheses supported the following conclusions:

(i) Older teachers do not perceive more participation in decision-making than do younger teachers.

(ii) Teachers with more formal educational preparation do not perceive more participation in educational decision-making than do teacher with less preparation.

(iii) Teachers within smaller faculties do not perceive more participation in educational decision-making than do teachers within large faculties.

Paul (1971) undertook "An Investigation of the Relationship between Principals' Decision-making Attitudes, Leader Behaviour and Teacher Grievances in Public Schools".

The purpose of this study was to determine whether principals' leader behaviour and attitudes about decision-making were related to the initiation of teacher grievances and principals' success in solving grievances. The two sub-problems examined were:

(i) Do principals in schools, which have had no grievances, differ from principals in schools with teacher grievances in respect to leader behaviour, attitudes about decision-making and selected demographic variables?

(ii) Was there a relationship among success in solving grievances, principals' leader behaviour and attitude about decision-making?

All contracts between Teachers' Associations and Boards of Education on file in the State Public Employees Relations Board were examined to determine the school district, which had accepted grievance procedures designating the principal as the individual who would decide the first appeal of a grievance.

Principals in those districts identified were asked to participate in the study. Principals in twenty-two schools with grievances and forty-three schools with no grievances agreed to participate. Of the forty-three schools, twenty-two were randomly selected and included in the sample.

In each of the forty-four schools in the sample, twelve randomly selected teachers were asked to answer the Leader Behaviour Description Questionnaire. The principals completed the Decision-Making Grid and provided information about the number of perceived difficulty of grievances filed in their schools. The data were complied and appropriate statistical tests were used to examine hypothesised relationships.

The findings of the study were:

(i) Principals in schools where no formal grievances had been filed had significantly higher mean consideration scores on the L.B.D.Q. than principals in schools with formal grievances.

(ii) There were no significant differences on the means of the L.B.D.Q. initiation of structure scores for the two groups of principals in the sample.

(iii) There were no significant differences between principals in schools with and without formal grievances on the four categories of leader behaviour as identified by the L.B.D.Q.

(iv) Principals in schools with no formal grievances did not differ significantly from principals in schools with grievances on the three decision-making styles as identified by the Decision-making Grid.

(v) Principals with different leadership styles did not differ significantly in their perceptions of the difficulty of teacher grievances, which were filed.

(vi) Principals with different leadership styles did not differ significantly in their success in solving grievances.

(vii) Principals with different styles of decision-making did not differ significantly in their success in solving grievances.

(viii) There were no significant differences between principals in schools with grievances and principals in schools with no grievances in regard to age, level of professional preparation, experience as a teacher or experience as a principal.

It was concluded that principals in the sample differed on one major dimension of leadership—consideration. Low consideration would seem to be an important factor in the initiation of grievances, but no definite evidence was found that suggested consideration was part of the principal's behaviour related to success in solving grievances. There were no differences on the initiation of structure scores, which seemed to indicate that consideration was a more important type of behaviour in relation to the initiation of teacher grievances than was initiation of structure.

It was theorised that a principal's desire to include teachers in the decision-making process and to use their ideas might be related to fewer grievances and more success in solving grievances. However, based upon the principals perceptions of his decision-making style, this was not supported by the findings of this study.

Roan (1971) studied "Decision-making as Perceived by Appointed and Elected School Superintendents in Florida."

The overall purpose of this study was to determine the decision-making processes as perceived by the school superintendents within the State of Florida for the academic year 1969-70. The study attempted to determine differences in decision-making in the five functional areas of school administration: business management, curriculum and instructional, pupil personnel, community relations, and staff management. Three aspects of decision-making were examined: first, differences as perceived between elected and appointed superintendents; secondly, differences according to size of the school system, and thirdly, differences and relationships between and among personal and situational variables of the superintendent and the school system in which he is employed.

Procedures

The information was gathered by use of a description of the superintendent's perception of his respective organisational structure as functioning for decision-making. All superintendents in the state of Florida were requested to participate in this study by letter and three sources of survey information.

(i) The latest biennial report compiled by the Florida State Department of Education was used to obtain information.

(ii) A personal Data Questionnaire developed and tested and designed for obtaining personal

information from superintendents. The writer relied on a study of similar types of questionnaires, advice of professionals and practising Florida school administrators both on the county and state level.

(iii) The Decision Point Analysis Research instrument originally developed in 1957 and continuously used and refined by researchers to identify functions essential in the development and support of an educational programme. It now consists of twenty-five decision items related to, and equally divided among, the five functional areas of business management, curriculum and instruction, pupil personnel, community relations and staff personnel. It also contains the titles of ten positions: business manager, principal, assistant principal, department head, special subject supervisor, director of instruction, guidance director, teacher, superintendent and board of education. The twenty-five decision items and ten positions recommend or influence the decisions, which provide information only and have nothing to do with making the decision.

Implications of the Findings

An analysis of the data contained implications for school administrators and researchers.

It has been shown that data about decision-making in the school system on all levels and modes can be obtained by use of various instruments.

(i) This research indicates that there are differences in types of amounts of involvement by various positions in the decision-making process.

(ii) In the area of functional administration between elected and appointed superintendents

there is considerable agreement in perception of decision-making. Only in the functional area of pupil personnel was there a significant difference.

(iii) Variations in decision-making practices within a school system may be used in self-evaluation of short and long-range objectives. More involvement within the framework of the school system of those who have shown a low profile in the decision processes should be considered. This may also include key school leaders in the community. This study reveals the importance of communication in school administration and the team concept of responsibility and authority.

Studies on Organisational Health

Snider (2000) studied "The Organisational Health of High School Departments and its Relationship to Departmental Effectiveness."

Educational decision-makers and researchers have long sought to identify the determinants of students' achievements and the overall effectiveness of schools. School health has been advanced as both a theoretical and practical explanation and empirical evidence is accumulating that this construct does have explanatory power. Healthy schools provide a necessary condition for meeting the instructional needs of goal achievement and adaptation and the expressive needs of integration and latency.

High schools are not monolithic structures, but rather they are characterised by decentralisation and specialisation. Given this reality, when one seeks to explain the role of the construct health in meeting the instructional and expressive needs, we should examine the role of the subject matter department. Subject matter departments are a ubiquitous feature of high schools in the United States. These departments are characterised by formidable social and psychological boundaries and are significant organisational structures within the school. It was hypothesised in this paper that healthier departments would have greater effectiveness and students achievement, The relationship between departmental health (as measured by a modified version of the Organisational Health Inventory) and departmental effectiveness (as measured by a modified version of the index of Perceived Organisational Effectiveness) was confirmed. However, the relationship of health to student achievement (as measured by Regents Comprehensive Examinations administered by New York State in content areas) was not confirmed. The results affirm a growing body of research on the importance of organisational health at all levels of education and suggest a need for further research on its effect on student achievement. The affirmation of the importance of establishing healthy organisations has practical importance for school administrators.

Holt (2000) studied "Relationship between the Organisational Health of Selected Public Schools in Texas and Strategies for Communicating with the Public."

The implementation of site-based management has required principals to involve more stakeholders with conflicting paradigms in decision-making, causing goal consensus to become more problematic in defining knowledge that reflects the values, commitments, and expectations of the entire community. Therefore, there is a need for principals to exhibit leadership in developing a positive organisational climate and communication strategies to strengthen public involvement in school reform in order to manage political pressures that may arise from activist groups. The purpose of this study was to determine if there is a relationship between the schools organisational health as perceived by the principals and the strategies utlilised by the schools to communicate with various stakeholders about school reform.

A survey containing 26 questions based on 5-point Likert rating scale was utilised 101 elementary principals responded to the survey from 26 school districts reflective of the varied demographics in the state of Texas. SPSS, a statistical package, was used to create, administer, and analyse the survey.

This study determined the degree to which principals perceived they utilised the following 12 indicators of organisational health: goal focus, communication, enterprise wholeness, power equalisation, human resource utilisation, cohesiveness/morale, innovativeness, diversity, autonomy, adaptation, accountability, and problem-solving. The scores for these indicators were totalled for each school, rank-ordered and divided into quartiles representing four levels of organisational health. Significant differences in relation to the degree or organisational health were exhibited between all groups.

This study determined the extent of the principals' utilisation of eight strategies to communicate with stakeholders about school reform. In addition, the study determined that there was a significant relationship between the schools' level of organisational health as perceived by the principals, and six of the eight communication strategies utilised by the schools, which included: involving stakeholders, understanding the community, informing the public about restructuring, establishing community allies, maintaining a relationship with the media, and dealing with opposition from activist groups. This study substantiated that the higher the level of organisational health, the more the principals perceived they utilised strategies for communication with stakeholders about school reform.

Bateman (1999) studied "Relationships Among Empowerment, Organisational Health, and Principal Effectiveness."

The purpose of this research was to analyse the difference between the levels of restructuring and organisational health in public high schools in Missouri. The level of restructuring for Relearning and Non-Relearning high school were based on survey responses of the high schools principals. The organisational health of those high schools was based on the survey responses from teachers.

The organisational health variables of institutional integrity, consideration, initiating structure, resource support, principal influence, morale and academic influence were tested.

High school principals responded to the Elements of Restructuring survey designed by Cawelti. Five teachers in each high school completed the Organisational Health Inventory designed by Hoy, Tarter and Kottkamp. Data from the surveys were analysed statistically using multivariate analysis of variance.

Hoy tested for differences in organisational health between Relearning high schools and non-Relearning high schools. Hoy tested for differences in organisational health among Relearning high schools and non-Relearning high schools, when those non-Relearning high schools were classified as low-level restructuring and high-level restructuring.

Non-Relearning high schools had significantly higher means than Relearning high schools on the variable of initiating structure. There were also sadistically significant differences on the variables of Initiating Structure, Resource Support and Academic Emphasis among the Relearning high schools, Low-level restructuring non-Relearning high schools, and High-level restructuring non-Relearning high schools, with the High-level restructuring non-Relearning schools having the highest mean scores on these variables.

The study is not an indictment of the Relearning efforts. It confirmed that the principals of these schools recognised a need for change and they turned to Relearning to provide the model for accomplishing change. In the early stages of change they were more like the non-Relearning schools that had not begun to make any changes. Schools involved in Relearning may be able to make some of the necessary changes given ample time to allow the organisational health to catch up with the administrative practices.

Finkelstein (1999) studied "The Effect of Organisational Health and Pupil Control Ideology on the Achievement and Alienation of High School Students."

One of the major challenges that public schools face is how to respond to the changing needs and interests of students. A greater understanding of the organisational dimensions that influence students achievement and alienation may allow teachers and administrators the opportunity to better control these variables.

These researchers focused on how two dimensions of school climate, Organisational Health and Pupil Control Ideology, affect a school's primary beneficiaries, the students. Further, the researcher sought to establish the usefulness of the dimensions as predictors of selected student outcomes.

The school was the unit of analysis in this study. The sample consisted of 41 New Jersey high schools. These schools represented a wide range of socio-economic status as well as rural, urban, and suburban areas. Data were collected from each faculty at a regularly scheduled faculty meetings or survey forms with instructions were placed in their mailboxes. The faculty members, selected at random filled out either the Organisational Health Inventory, Pupil Control Ideology form or the Student Control Ideology form, a revision of the PCI. Each of these instruments was designed to measure selected dimensions of school climate.

Descriptive statistics were calculated for all variables used in this study. Correlation Coefficients were computed for each measure of school climate with the indicators of student achievement and alienation. Further testing of variables was conducted using multiple regressions.

Eight hypotheses tested in this study. Three were supported by the data: Organisational Health is related to student achievement, Organisational Health and Pupil Control Ideology are related to student alienation and the discovery of an inverse relationship between Organisational Health and Pupil Control Ideology. As health rises, custodialism decreases. There was no relationship found between Pupil Control Ideology and student achievement, and Student Control Ideology did not correlate with either Pupil Control Ideology or Organisational Health.

Frueauff (1998) studied "Organisational Health and the Influences that Enable and Constrain the Development of Healthy Schools."

Educational leaders have been challenged in recent years to recognise the importance of organisational health for their school systems. The purpose of this study was to determine what enables and what constrains the development of healthy schools. Two widely divergent schools were selected from among five schools following an analysis of the Organisational Health Inventory that was administrated to teachers at those schools. The qualitative component of the study examined these two schools through open-ended interviews with 12 teachers at each school.

An analysis of these interviews identified enabling and constraining influences to the development of healthy schools. Further investigation of the interview data was used to ascertain the impact of the enablers and constraints on the institutional level, managerial level and technical level of the schools.

The school determined to be the most healthy exhibited the following enabling conditions: extensive support by parents and community; a strong system of communication within the school and outside the school; a welcoming school atmosphere; a supportive environment for staff; a proactive problem solving process; a collegial workplace; provision of adequate supplies and materials; a tone of trust, loyalty and commitment; an ability to influence superiors; and a focus on the academic purpose of the school. The school determined to be the least healthy exhibited conditions that inhibited or constrained the development of good health.

This study supports the powerful effect of the work atmosphere on teacher behaviour, as well as the distinctiveness and importance of utilising the organisational health construct in describing the school environment. This study also supports specific recommendations for principal actions that might improve the health of a school.

Watts (1997) studied "The Relationships of School Organisational Health and Teacher Commitment to Student Achievement in Selected West Virginia Elementary Schools".

This study was designed to access the relationships between school organisational health, teacher commitment, and student achievement as measured by third and sixth grade CTBS test scores. The purposes of the study were to determine whether relationships existed between school health and achievement, teacher commitment and achievement, and the combined variables of school health and teacher commitment and student achievement.

A sample of 504 teachers in 29 identified schools in four countries of south-western West Virginia was chosen. Each participant was provided a packet, which contained a cover letter, a sheet with five demographic questions, the Organisational Health Inventory for Elementary Schools (OHI-E), and the Organisational Commitment Questionnaire (OCQ). The return rate was 71%.

The data were analysed using regression analysis to determine if any significant relationships existed. The level of significance was set at $p<.05.$ The following findings resulted:

A statistically significant relationship was found between school health and achievement for sixth graders, but not for third graders. However, on subscales of the OHI-E, a significant relationship was found between collegial leadership and achievement at the third grade level and between academic emphasis and achievement at the sixth grade level.

No significant relationships existed between teacher commitment and student achievement at either grade level.

A significant relationship was established between the combined measures of health and commitment and achievement at the sixth grade level, but not at the third grade level.

The results of this study provided confirmation to the existing literature, which suggests the importance of school climate or health on student achievement. The results did not confirm some literature and the hypothesis of the study pertaining to a significant and positive relationship between teacher commitment and achievement.

The study concludes that the creation and maintenance of a healthy school climate, especially the presence of principal leadership that emphasises both consideration and task initiation and an academic climate that creates a press for achievement, will increase student achievement. While commitment and achievement were not significantly related in the study, further investigation is recommended. The study also found a strong relationship between SES and achievement in the identified schools.

Darji and Dongre, (1982) undertook "A Study of School Renewal with respect to Organisational Health."

The objectives of the study were: (i) to identify the leadership behaviour patterns of school principals of Baroda district and Baroda city, (ii) to identify the organisational climate types of the schools, (iii) to identify the nature of organisational health of the schools, and (iv) to look into the organisational health of the schools through the leadership behaviour patterns of principals and organisational climate of the schools.

The investigation was basically a survey type of study confined to the secondary schools of Baroda district. Necessary data were collected from twenty-five schools of Baroda city and twenty-five schools of Baroda district. The tools used in the study were the Leadership Behaviour Description Questionnaire developed by Halpin and Winer, the Organisational Climate Description Questionnaire of Halpin and Croft and the Organisational Health Description Questionnaire developed by the investigators.

The findings of the study were: (i) Among the schools studied, 44 per cent had principals manifesting HH pattern of leadership behaviour and 34 per cent had principals with LL pattern. (ii) Closed organisational climate was prevalent in 32 per cent schools, open climate in 19 per cent schools and autonomous climate in another 18 per cent schools. (iii) Open as well as closed climates were more in district schools than in city schools. (iv) The mean scores on various dimensions of organisational health ranged from 24 to 29. The highest scores were on goal focus, cohesiveness, problem solving adequacy, and the lowest scores were on communication adequacy and optimum power equalisation. From an organisational health point of view the picture was encouraging. (v) The teachers in district schools were more cohesive than those in the city schools. (vi) The schools with principals manifesting HL pattern of leadership behaviour were the best in goal focus, innovativeness and problem-solving adequacy. (vii) The schools with principals of HH pattern of leadership had the best innovativeness. (viii) The schools having principals manifesting LH pattern of leadership were poorer than the other schools. (ix) As one moved from openness to closedness, the mean scores on almost all the dimensions of organisational health decreased. The autonomous schools were the highest on goal focus and resource utilisation. (x) Communication adequacy was poor in the paternal and closed schools.

Sharma (1982) undertook "A Study of Management of Education System with Special reference to Decision-making and Organisational Health."

The main objectives of the investigation were:

(i) To study the management of a technological university with respect to governance, decisional participation of faculty members and organisational health.

(ii) To study the management of a technically oriented university with respect to three aspects.

(iii) To study the management of Indian Institute of Technology with respect to the three aspects.

(iv) To compare the three systems, namely Technological University, Technologically-oriented University, and Indian Institute of Technology, with respect to the three aspects.

(v) To study the relationship between the existing decisional participation of faculty members and organisational health.

(vi) To study the relationship between the expected decision participation and the organisational health.

(vii) To study the relationship between the existing decisional participation and the expected decisional participation.

The study was limited to Technical Educational Systems—Technological Universities, Technically-oriented Universities and five Indian Institutes of Technology. Final data for the study were collected from three situations one each belonging to the three categories. Sample for the study consisted of 400 Professors, Readers, and Lecturers, of whom 200 belonged to the Technological University. 70 to the technologically-oriented university, and 130 to the Indian Institute of Technology. The tools used for data collection were two instruments related to decision-making participation and questionnaire on organisational health all developed by the investigator. The data were analysed using percentage. Mean standard deviation t-test and product moment correlation also give organisational health questionnaire developed under the study was factor analysed.

The major findings of the investigation were:

(i) The three educational systems, namely technological university, technically-oriented university and Indian Institute of Technology, were different from the governance point of view. Technological university had syndicate as its top-most governing body. Technically-oriented University consisted of senate as the top-most body for governance though executive powers were with the syndicate. In the case of Indian Institute of Technology the top-most body for all the institutes was the IIT council with a Board of governors in each institute. In Technically-oriented University the governing body had got representation from staff, students and community members.

(ii) Existing decisional participation of the faculty members was less than the considerable participation for the three education systems studies.

(iii) In all the three educational systems faculty members wanted more participation in different situations.

(iv) There was significant difference between the existing and the expected decisional participation for all the three educational systems.

(v) Relationship between organisational health and existing decisional participation of the faculty members was significant.

(vi) There was no significant relationship between organisational health and expected decisional participation.

(vii) The existing decisional participation and the expected decisional participation were related with each other.

Factor analysis revealed that all the ten dimensions of the organisational health questionnaire were related with one another. Only one dominated factor was found out, which was named as organisational effectiveness.

Studies on Teacher Morale

Killum (1993) studied "The Relationship Among Principal Leadership, School Effectiveness, Teacher Morale, and Selected Demographic Variables in Secondary Schools with different Organisational Structures".

Fourteen schools, representing 82% of the population of secondary schools in a large metropolitan school district, were the units of analysis for this study. The schools were classified as having bureaucratic or loosely coupled structures relative to the organisational dimensions of goal consensus and horizontal and vertical communication. The results indicated that there were no significant differences in the characteristics of the two groups of schools in principals leadership, school effectiveness, teacher morale, and selected demographic variables. Eight schools in the sample were classified as loosely coupled and six schools were bureaucratic based on the images of the two organisational types described in the literature. However, a comparative analysis of the two groups indicated no significant differences in characteristics of principal leadership effectiveness, school effectiveness, teacher morale, and selected demographic variables.

Narulla (1986) made "An Analysis of Common Factors of Teacher Morale".

The objectives of the study were: (i) to identify through factor analysis of fundamental dimensions of teacher morale, and (ii) to devise and standardise a teacher morale inventory based on the dimensions discovered through factor analysis.

The fundamental dimensions of teacher morale were identified with the help of a hundred experts. For a preliminary draft of the inventory, a sample of 239 teachers was taken. The final form of the inventory was tried on 640 teachers. For reliability and validity a sample of 500 teachers was taken. The sample of teachers was taken from government and non-government recognised high/higher secondary schools of 12 districts of Haryana. The 18 dimensions identified for the teacher morale inventory were linked with areas like self-confidence in teaching, work-load in teaching and non-teaching, salary, facilities (academic and non-academic), relationship with colleagues, parents, headmasters and students, social status, discipline, co-curricular activities, and attitude towards the teaching profession. Based on these dimensions, 263 items were constructed. These items were scored on a three point scale ranging from 'strongly agree' to 'strongly disagree'. After the item analysis, 168 items were retained which were further subjected to factor analysis.

The study revealed: 1. After the factor analysis of the scores on the inventory five factors were extracted, viz., (a) morale based on teacher self-confidence, work-load and job satisfaction, (b) morale based on educational and social support, (c) morale based on human and social relationships among the staff, discipline and facilities for co-curricular activities, (d) morale based on service conditions and rapport with students and colleagues, (e) morale based on professional adjustment. The items were readjusted under these factors and a final form of the inventory was prepared which was standardised. 2. The characteristics of the inventory were: (a) It had 168 items divided into five areas (based on factor analysis); (b) The scoring was done on a three-point scale by giving a 3, 2 or 1 score to 'strongly agree', 'no opinion', and 'strongly disagree', respectively; (c) The test-retest reliability of the inventory was 0.97 for the whole inventory and for the five different dimensions of the inventory the reliability coefficient ranged from 0.12 to 0.97; (d) The inventory was validated for content, construct and factorial validity. The validation against the ratings of headmasters revealed a validity coefficient of 0.81 for the whole inventory. The validity coefficient for different dimensions ranged from 0.69 to 0.86; (e) Percentile norms were established for Haryana school teachers; (f) The teachers, on the basis of scores, were categorised into five categories. Those obtaining scores 454 and above were considered very good, those with a score ranged of 430 to 453 as good, and those with a score range of 416-429 as average, those with a score range of 404-415 as poor, and those with a score of 403 and below having very poor morale.

Pandey (1985) undertook "A Study of Leadership Behaviour of the Principal, Organisational Climate and Teacher Morale of the Secondary Schools".

The study aimed (i) to find out the relationship between the leadership behaviour of principals and the organisational climate of schools, (ii) to investigate the relationship between the leadership behaviour of principals and teacher morale, and (iii) to investigate the relationship between organisational climate and teacher morale. In order to attain these objectives, several hypotheses were formulated.

The study belonged to the category of descriptive survey of a correlational nature. The sample in this study included 34 secondary schools drawn from a population of 138 secondary schools of Allahabad district through the stratified random sampling technique. A total of 404 teachers of these schools participated in this study. A Hindi adaptation of Halpin and Winer's Leadership Behaviour Description Questionnaire, the School Organisational Climate Description Questionnaire by Motilal Sharma and the Teacher Morale Inventory (TMI) developed by the investigator herself were used for data collection. The Mann-Whitney U-test, chi-square with Yate's correction and Rank difference correlation coefficient with tied observations were the statistical techniques used to examine the hypotheses.

The major findings were:

(i) No significant difference was found between the leadership behaviour of rural and urban principals.

(ii) Rural schools were more open than those in urban areas.

(iii) A positive and significant relationship at 0.05 level was found between the initiating structure dimension of leadership behaviour and esprit, psycho-physical hindrance, controls, production emphasis and humanised thrust dimensions of organisational climate.

(iv) The consideration dimension of leader behaviour was found positively and significantly related to psycho-physical hindrance, controls and humanised thrust dimensions of organisational climate.

(v) Teacher morale was positively and significantly related to the initiating structure and consideration dimensions of leadership and controls, production emphasis and humanised thrust dimensions of organisational climate.

(vi) Chi-square value was found significant at 0.05 level between high vs. low teacher morale and open vs. closed climate.

Mahatma (1980) studied "Classroom Ethos and their Relationships with Teacher Behaviour Characteristics and Teacher Morale".

The major objectives of the study were:

(i) To make a survey of classroom ethos as perceived by the tenth grade students of Bikaner and Jodhpur ranges of Rajasthan,

(ii) To identify the characteristic patterns, ALP themes and educativeness of tenth grade actual and ideal classrooms,

(iii) To identify the actual and ideal ethos patterns of Hindi, social studies, mathematics and general science subjects,

(iv) To predict the educative life of different classrooms of tenth grade in the light of educational ethos,

(v) To find out the relationship between the A, L, and P scores and characteristics of the teachers classroom behaviour, and

(vi) To examine the relationship between the A, L, and P scores of classroom ethos and the different dimensions of the teacher's morale.

The study included 1,134 boys and 480 girls selected from schools belonging to five districts of Bikaner and Jodhpur ranges. Using Thelen's ALP Classroom Ethos Instrument, Teacher Behaviour Characteristics Scale, and Teacher Morale Inventory collected the data. The data were analysed by using descriptive statistics such as mean, standard deviation, and product moment correlation.

The major findings of the study were:

(i) Classrooms were generally characterised as personally supportive milieu, less interactive and less democratic in the real teaching-learning situations.

(ii) Students desired more autonomy for decision-making and interpersonal cooperation or support for effective group actions in the teaching-learning situations.

(iii) Three basic elements which emerged into a characteristic pattern of tenth grade actual classroom could be described as (a) the individually interpersonal meaningful quest for personal cognitive outcomes rather than emphasising on group achievement in the imposed formal group structure, (b) the teacher-defined learning directions for group actions, and (c) the apathetic attitude towards the reality orientation of societal ideological awareness which was not conducive to striking a balance between theory and practice during the teaching-learning process.

(iv) The classrooms of mathematics were generally characterised as a co-operative, supportive milieu interpersonally. The classrooms were oriented to the desired accomplishment of group tasks and the clarification of personal experience.

(v) The authenticity aspect of tenth grade actual classrooms was significantly related to autocratic-democratic, harsh-kindly, evading-responsible, etc., characteristics of the teachers' classroom behaviour.

(vi) An attempt was made to study the relationship between the A, L, and P ethos in general and the fourteen dimensions of the teacher's morale in general. Out of the 42 relationships tested only one between 'productivity' and 'material and equipment' dimension of the teacher's morale was significant.

Vyas (1980) studied "Factors Affecting Teacher Morale".

The major purpose of the study was to determine the factors affecting teachers' morale. The specific objectives were: to study the teachers' morale in relation to age, sex, material status, teaching experience, and qualifications and to study teachers' morale in relation to their self-concept, attitude and adjustment.

The sample for the study comprised 56 secondary schools selected on a stratified random basis from the 215 secondary schools of Baroda district. The tools for data collection were: the Teacher Morale Inventory by Dekhtawala, the Personality Word List by Pratibha Deo, the MTAI and the Adjustment Inventory of Bell. The Teacher Morale Inventory had five components, namely, individual characteristics, behavioural characteristics, group spirit, attitude towards the job and community investment. The statistical techniques used for data analysis were: the use of descriptive statistics, t-test, product moment coefficient of correlation, factor analysis by principal components axis using varimax rotation for factor interpretation.

The major findings of the study were:

(i) Teachers' morale was not related to their age or sex.

(ii) The two components of morale, group spirit and attitude towards the teaching job, were significantly different for teachers in the age groups 21 to 25, 31 to 35 and 36 to 40. In the case of community involvement, two age groups, 41 to 45 and above 45, differed significantly.

(iii) Marital status did not influence teachers' morale.

(iv) The teachers with less teaching experience had a higher level of morale than those with more experience.

(v) The postgraduate teachers had a significantly lower morale than the undergraduate. The trained graduates and the untrained postgraduates differed significantly in their morale. The trained postgraduate teachers had a higher morale than the untrained postgraduate teachers.

(vi) Teachers' morale and teachers' self-concept had no relationship.

(vii) Teachers' attitude and teacher morale were not significantly related.

(viii) Teachers' adjustment and teachers' morale were significantly related.

(ix) The scores on the teacher morale inventory. When factor analysed, yielded nine patterns.

Dekhtawala (1977) studied "Teacher Morale in Secondary Schools of Gujarat".

The important objectives of the study were:

(i) Construct and standardise a teacher morale inventory to measure morale of the secondary schools of Gujarat State;

(ii) To study the morale of teachers in schools of Gujarat in relation to various regions, areas, types of schools, size, and achievement of schools; and

(iii) To subject the results of the developed inventory to factor analysis.

A teacher morale inventory was standardised. The sample comprised 1220 secondary teachers. Means, standard deviations and to values were found out. The data were subjected to factor analysis by the principal's axis method.

The major findings of the study were:

(i) South Gujarat region possessed highest morale (362.19), whereas Kutch-Saurashtra manifested lowest morale (330.97).

(ii) There was significant relationship between teacher morale and achievement of students, but no significant relationship was found in relation to size of the schools, types of the schools, and area of the schools.

(iii) The male teachers, older teachers, and married teachers had higher morale than their counterparts. But no significant relationship was found between teacher's morale and teacher's experience.

(iv) Through factor analysis thirteen factors were extracted. They were: Teacher Characteristics and Leadership Behaviour, Teacher Feelings towards Teaching Profession, Teacher Cheerfulness, Group Cohesiveness, Rationality and Efficiency towards the Teaching Profession, Leadership Behaviour and Teaching Profession, Leadership Behaviour and Teaching Efficiency, Satisfaction with the School Climate, School Climate and Teacher Workload, Feelings towards the Institution, Community Support,

Teacher Zeal and Extra Effort, Satisfaction towards the Job, and Attitude towards the Job.

Franklin, I. (1975) undertook "A Study of Organisational Climate and Teacher Morale in Colleges of Education in Gujarat".

The specific objectives of the study were:

(i) To identify the types of climate of the colleges of education of Gujarat;

(ii) To investigate into the relationship between organisational climate of the colleges and morale of the teacher educators working in them;

(iii) To delineate the leadership behaviour patterns of college principals; and

(iv) To examine and assess the impact of variables of organisational climate, teacher morale and leadership of organisational climate, teacher morale and leadership behaviour on the effectiveness of teacher education programme at the B.Ed. level.

Three standardised instruments—the OCDQ (Halpin and Croft), the LBDQ (Halpin and Winer) and the PTO (Bentley)—were used besides a self-devised questionnaire on 'effectiveness of teacher education programme.' A proforma on personal data was also developed by the investigator to collect further data. Other data gathering techniques employed were participant and non-participant observation and interview. The data were collected from a sample of thirty-five colleges, which constituted 87.50 per cent of the population of the study. The respondents were 300 college teachers working in colleges of education. The statistical measures employed were contingency coefficient, coefficient of correlation by product moment method analysis of variance and t-test.

Some of the major findings of the study were as follows:

(i) The openness of climate in contrast to closedness of the climate did not lead to 'high' or 'low' effectiveness of the teacher education programme. However, the dimension Esprit' indicated a significant effect on the low side.

(ii) The teachers' rapport with the principal and the teacher educators the teachers, job satisfaction, the teacher's salary, the teacher educators' satisfaction with work load, the community support and pressure, and the curriculum issues had a significant and contributing effect making the teacher education programme less effective in the state of Gujarat.

(iii) There was no significant difference in morale of teacher educators with an urban background and those with rural background.

(iv) Morale of teacher educators was not significantly related to the number of years of teaching experience of the teacher educators.

(v) The background data of the teacher educators in colleges of education in Gujarat did not show any marked difference under the six climate categories, viz., the open, the autonomous, the controlled, the familiar, the paternal and the closed.

Shelat (1975) undertook "A Study of Organisational Climate, Teacher Morale and Pupil Motivation Towards Institution in Secondary Schools of Baroda District".

Major objectives of the study were:

(i) To measure and identify organisational climate, teacher morale and academic motivation of pupils;

(ii) To find out interrelationship between organisational climate and leadership behaviour, organisational climate and teacher morale, organisational climate and pupil motivation, organisational climate and pupil achievement at the S.S.C. Examination.

(iii) To find out interrelationship between teacher morale and pupil achievement, teacher morale and leadership behaviour, teacher morale and academic motivation of pupils; and

(iv) To examine the relationship between organisational climate and its correlates with reference to the location, size and effectiveness of schools.

The sample consisted of 100 high schools selected from the thirteen Talukas of Baroda district. Tools employed for the collection of data were the adapted Gujarati version of (i) the Organisational Climate Description Questionnaire by Halpin and Croft; (ii) the Leadership Behaviour Description Questionnaire by Halpin and Winer; (iii) the School Survey by Robert Coughalan; (iv) the Junior Index of Motivation by Jack Frymier; (v) Personal Data Sheet; and (vi) External Criteria Sheet.

Major findings of the study were:

(i) The organisational climate in rural schools was autonomous and paternal, whereas in urban schools, closed and open types were predominant.

(ii) Greater percentage of small size schools had open and autonomous climate as against greater percentage of large size schools having controlled and familiar climate.

(iii) Most of the high achievement schools had closed climate and low achievement schools had open climate.

(iv) Schools having closed climate had low teacher morale, whereas schools of open climate had high teacher morale.

(v) Open and autonomous climate contributed to boys' academic achievement, whereas controlled and familiar climate contributed to girls' academic achievement, and paternal climate contributed to the achievement of both boys and girls.

(vi) No relationship existed between the age of the teachers and school climate.

(vii) Leadership behaviour did not influence pupils' academic achievement.

Pillai (1974) studied "Organisational climate, Teacher Morale and School Quality".

The present study was planned to determine the extent to which the organisational climate of schools and faculty morale in the school were related to the quality of schools. The specific objectives were (i) to investigate the relationship climate and pupil performance; (ii) to investigate the relationship between organisational climate and invectiveness of schools; (iii) to investigate the relationship between faculty morale of school with the pupil performance; (iv) to investigate the relationship between faculty morale and the innovativeness of schools.

The sample consisted of 190 secondary schools, selected from Tamil Nadu State. The tool administered were: (i) the Organisational Climate Description Questionnaire of Halpin and Croft; (ii) the Bentley and Rempell's Purdue Teacher Opinionnaire; (iii) an inventory scale prepared by the investigator to assess the innovative ability of the school; and (iv) a questionnaire for demographic data and pupil performance data. Person product-moment correlation was used to analyse the data.

The major findings of the study were as follows:

(i) Performance of pupils was significantly better in open and autonomous climate schools than in schools of other climate types.

(ii) Performance of pupils in high morale school was superior to that of the average morale schools which in turn was better than the low morale schools.

(iii) The ability of the school to introduce innovation in educational practices was higher in high morale schools than the average or low morale schools.

(iv) Higher the faculty morale, quicker and better was the school introducing newer practices.

(v) Both climate and morale were positively and highly related to both criteria, namely, pupil performance and innovative ability of the schools.

(vi) Esprit, thrust, disengagement and hindrance were found to significantly influence the level of performance of pupils in schools.

(vii) Curricular issues, school facilities and services, community support of education, rapport among teachers, teacher salary, satisfaction with teaching, teacher rapport with principal, community pressures, teacher status and teacher load were found to contribute to pupils performance in schools.

(viii) The innovative ability of the school was significantly related to the three climates, namely, esprit, thrust and disengagement.

(ix) The four morale dimensions, namely, school facilities and services, curricular issues, teacher

salary and community pressures were found to influence the innovative ability of the schools.

(x) There was a high correlation between climate and morale.

Studies on Leadership Behaviour

Hennessey (2000) made "An analysis of Leadership Decisions in Implementing Middle School Standards Based on Foreign Language Programmes".

The purpose of this study was to analyse the decision-making process of school leaders in implementing standards in the foreign language programs at the middle school level. Based on the relevant literature, a conceptual framework for the study provided the contexts in which the decisions were made, namely, the development of standards driven state and district curriculum guides in the area of foreign languages, middle school philosophy and reform efforts, and foreign language programme models and theories. The inquiry about the leadership decision for the study focused on three areas: (1) to determine what decisions were being made in implementing the foreign language programme in the sample middle schools;(2) to determine what factors influenced the decision-making for foreign language programme reform at the school levels; and (3) to compare documents that guided the decisions for implementation of the standards driven foreign language programs.

To examine the elements of leadership decision-making, a qualitative, cross-case study was conducted. The comparison of documents and the use of oral interviews of educational leaders and foreign language teachers provided sufficient data to analyse what and how decisions were being made in a large, urban school district in Georgia. The finding indicated that the decisions were influenced by the development of the state curriculum guide called the Georgia Quality Core Curriculum, and that leaders were involved in decision-making with the collaboration of the district foreign language coordinator and the school foreign language teachers.

Considering the complexity of the decision-making process and the role leaders played in varied relationship among constituencies, the conclusions of the study disclosed the following results of leadership decision-making for foreign language programs in this school district: (1) The decisions were made basically through the collaboration of the district level foreign language coordinators and the middle school foreign language teachers. (2) Foreign language programs aligned with district, state, and national standards. (3) The influence of the broader context and characteristics of middle school curriculum helped shape the foreign language middle school programs. The designation of a school based instructional leader to ensure that standards were infact being implemented into the classroom practices was needed.

Lin (1999) undertook "A Study of Principal's Leadership Style and School Effectiveness in Selected Secondary Schools in New Jersey."

This study attempted to investigate the principal's leadership style, leadership flexibility, and leadership effectiveness as identified by LBA II Self, an instrument developed by Blanchard Training and Development Incorporated, and to determine their correlation with school effectiveness as measured by student's academic achievement in HSPT, SAT, graduation rate, and post-graduation plans in selected public secondary schools in New Jersey.

This research project also included the socio-economic status of the school and school size to study the principal's leader behaviour patterns, school effectiveness, and their inter-relationship.

The research findings based on the results of Pearson correlation co-efficient, chi-square, t-test, and ANOVA suggested that the principal's leadership did not have a significant correlation with school effectiveness as measured by student's academic achievement. Moreover, the principal's leadership style, leadership effectiveness, and leadership flexibility were independent of the socio-economic status of the school or school size. A highly significant correlation was found between the socio-economic status of the school and student's academic achievement in SAT (r=.7592, p<.001) HSPT (r=.706, p<.001), and post-graduation plans (r=.7144, p<. 001). The school size had some negative effect on students' academic performance in SAT (r=-.3772, p<.017), HSPT (r=-.4137, p<.007), and post-graduation plans (r=-.3679, p<. 017), but not on graduation rate (r=-.3479, p<.204).

Stringham (1999) undertook "A Study of Leadership Styles of Principals and the Organisational Climate in Successful Public Secondary Schools in New Jersey."

This study analysed the preferred leadership styles of principals in successful public high schools in New Jersey and the organisational climates found in these public schools. In addition, this study examined the relationship between the preferred leadership styles of principals in successful public high schools in New Jersey and the characteristic traits of transformational leadership. The staff and principals of eight New Jersey high schools that were awarded the United States Department of Education's Blue Ribbon Award were surveyed using two quantitative instruments. The first survey, called the Organisational Climate Description Questionnaire-Revised for Secondary Schools (OCDQ-RS) developed by Halpin and Croft (1963) and later revised by Hoy and Tarter (1997), presents an in-depth analysis of teachers' perceptions of the organisational climates found in their schools. The thirty-four item climate instrument measures five dimensions: (1) supportive principals, (2) directive principals, (3) engaged teacher behaviour, (4) frustrated teacher behaviour, and (5) intimate teacher behaviour. This instrument also measures openness of school climate. The second quantitative instrument called the Leadership Assessment Inventory (LAI) created by Burke (1994) contains eighteen pairs of statements. The LAI identifies transformational leadership and transactional leadership styles. The dimensions of the LAI are: (1) determining direction, (2) influencing followers, (3) establishing purpose, (4) inspiring followers, and (5) making things happen. The results indicated a relationship between school climate, transformational leadership, and successful public high schools in New Jersey.

Morrison (1999) undertook "An Investigation of Leadership Practices Demonstrated by two Women Principals Identified by their Supervisors as Risk Takers in one North Carolina County".

The purpose of this study was to investigate the leadership practices of two successful women principals identified as risk-takers by their supervisors. The investigation sought to understand the characteristics and practices of principals willing to take risks in schools and how these practices influence school culture. As a result of the investigation, a preliminary risk-taking framework was developed. Through the development of two case studies, the study was designed to reveal whether or not the principals identified as risk-takers engage in practices which "make a difference" in their schools and the lives of children.

Qualitative research methodology was used to investigate the two women principals. Six women principals, identified as risk-takers by their supervisors, were initially interviewed by the researcher. Upon analysing this data and the results of risk attitudes inventory each principal was administered, the sample was narrowed to two principals for further study. In the development of the case studies, multiple data sources were utilised, providing triangulation. In addition to interviewing each principal twice, asking about their risk-taking practices and school cultures, parents and teachers were interviewed and asked to describe their principal's risk-taking practices and the culture of their respective schools. The investigation also included observations and document reviews for each school.

Several themes emerged from the data, which confirmed that these two principals are indeed taking risks which "make a difference" in their schools. The data revealed that both principals have a strong sense of purpose that influences their respective school cultures. Both principals are straightforward in communicating to all stakeholders and the community that schools are for developing children and that we must do "whatever it takes" to assure their development. In addition, both principals exhibit a bias toward action and risk-taking. These principals and their schools write grants, explore and implement new programs, and continually seek innovative ways to secure the resources and knowledge necessary to support the development of children. Both principals speak of the importance of community in supporting and developing children, and their schools are recognised as successful School Development Programme (Comer) schools. Through practice and words, these principals communicate the power we have in schools to "make a difference" in the lives of children.

Patel (1983) undertook "A Study of the Leadership Behaviour of Principals of Higher Secondary Schools of Gujarat State".

The major objectives of the study were: (i) to identify leadership behaviour patterns of principals of higher secondary schools of Gujarat State as perceived by principals and teachers in reality and according to their ideals, (ii) to identify the organisational climate of the schools, (iii) to measure professional development status of the teachers working in these schools, and (iv) to study the interrelationship among leadership beahviour of the principals, organisational climates of schools and professional development of teachers.

This was, by and large, a survey type of study. One hundred higher secondary schools were selected out of 949 higher secondary schools on the basis of stratified random sampling. The investigation was based on the responses of 1000 higher secondary school teachers and 100 principals. LBDQ developed by Halpin and Winer, OCDQ developed by Helpin and Croft, a Professional Development Inventory (controlled and open response type) and a personal data sheet for principals were used as tools for collecting the data. T-test and correlation techniques were used to draw conclusions.

The major findings were (i) There was a positive relationship between the two dimensions of leadership behaviour of the school principal, viz., initiating structure and consideration. (ii) The principals of the schools manifested mostly the high consideration (HH) and low consideration (LL) pattern of leadership behaviour leaving middle positions sufficiently vacant. (iii) The HH pattern of leadership behaviour was associated with open, autonomous and controlled climates; the LL pattern of leadership behaviour was associated with closed climates. (iv) Morale of teachers increased when the actual leadership behaviour of the leader approximated the desired behaviour as perceived by teachers. (v) Significant mean differences were found between leaders; self-perception and faculty perception of his actual leadership behaviour. (vi) Male and female principals perceived their own leadership behaviour is being significantly different on the 'consideration' dimension. (vii) No significant differences were found between male and female administrators as perceived by teachers and by themselves on 'initiating structure' and 'consideration'. (viii) The principal's effectiveness was a significant predictor of organisational climate. (ix) The professional development of teachers of higher secondary schools was quite encouraging because on no dimensions was the score less than sixty per cent. (x) The schools showed a tendency towards being closed rather than open. (xi) The teachers scored highest on professional development under the leadership of principals manifesting the HL pattern of leadership behaviour in contrast to teachers working under the leadership of principals manifesting the LL pattern. (xii) The teachers working in schools where a paternal climate prevailed scored highest on their professional development and lowest in schools with familiar climate. (xiii) The rural-urban dimension did not play any significant role in case of any of the dimensions of leadership behaviour. (xiv) Professional qualifications of principals did not play any significant role in the professional development of teachers and in shaping the climate of the schools. (xv) Professional qualities significantly correlated with values, attitudes and motivation and negatively correlated with 'condition'.

(xvi) Esprit significantly correlated with 'intimacy', 'thrust' and 'aloofness'. (xvii) Aloofness significantly correlated with 'production emphasis' and 'thrust'.

Naik (1982) made "An Inquiry into the Relationship between Leadership Behaviour of Secondary School Headmasters and Teacher Morale."

The objectives of the investigation were: (i) to study the leadership behaviour of the headmasters of the secondary schools of South Gujarat, (ii) to study the morale of the teachers of the secondary schools of South Gujarat, (iii) to examine the relationship between different dimensions of leadership behaviour of the headmasters and different dimensions of the teachers' morale, (iv) to find out the relationship between the leadership behaviour of the headmasters and the area, sex, size and management of the school, and (v) to study the relationship between the teachers' morale and the area, sex, size and management of the school.

The sample for the study consisted of 100 schools drawn from the five educational districts of South Gujarat. The sample included all types of schools, viz., boys', girls', urban, rural, large, small, government and private. Using Leadership Behaviour Descriptive Questionnaire (LBDQ) and Teacher Morale Inventory the data were collected. Coefficients of correlation were computed between twelve dimensions of leadership behaviour and fourteen dimensions of teachers' morale. Relationship between leadership behaviour, teachers' morale and certain biographical variables were studied by analysing the collected data using univariate analysing of variance.

The major findings of the investigation were: (i) There was significant and positive relationship between building facilities, evaluation of students, special services, supervisory relations and colleague relations. (ii) Integration (leadership behaviour dimension) was significantly related to material and equipment, special services and to supervisory relationships. (iii) There was no significant relationship between the twelve dimensions of LBDQ and the experience of the headmaster. (iv) Teachers' morale had no significant relationship with the type of school, area of the school, and size of the school. (v) LBDQ had no significant relationship with the type of school, area of the school, and size of the school.

Gupta (1978) studied "Leadership Behaviour of Secondary School Headmasters in Relation to their Personality and the Climate of their Schools".

The major objectives of study were: (i) to identify and classify the organisation climate of the secondary schools of Rajasthan; (ii) to study the leadership behaviour dimensions of the headmasters of secondary schools in Rajasthan having different types of school climates; (iii) to study the personality factors of the headmasters of schools having different types of school climates, and (iv) to examine the dimensions of leadership behaviour and the factors of personality of secondary school headmasters which may be used as predictors of the school climate.

Using stratified two stages random sampling technique drew a sample of hundred secondary schools from Rajasthan State. The Sharma's School Organisational Climate Description Questionnaire, the Stogdil's Leadership Behaviour Description Questionnaire (LBDQ) and 16 PF Test From A of Cattell and Eber (standardised for Indian adults by S.D. Kapoor, 1962) were used as tools for data collection. Correlation, chi-square, Kolmogorov Smirnov two sample tests, analysis of variance and Scheffe's test were used for the analysis of data.

The major findings of the study were as follows: (i) Out of the 100 schools, 15, 15, 14, 20, 26, and 10 schools were perceived by their respective staff as open, autonomous, familiar, controlled, paternal, and closed, respectively. (ii)Headmasters of different climate type schools were found to differ significantly on eight dimensions of LBDQ, viz., 'Demand Reconciliation', Tolerance of Uncertainty', 'Initiation of Structure', 'Tolerance of Freedom', 'Role-Assumption'. 'Consideration', 'Production-Emphasis', and

'Superior-Orientation'. (iii) 'Tolerance of Uncertainty' mean score was reported highest for headmasters of 'Paternal' type climate schools and lowest for the 'Closed' climate type schools. (iv) Headmasters of 'Open' climate type schools scored highest 'Integration' mean score, whereas the same was lowest in case of 'Closed' climate type schools. (v) There were significant positive relationships between school climate and all the different dimensions of LBDQ. (vi) There were no significant relationship between school climate and factors A,C,E,H,N,O,Q_1,Q_3, and Q_4 of 16 PF. (vii) The following predictor variables for predicting the school climate were located: (a) Consideration (leadership behaviour dimension), (b) Predictive-Accuracy (leadership behaviour dimension), (c) Expedient vs. Conscientious (personality factor), (d) Tough-minded vs. Tender-minded (personality factor), (e) Practical vs. Imaginative (personality factor), and (f) Group-dependent vs. Self-sufficient (personality factor).

Singh (1978) undertook "A study of Leadership Behaviour of Heads of Secondary Schools in Haryana and its Correlates".

The study proposed: (i) to investigate into the leadership behaviour of the school headmasters in Haryana as described by their teachers, and to compare their leadership behaviour with some other professional leaders; and (ii) to explore the relationship of variable such as personality factors, sex, age, teaching and administrative experience with leadership.

From each of the ten districts of Haryana State, ten schools were selected. Five teachers from each of these 100 schools were selected. Thus 100 heads as perceived by their 500 teachers were included in the study. The sample for the professional leaders consisted of seven factory managers as perceived by their twenty-eight factory superintendents, seven army officers as perceived by twenty-eight junior commissioned officers, seven college principals as perceived by their twenty-eight lecturers, and seven municipal committee presidents as perceived by twenty-eight municipal committee members. The

Leadership Behaviour Description Questionnaire and the Cattell's 16PF Inventory were used to collect data.

It was found that (i) out of five professional leaders, headmasters occupied the third position on the leadership scale; (ii) total leadership was significantly related to the four personality factors, viz., outgoingness, intelligence, emotional stability, and assertiveness; (iii) the leadership behaviour of the heads was not related to sex, except on 'integration' in which women heads exceeded men heads; (iv) the leadership behaviour of heads was not related to their age between twenty-five and sixty-two years; (v) total leadership behaviour of heads was not related to their teaching experience between six and thirty-five years; and (vii) the leadership behaviour of heads was not significantly related to their administrative experience.

Darji (1975) undertook "A Study of Leadership Behaviour and its Correlates in the Secondary Schools of Panchmahals District".

The study was undertaken with a view to (i) identifying the leadership behaviour patterns of principals of sampled schools of the selected district; (ii) identifying the organisational climate of the sampled schools; (iii) measuring teacher morale in the sampled schools; (iv) studying interrelationship among leadership behaviour of the principals of secondary schools, organisational climate, teacher morale, innovativeness of the school, and motivation of pupils towards the schools and ultimately building up a picture of the achievement of the pupils in terms of the S.S.C. Examination results; (v) measuring academic motivation of pupils of the sampled schools; and (vi) studying the significance of relationship between each of the two dimensions of leadership behaviour, namely, 'initiating structure' and 'condition' with (a) the nature of management of the school, (b) location of the school, (c) size of the school, (d) sex type classification of the school, (e) academic status of the school, (f) socio-economic status of the school, (g) innovativeness of the school, (h) age of the principal, (i) sex of the principal, (j) experience of the principal as a principal, (k) leadership behaviour patterns of the principal, (l) teacher morale, (m) organisational climate of the school, and (n) motivation of pupils towards their schools.

The necessary data were collected from 400 teachers and 1000 pupils of 100 schools selected on stratified bases from the Panchmahals District. The tools used were: (i) the Leadership Behaviour Description Questionnaire (LBDQ), (ii) the Organisational Climate Description Questionnaire (OCDQ), (iii) the tool for measuring Teacher Morale by Robert Coughlan (School Survey), (v) the Innovativeness Scale prepared by Doctor, and (v) the Junior Index of Motivation (JIM) Scale.

It was found that (i) the leadership behaviour dimensions and patterns were critical indicators of organisational climate, staff morale, academic motivation, school innovativeness and academic status; (ii) the percentage of principals manifesting the HH pattern of leadership behaviour was the highest (forty-nine per cent); (iii) all the principals of the open climate schools manifested the HH leadership behaviour pattern; (iv) the percentage of the principals manifesting the HH pattern went on decreasing from high morale schools to low morale schools; (v) there was no direct relationship between pupil motivation and the leadership behaviour of the principals; (vi) most of the schools having 'high innovativeness' had principals who manifested the HH and the HL leadership behaviour patterns; (vii) most of the schools of high academic status had principals with HH leadership behaviour pattern, and (viii) the leadership behaviour dimensions and patterns were found to be significant in relation to variables of climate, morale, and innovativeness but not in relation to pupil motivation towards schools and academic status of schools.

Cornell (1972) studied the "Relationship between Negotiation Function and Leadership Behaviour of Superintendents of School Districts in the State of New Jersey."

This investigation sought to determine and compare the school superintendent's negotiation function as stated by school superintendents and the leadership behaviour of the superintendent as perceived by school board presidents and teacher association presidents in school districts in the State of New Jersey in 1971. In addition, the investigation sought to ascertain the relationship between the perceived leadership behaviour and the negotiation function of the superintendent and each of the three variables: (1) district size; (2) experience as a superintendent; and (3) negotiation experience.

The sample for this study consisted of a superintendent, a school board member and a teacher association president in two hundred selected school districts in the State of New Jersey. Responses, considered valid, were received from 194 superintendents, 136 school board presidents and 159 teacher association presidents. The major materials used to collect data for this study were the Leadership Behaviour Description Questionnaire and the Negotiation Function Questionnaire. Questionnaires were returned from 81.5 per cent of the total population samples selected for the study.

The statistical techniques employed in the analysis of the study included mean, standard deviations, percentages, t-test for independent samples, chi-square technique and analysis of variance.

Findings and conclusions: Analysis of the data led the investigator to the following findings and conclusions.

Superintendents were perceived by school board presidents as engaged in leadership behaviour relating to the dimensions of initiating structure and consideration significantly more frequently than teacher association presidents. It was concluded that specific action on the part of superintendents was necessary if they were to strengthen the leadership behaviour perceptions of the teacher group. Further, superintendents should be as visible to their staff as they are to the school board or any community group.

The study revealed that superintendents have successfully developed skills in sensitivity, communication, empathy, motivation and goal involvement in their relationships with school boards, but have not exhibited the same success with professional staff.

Superintendents' responses revealed a lack of consensus as to a singular negotiating position. The functions of non-participant negotiator for the board and consultant to teachers were perceived as least acceptable to superintendents in this study.

The investigation revealed that the superintendent's negotiation function had little effect on the dimension of initiating structure yet, it was revealed that the superintendents' negotiation function affected the respondents' perceptions for the dimension of consideration especially in the areas of employment and salary. It was concluded that situational factors, peculiar to any given school district would be the best determinants of the superintendent's negotiation function in all areas except those consisting of monetary, welfare or bilateral decision-making considerations. In those areas the function of either dominant third party or team member seemed to enhance leadership perceptions most consistently. It was further noted that the function of consultant to the board was least favourable to the leadership dimension scores of superintendents. Support for the middleman role was not evident in this investigation.

Relationships between negotiation function and leadership behaviour were not significant. It was concluded that superintendents were relatively free to select a position in negotiations as their particular situation demanded.

Significant relationships did exist between the superintendents' negotiation functions and the variable of district size. The variables of experience as a superintendent and negotiation experience had almost no effect on the negotiation function of superintendents.

The possibility that factors such as size of administrative staff, school financial status or academic training, peculiar to the superintendent's role of a particular school district, led the investigator to conclude that an in-depth investigation of these possibilities was necessary.

CONCLUSION

There are very few studies conducted in India relating decision-making with organisational health, teacher morale and leadership behaviour.

The present study makes an earnest attempt to study the relationship between decision-making, organisational health, teacher morale and leadership behaviour.

The succeeding chapter spells out the details of the research procedure.

4

Research Procedure

INTRODUCTION

This chapter signifies the methodological framework of the study, which consists of the following aspects:

(i) Method of the Study

(ii) Population and Sample of the Study

(iii) Hypotheses

(iv) Tools and Techniques Used

(v) Data Collection

(vi) Statistical Techniques Used

(vii) Method of Analysis and Interpretation

Each of the above aspects are briefly described below:

METHOD OF THE STUDY

Present study involved a descriptive survey (expost facto) method of research.

POPULATION AND SAMPLE OF THE STUDY

The data required for the present study is collected from the Heads of Schools and Assistant Teachers of Secondary Schools working in Dharwad Taluka. The population and sample of the study is presented in the following Table.

Karnataka State has 27 districts. Out of these 27 districts Dharwad district is known for academic activities

Table 4.1: Population and Sample of the Study

Sl. No.	*Name of the School*	*Total Number of Head Masters*	*Respondent Heads of Schools*		*Respondent Assistant Teachers*		*Total Respondent Assistant Teachers*
			Male	*Female*	*Male*	*Female*	
1	*2*	*3*	*4*	*5*	*6*	*7*	*8*
1.	Govt. High School, Navalur	1	1		3	2	5
2.	Govt. High School, Karadigudda	1		1	3	2	5
3.	Govt. High School, Narendra	1		1	5	-	5
4.	Govt. High School, Kotur	1		1	3	2	5
5.	Govt. High School, Tadakod	1	1		-	5	5
6.	Govt. High School, Yarikoppa	1	1		3	2	5
7.	Govt. High School, Yadwad	1	1		3	2	5
8.	Govt. High School, Devarahubballi	1	1		3	2	5
9.	Urdu Govt. High School, Dharwad	1	1		3	2	5
10.	Govt. High School, Dharwad	1		1	3	2	5
11.	U.P.S. Dharwad	1		1	5	-	5
12.	Aadarsha Balika High School, Dharwad	1	1		2	3	5
13.	Presentation High School, Dharwad	1		1	3	2	5
14.	Aalur Ventakaraman, High School, Dharwad	1	1		3	2	5

1	*2*	*3*	*4*	*5*	*6*	*7*	*8*
15.	Mrutunjaya High School, Dharwad	1	1		3	2	5
16.	Basel Mission Jr. College, Dharwad	1	1		2	3	5
17.	Vidyaranya High School, Dharwad	1		1	3	2	5
18.	K.E. Board High School, Dharwad	1	1		3	2	5
19.	K.N.K. Girls High School, Dharwad	1	1		4	1	5
20.	Karnataka High School, Dharwad	1	1		3	2	5
21.	Basel Mission Girls High School, Dharwad	1		1	3	2	5
22.	Jayadevitai Ligade High School, Dharwad	1	1		3	2	5
23.	Sharadha Girls High School, Dharwad	1		1	1	4	5
24.	RIS High School, Dharwad	1	1		3	2	5
25.	Bharat High School, Dharwad	1	1		3	2	5
26.	Anjuman High School, Dharwad	1	1		5	-	5
27.	Vanita High School, Dharwad	1	1		2	3	5
28.	St. Joseph English High School, Dharwad	1	1		5	-	5
29.	New High School, Dharwad	1	1		4	1	5

Table 4.1: Contd...

1	*2*	*3*	*4*	*5*	*6*	*7*	*8*
30.	Budharakkitha High School, Dharwad	1		1	2	3	5
31.	Nehru High School, Hebballi	1	1		5	-	5
32.	SGM, High School, Garag	1	1		5	-	5
33.	SGV High School, Uppinabetageri	1	1		3	2	5
34.	SS High School, Somapur	1	1		3	2	5
35.	S.S. High School, Nigadi	1	1		4	1	5
36.	M.G. High School, Mugad	1	1		3	2	5
37.	New High School, Tegur	1		1	3	2	5
38.	S.S. High School, Amminabhavi	1	1		3	2	5
39.	S.S.T. High School, Alnavar	1	1		2	3	5
40.	Urdu High School, Uppinabetageri	1	1		5	-	5
41.	Urdu High School, Alnavar	1	1		4	1	5
42.	S.S.T. Girls High School, Alnavar	1		1	2	3	5
43.	Channabasaveshwar High School, Dharwad	1	1		5		5

1	*2*	*3*	*4*	*5*	*6*	*7*	*8*
44.	Basel Mission English High School, Dharwad	1		1	2	3	5
45.	Sarasaganga High School, Dharwad	1		1	3	2	5
46.	Jayakiriti High School, Garag	1	1		5	-	5
47.	Prabhudeva High School, Honnapur	1	1		3	2	5
48.	S.D.N. High School, Managundi	1	1		3	2	5
49.	St. Theresa High School, Alnavar	1		1	-	5	5
50.	A.E.S. High School, Alnavar	1	1		3	2	5
51.	Jai Hind High School, Dharwad	1		1	5	-	5
52.	KPES High School, Dharwad	1	1		-	5	5
53.	Maruti High School, Dharwad	1		1	4	1	5
54.	Pavan English High School, Dharwad	1	1		3	2	5
	Total	54	54				270

and educational institutions. Dharwad district has 5 talukas, from among these talukas Dharwad taluka was selected as the locale of the study. Finally the data was collected from 54 heads of schools and 270 assistant teachers. From each school five teachers were selected. All the Heads of schools of 54 schools were involved in the study.

HYPOTHESES

1. **Major Hypothesis:** There is no significant difference between schools under Heads with different decision-making styles (Routine, Compromise, Heuristic) and organisational health as a whole.

   Sub-hypothesis: There is no significant difference between schools under Heads with different decision-making styles (Routine, Compromise, Heuristic) in integrity.

   Sub-hypothesis: There is no significant difference between schools under Heads with different decision-making styles (Routine, Compromise, Heuristic) in consideration.

   Sub-hypothesis: There is no significant difference between schools under Heads with different decision-making styles (Routine, Compromise, Heuristic) in initiating structure.

   Sub-hypothesis: There is no significant difference between schools under Heads with different decision-making styles (Routine, Compromise, Heuristic) in resource support.

   Sub-hypothesis: There is no significant difference between schools under Heads with different decision-making styles (Routine, Compromise, Heuristic) in principal influence.

   Sub-hypothesis: There is no significant difference between schools under Heads of the schools with different decision-making styles (Routine, Compromise, Heuristic) in morale.

   Sub-hypothesis: There is no significant difference between schools under Heads with different decision-making styles (Routine, Compromise, Heuristic) in academic emphasis.

2. **Major Hypothesis:** There is no significant difference between schools under Heads with different leadership

styles (Initiating Structure, Consideration) in organisational health as a whole.

Sub-hypothesis: There is no significant difference between schools under Heads with different leadership styles (Initiating Structure, Consideration) in integrity.

Sub-hypothesis: There is no significant difference between schools under Heads with different leadership styles (Initiating Structure, Consideration) in consideration.

Sub-hypothesis: There is no significant difference between schools under Heads with different leadership behaviour styles (Initiating Structure, Consideration) in initiating structure.

Sub-hypothesis: There is no significant difference between schools under Heads with different leadership styles (Initiating Structure, Consideration) in resource support.

Sub-hypothesis: There is no significant difference between schools under Heads with different leadership styles (Initiating Structure, Consideration) in principal influence.

Sub-hypothesis: There is no significant difference between schools under Heads with different leadership styles (Initiating Structure, Consideration) in morale.

Sub-hypothesis: There is no significant difference between schools under Heads with different leadership styles (Initiating Structure, Consideration) in academic emphasis.

3. **Major Hypothesis:** There is no significant difference between schools with male and female Heads in organisational health as a whole.

Sub-hypothesis: There is no significant difference between schools under male and female Heads in integrity.

Sub-hypothesis: There is no significant difference between schools under male and female Heads in consideration.

Sub-hypothesis: There is no significant difference between schools under male and female Heads in initiating structure.

Sub-hypothesis: There is no significant difference between schools under male and female Heads in resource support.

Sub-hypothesis: There is no significant difference between schools under male and female Heads in principal influence.

Sub-hypothesis: There is no significant difference between schools under male and female Heads in morale.

Sub-hypothesis: There is no significant difference between schools under male and female Heads in academic emphasis.

4. **Major Hypothesis:** There is no significant difference between schools under Head with varying experience (below 15, 15-25, above 25 years) in organisational health as a whole.

   Sub-hypothesis: There is no significant difference between schools under Heads with varying experience (below 15, 15-25, above 25 years) in integrity.

   Sub-hypothesis: There is no significant difference between schools under Heads with varying experience (below 15, 15-25, above 25 years) in consideration.

   Sub-hypothesis: There is no significant difference between schools under Heads with varying experience (below 15, 15-25, above 25 years) in initiating structure.

   Sub-hypothesis: There is no significant difference between schools under Heads with varying experience (below 15, 15-25, above 25 years) in resource support.

Sub-hypothesis: There is no significant difference between schools under Heads with varying experience (below 15, 15-25, above 25 years) in principal influence..

Sub-hypothesis: There is no significant difference between schools under Heads with varying experience (below 15, 15-25, above 25 years) in morale.

Sub-hypothesis: There is no significant difference between schools under Heads with varying experience (below 15, 15-25, above 25 years) in academic emphasis.

5. **Major Hypothesis:** There is no significant difference between schools under Heads with different decision-making styles (Routine, Compromise, Heuristic) in teacher morale as a whole.

Sub-hypothesis: There is no significant difference between schools under Heads with different decision-making styles (Routine, Compromise, Heuristic) in individual characteristics.

Sub-hypothesis: There is no significant difference between schools under Heads with different decision-making styles (Routine, Compromise, Heuristic) in behavioural characteristics.

Sub-hypothesis: There is no significant difference between schools under Heads with different decision-making styles (Routine, Compromise, Heuristic) in group spirit.

Sub-hypothesis: There is no significant difference between schools under Heads with different decision-making styles (Routine, Compromise, Heuristic) in attitude towards job.

Sub-hypothesis: There is no significant difference between schools under Heads with different decision-making styles (Routine, Compromise, Heuristic) in community involvement.

6. **Major Hypothesis:** There is no significant difference between schools under Heads with different leadership

styles (Initiating Structure and Consideration) in teacher morale as a whole.

Sub-hypothesis: There is no significant difference between schools under Heads of schools with different leadership styles (Initiating Structure and Consideration) in individual characteristics.

Sub-hypothesis: There is no significant difference between schools under Heads with different leadership styles (Initiating Structure and Consideration) in behavioural characteristics.

Sub-hypothesis: There is no significant difference between schools under Heads with different leadership styles (Initiating Structure and Consideration) in group spirit.

Sub-hypothesis: There is no significant difference between schools under Heads with different leadership styles (Initiating Structure and Consideration) in attitude towards the job.

Sub-hypothesis: There is no significant difference between schools under Heads with different leadership styles (Initiating Structure and Consideration) in community involvement.

7. **Major Hypothesis:** There is no significant difference between schools under male and female Heads in teacher morale as a whole.

   Sub-hypothesis: There is no significant difference between schools under male and female Heads in individual characteristics.

   Sub-hypothesis: There is no significant difference between schools under male and female Heads in behavioural characteristics.

   Sub-hypothesis: There is no significant difference between schools under male and female Heads in group spirit.

Sub-hypothesis: There is no significant difference between schools under male and female Heads in attitude towards job.

Sub-hypothesis: There is no significant difference between schools under male and female Heads in community involvement.

8. **Major Hypothesis:** There is no significant difference between schools under Heads with varying experience (below 15, 15-25, above 25 years) in teacher morale as a whole.

   Sub-hypothesis: There is no significant difference between schools under Heads with varying experience (below 15, 15-25, above 25 years) in individual characteristics.

   Sub-hypothesis: There is no significant difference between schools under Heads with varying experience (below 15, 15-25, above 25 years) in behavioural characteristics.

   Sub-hypothesis: There is no significant difference between schools under Heads with varying experience (below 15, 15-25, above 25 years) in group spirit.

   Sub-hypothesis: There is no significant difference between schools under Heads with varying experience (below 15, 15-25, above 25 years) in attitude towards job.

   Sub-hypothesis: There is no significant difference between schools under Heads with varying experience (below 15, 15-25, above 25 years) in community involvement.

9. **Major Hypothesis:** There is no interaction effect of Heads decision-making styles (Routine, Compromise, Heuristic) and leadership styles (Initiating Structure and Consideration) on organisational health.

10. **Major Hypothesis:** There is no interaction effect of decision-making styles (Routine, Compromise, Heuristic)

and leadership styles (Initiating Structure and Consideration) on teacher morale.

11. **Major Hypothesis:** There is no association between decision-making styles (Routine, Compromise, Heuristic) and leadership styles (Initiating Structure, Consideration) of Heads of Schools.

12. **Major Hypothesis:** There is no association between decision-making style (Routine, Compromise, Heuristic) and organisational health (High, Average, Low).

13. **Major Hypothesis:** There is no association between decision-making style of Heads of Schools (Routine, Compromise, Heuristic) and teacher morale (High, Average, Low).

14. **Major Hypothesis:** There is no association between decision-making style (Routine, Compromise, Heuristic) and sex (Male, Female) of Heads of schools.

15. **Major Hypothesis:** There is no association between decision-making style (Routine, Compromise, Heuristic) and teaching experience (below 15, 15-25, above 25 years) of Heads of schools.

16. **Major Hypothesis:** There is no association between decision-making style of Heads of schools (Routine, Compromise, Heuristic) and type of management (Govt. aided, unaided) of schools.

17. **Major Hypothesis:** There is no association between leadership style of Heads of schools and organisational health (High, Average, Low).

18. **Major Hypothesis:** There is no association between leadership style of Heads of schools (Initiating Structure and Consideration) and teacher morale (High, Average, Low).

19. **Major Hypothesis:** There is no association between leadership style and sex (Male, Female) of Heads of schools.

20. **Major Hypothesis:** There is no association between leadership style and experience of Heads of schools.

21. **Major Hypothesis:** There is no association between leadership style of Heads of schools and type of management (Govt. aided, unaided) of schools.

22. **Major Hypothesis:** There is no significant relationship between organisational health and teacher morale in high schools.

23. **Major Hypothesis:** There is no significant relationship between dimensions of organisational health and components of teacher morale.

24. **Major Hypothesis:** There is no significant relationship between dimensions of organisational health.

25. **Major Hypothesis:** There is no significant relationship between dimensions of teacher morale.

26. **Major Hypothesis:** There is no significant influence of leadership style (Initiating Structure), decision-making style (Routine, Compromise, Heuristic), teacher morale sex, experience and type of management on organisational health.

27. **Major Hypothesis:** There is no significant influence of leadership style (Initiating Structure and Consideration), decision-making style (Routine, Compromise, Heuristic.), organisational health, sex, experience, type of management on teacher morale.

TOOLS

For collection of the data required for the present study the following tools were used:

(i) Decision-making Style Questionnaire (DMSQ).

(ii) Teacher Morale Inventory (TMI)

(iii) Organisational Health Inventory (OHI)

(iv) Leadership Behaviour Description Questionnaire (LBDQ).

The Decision-making Style Questionnaire

This tool was developed by the investigator in consultation with the guide, which covers four areas of decision-making.

(i) Entrepreneurial problems.

(ii) Administrative problems.

(iii) Academic problems.

(iv) Personnel problems.

Lipham and Hoeh (1974) have given a sound classification of decision-making styles which envelop the ingredients of all the aforesaid classifications. Their typology has concern for the structure of the relationship between individuals. The behaviour required facilitating decision-making. The manner of proceeding in decision-making and the social, emotional tone of the Inter-personal relationships. This typology includes routine, compromise and heuristic decision-making styles.

Routine, Compromise and Heuristic Decision-making

Routine decisions are taken to keep the institution going. In the words of Lipham and Hoeh (1974) "In routine decision-making, the situation is usually structured hierarchically, the role behaviour is characterised by specialised yet co-ordinated effort, the processes utilised are largely formal and the relationships themselves are likely to be somewhat stressful". In short, it is programmed type of decision.

Ideas clash occasionally under a competent Head of School. The Head of School must be capable of arriving at a compronising formula without offending either party. The Head of School must be a human relations facilitator and see that occasional ill-feelings and feelings of an animosity and jealousy among the faculty as a result of clashes are adequately diagnosed and analysed and remediation taken. In short, it is a compromise type of decision.

In heuristic decision-making, there is a lack of emphasis on hierarchical structure, role behaviour is characterised by freedom for each individual to explore all ideas. The emotional and social tone is relatively relaxed; openness, originality and seeking of consensus are the essentials of heuristic decision-making. In a nutshell it is a creative type of decision.

The Decision-making Style Questionnaire has four main problem areas:

(i) Entrepreneurial Problems.

(ii) Administrative Problems.

(iii) Academic Problems.

(iv) Personnel Problems.

Each problem area had 12 problems followed by three alternative solutions representing heuristic, routine and compromise decision-making styles of Heads of schools.

Those solutions were arranged in an orderly manner for all the three styles as Routine, Compromise and Heuristic.

Scoring Technique

The responses of the Heads of schools to the 48 items were collected and 14 frequencies of Routine, Heuristic and Compromise were calculated. The respondent is assigned to 3 categories in which he or she had 12 maximum frequencies.

Validity and Reliability

The reliability of the Decision-making Style Questionnaire was computed using split-half method of reliability. The area-wise reliability and validity of the questionnaire are:

Sl. No.	*Components*	*Reliability*	*Validity*
1.	Entrepreneurial	0.78	0.88
2.	Administrative	0.88	0.94
3.	Academic	0.80	0.89
4.	Personnel	0.98	0.99

The overall reliability of the questionnaire was 0.86 and overall validity of the questionnaire was 0.92.

Organisational Health Inventory

To collect the relevant data the organisational Health Inventory (OHI) of W.K. Hoy, C.J. Tarter and R.B. Kottamp (1991) is adopted. This inventory consists of 44 items under seven dimensions that capture the critical instrumental and expressive aspects of organisational function on three levels of organisational health. The details regarding these dimensions and number of items under each are given in Table 4.2.

Table 4.2: Dimensions of Organisational Health in Terms of Organisational Levels and Dimensions

Sl. No.	*Level*	*Function*	*Dimension*	*Number of items.*
1.	Institutional	Instrumental	Institutional Integrity	7
2.	Managerial	Expressive	Consideration	5
		Instrumental	Initiating Structure	5
		Instrumental	Resource Support	5
		Instrumental	Principal Influence	5
3.	Technical	Expressive	Morale	9
		Instrumental	Academic Emphasis	8
			Total	44

This inventory has been revalidated by calculating the reliability and validity co-efficients.

Organisational Health

Institutional Level: Institutional level is the high schools ability to cope with its environment in a way that maintains the educational integrity of its programme. Assistant teachers are protected from unreasonable community and parental demands.

Institutional Integrity: Institutional integrity describes an institution that has integrity in its educational program. The college is not vulnerable to narrow, vested interests of community groups: indeed, teachers are protected from unreasonable community and parental demands. The high school is able to cope successfully with destructive outside forces.

Managerial Level

Initiating structure, consideration principal influence and resource support provide measure of the organisational health at the managerial level.

Consideration: Consideration is principal behaviour that is friendly, supportive and collegial. The principal looks out for the welfare of faculty members and is open to their suggestions.

Initiating Structure: Initiating structure is task and achievement-oriented behaviour. The principal makes his or her attitudes and expectations clear to the faculty and maintains definite standards of performance.

Resource Support: Resource support refers to an institution where adequate classroom supplies and instructional materials are available and extra materials are easily obtained.

Principal Influence: Principal influence is the principal's ability to affect the actions of superiors. The influential principal is persuasive, works effectively with the superintendent. Simultaneously demonstrates independence in thought and action.

Technical Level

Morale and Academic Emphasis are the indices of organisational health of the technical level.

Morale: Morale is the sense of trust, confidence, enthusiasm and friendliness among teachers. Teachers feel good about each other and, at the same time, feel a sense of accomplishment from their jobs.

Academic Emphasis: Academic emphasis refers to the school's press for achievement. High but achievable goals are set for students: the learning environment is orderly and serious, teachers believe students can achieve, and students work hard and respect those who do well academically.

RO = Rarely Occurs

SO = Some times Occurs

O = Often Occurs

VFO = Very Frequently Occurs

Weighted scores 4, 3, 2 and 1 are associated to the responses and reverse scoring is adopted for negative items.

Reliability and Validity

The inventory has been revalidated by calculating the reliability and validity coefficient reliability of tool has been established by calculating the reliability co-efficient by split of method (r = .7982) and validity was established by taking the square root of reliability $\sqrt{0.7982} = 0.89$

Thus this tool is found to be reliable and valid.

Teacher Morale Inventory

Morale is intangible; it cannot be seen or isolated. But it is possible to determine the quality of morale by observation of the way people act.

Teacher Morale Inventory adopted by Dektawala (1977) was used which is validated in Indian context.

The Teacher Morale Inventory used in this study has five components, which are further divided into sub components.

Components

(i) Individual Characteristics

(ii) Behavioural Characteristics

(iii) Group Spirit

(iv) Attitude towards job

(v) Community involvement

On the basis of the above five components, one hundred statements have been framed and they cover the opinions and attitudes about the teachers' work in educational institutions. All the selected assistant teachers were asked to indicate their responses, to each of the hundred statements on a five-point scale. These are:

A = Fully Agree

B = Agree

C = Undecided

D = Disagree

E = Fully Disagree

If the respondent fully agree with the item, he had to mention 'A'; if he agreed with the item, he had to mention 'B'; if he was undecided with the item, he had to mention 'C'; if he disagreed with the item, he had to mention 'D'; if he fully disagreed with the item, he had to mention 'E'. For each item there is a rating scale.

Firstly responses are checked with the key and weightages are as follows.

A	B	C	D	E
5	4	3	2	1

For negative items, the scoring for the responses follow the scheme given below:

A	B	C	D	E
1	2	3	4	5

The responses were hand scored and the morale score for each high school was calculated by finding the average total score and average scores for each of the five-component, viz., individual characteristics, group spirit, attitude towards job and community involvement were also calculated. The high schools mean total scores gave an idea as to what was the average morale of the assistant teachers of a particular high school.

Reliability and Validity

Dekhtawala measured the concerned validity of the tool by correlating the score of the teachers with the principal's rating. The product moment coefficient of correlation between the two sets of sources was. 77 which is quite high.

Reliability

The investigator established reliability of the instrument by test-retest method. The correlation coefficient obtained is .89. Split half method was also used to further test reliability. Scores on the odd items of the inventory were correlated with the even item scores and the correlation was found to be .99 indicating the instrument's high reliability. The validity calculated through reliability worked out to $\sqrt{0.89} = 0.94$.

Leadership Behaviour Description Questionnaire

The leadership behaviour description questionnaire, popularly known as L.B.D.Q., developed by E.A. Fleishman (1973) has been employed for the purpose of collecting data on leadership styles of secondary school Heads as perceived by their respective teachers.

This is a 48 item questionnaire divided into two independent areas of leadership called 'Consideration' and 'Initiating Structure'. The first area includes 28 items and the second area is made up of 20 items. The scale is designed to find answer to the question, what does your own head of the school actually do? All the 48 items are presented with a 5-point scale (continuous answer) that has scoring weights of 1 to 5, depending on the item orientation to the total dimension. The highest score is 112 for 'Consideration' and 80 for 'Initiating Structure'.

By using this questionnaire it is possible to get a view of how a Head of the school thinks he should lead and compare this view with an assessment by his subordinate (teachers) of his actual leadership performance.

(i) **Consideration:** That is being friendly and approachable creating pleasant group members, treating them as equals, giving advance information about changes, concern for personal welfare of their respective teachers, willingness to make changes and explain the rationale of decision accompanied by consultative actions.

(ii) **Initiating Structure:** That is clearly defining own role and letting group members know what is expected of them, planning and organising the group tasks, encouraging use of uniform procedure, trying out own ideas in the group, clarifying own attitude to the group, deciding for the group members what they should do and how, assigning specific tasks to them, ensuring that their own role in the group is understood by the members, scheduling work and maintaining performance schedules.

The scoring scheme of the tool is of 5 anchoring points of 5, 4, 3, 2, 1 and reverse scoring was adopted for negative items.

Validity and Reliability

Reliability co-efficient was established by split half method (r = 0.7901) and validity was established by taking the square root of reliability $\sqrt{0.7901}=0.98$. Thus this tool is found to be reliable and valid.

The description of the tools is given in table 4.3.

Data Collection

The investigator personally collected the data form 54 Heads of secondary schools and 270 assistant teachers of

Table 4.3: Description of the Tools Used in the Study

Sl. No.	*Name of the Tool*	*Dimensions*	*Total Statements*		*Scoring Technique*			
			Positive	*Negative*	*R*	*C*	*H*	
1.	Decision-Making Style Questionnaire	Entrepreneurial Problems	12		R	C	H	
		Administrative Problems	12		R	C	H	
		Academic Problems	12		R	C	H	
		Personnel Problems	12		R	C	H	
		Total	48					
			Positive	*Negative*	*RO*	*SO*	*O*	*VFO*
2.	Organisational Health Inventory	• Institutional Level						
		1. Integrity	1	6	4	3	2	1
		• Managerial Level						
		1. Consideration	5	-	4	3	2	1
		2. Initiating Structure	5	-	4	3	2	1
		3. Resource Support	5	-	4	3	2	1
		4. Principal Influence	4	1	4	3	2	1
		• Technical Level						
		1. Morale	7	2	4	3	2	1
		2. Academic emphasis	8	-	4	3	2	1
		Total (Positive and Negative)	35	9				
		Total	44					

				Positive	Negative	A	B	C	D	E
3.	Teacher Morale Inventory		Individual characteristics	8	8	5	4	3	2	1
			Behavioural Characteristics	12	13	5	4	3	2	1
			Group Spirit	13	12	5	4	3	2	1
			Attitude towards the job	14	12	5	4	3	2	1
			Community Involvement	4	4	5	4	3	2	1
			Total (Positive and Negative)	51	49					
			Total	100						

				Positive	Negative	A	B	C	D	E
4.	Leadership Behaviour Description Questionnaire	1.	Consideration	17	11	5	4	3	2	1
		2.	Initiating Structure	18	2	5	4	3	2	1
			Total (Positive and Negative)	35	13					
		Total		48						

Dharwad Taluka. Heads of schools and assistant teachers were personally administered the tools. Clear-cut instructions were given to fill up the responses to the items in the tools. The filled in proformas and tools were collected. The Heads of schools and assistant teachers were informed the purpose of the study. The Decision-making Style Questionnaire was administered to the Heads of schools. The Teacher Morale Inventory, Organisational Health Inventory and Leadership Behaviour Description Questionnaire were administered to the assistant teachers. The confidentiality of the responses was assured. The collected data was systematically pooled for analyses.

DATA ANALYSIS

For the purpose of analysis of the empirical data, the following statistical techniques were used:

(i) Descriptive statistics

(ii) Differential statistics

(iii) Correctional analysis

(iv) Regression analysis

The analyses and interpretation of results are presented in Chapter 5.

5

Data Analyses and Results

Method of Analyses and Interpretation

However valid, reliable and adequate the data may be, it does not serve any useful purpose unless it is carefully processed, systematically classified and tabulated, scientifically analysed, intelligently interpreted and rationally concluded.

After the data had been collected, it was processed and analysed using Microsoft Excel-97 and SPSS Software to draw exact conclusions. In the present study correlates of decision-making styles are measured using the relevant tools.

The data collected from the heads of high schools and their assistant teachers with regard to Decision-making Style, Leadership Style, Organisational Health and Teacher Morale were analysed with reference to the objectives and hypotheses. The raw scores were converted into percentages on the basis of number of items in each dimension/component of a variable. Then the data have been subjected to the following statistical analyses, namely descriptive, differential, correlation, and multiple regression analysis. The results of statistical analyses have been summarised, tabulated and interpreted appropriately in the following sections.

Descriptive Analysis

The study is on decision-making style of heads of schools, leadership behaviour, organisational health and teacher morale and their dimensions. For each main variable and their dimensions separate scores are calculated. From these scores the relevant statistics were calculated to describe the variables to compare the groups and to find out the correlation between variables.

Table 5.1: Categorisation of Heads of Schools on the Basis of Decision-making Style

Decision-making Style	*No.*	*Percentage*
Routine	29	53.70
Compromise	14	25.92
Heuristic	11	20.38
Total	54	100

From table 5.1 it can be seen that 53.70% of the Heads of schools perceive themselves to be routine decision-makers. That is, they see themselves as adapting programmed type of decisions. Their schools are usually hierarchically structured. The functioning of the schools and the relationship among the people are more formal and they are following a rigid routine. 25.92% of the Heads perceive themselves to be a compromise decision-maker, that is, they see their role as negotiators. They are concerned with a strategy for dealing with conflicts that may occur because of differences among school personnel. They serve as the impartial mediators in the decision-making process. Only 20.38% of the Heads perceive themselves to be heuristic, that is, creative in decision-making. It implies that there is not a

Table 5.2: Category of Heads of Schools on the Basis of Leadership Style

Style	*No.*	*Percentage*
Initiating Structure	39	72.00
Consideration	15	28.00
Total	54	100.00

rigid hierarchical structure in their schools. It means that, there is freedom for the faculty and there is an emotional and social tone in their role as negotiators.

The table 5.2 results clearly indicate that, out of 54 school Heads 72.00% have initiating structure leadership style and 28.00% consideration leadership style.

Table 5.3: Categories of Heads of Schools on the Basis of Sex (Male and Female)

Style	*No.*	*Percentage*
Male	37	68.25
Female	17	31.48
Total	54	100

The table 5.3 results clearly indicate that, out of 54 Heads of schools, 68.52% are male and only 31.48% female.

Table 5.4: Categories of Heads of Schools on the Basis of Educational Qualification

Qualification	*No.*	*Percentage*
Graduate	29	53.70
Post-graduate	25	46.30
Total	54	100

In the present study 53.70% of the school Heads have graduate degree compared to 46.30% of the Heads of schools

Table 5.5: Categories of Heads of Schools on the Basis of Age (in years)

Age (in years)	*No.*	*Percentage*
30-40	11	20.37
41-50	12	22.22
51-60	31	57.41
Total	54	100

who have a post-graduate degree. But in general nearly equal percentage of the Heads have graduate and post-graduate educational qualification.

The table 5.5 results clearly show that 57.41% of the Heads of schools are in the age category of 51-60 years, 22.22% in 41-50 years and 20.37% of the Heads of schools in the lower age category, i.e., 30-40 years.

Table 5.6: Categories of Heads of Schools on the Basis of Experience (in years)

Experience	*No.*	*Percentage*
Below 15	14	25.93
15-25	11	20.37
Above 25	29	53.70
Total	54	100

In the present study, 53.70% of the Heads of schools have more than 25 years teaching experience, 25.93% with below 15 years teaching experience and 20.37% with 15-25 years teaching experience.

Table 5.7: Categories of Heads of Schools on the Basis of Type of Management

Type of Management	*No.*	*Percentage*
Government	10	18.25
Aided Private	33	61.11
Unaided Private	11	20.37
Total	54	100

Out of 54 school Heads 61.11% belong to aided schools, 18.52% to government schools and 20.37% to unaided schools.

From the table 5.8 we can observe the following:

(i) Out of 54 heads of schools 40.74% of the school Heads perceive themselves to be routine

Table 5.8: Distribution of Heads of Schools on Decision-making Style

Problems	*Routine*	*%*	*Compromise*	*%*	*Heuristic*	*%*	*Total*
Entrepreneurial Problems	22	40.74	14	25.93	18	33.33	54
Administrative Problems	29	53.70	15	27.28	10	18.52	54
Academic Problems	28	51.85	15	27.28	11	20.37	54
Personnel Problems	29	53.70	14	25.93	11	20.37	54
Total	29	53.70	14	25.93	11	20.37	54

decision-makers, 33.3% of Heads of schools perceive themselves to be heuristic decision-makers and 25.93% of the school Heads perceive themselves to be compromise decision-makers in the area of entrepreneurial problems.

(ii) In the area of administrative problems, 53.70% of the Heads of schools perceive themselves as routine decision-makers, 27.28% as compromise decision-makers and 18.52% as heuristic decision-makers.

(iii) But in the area of academic problems, 51.85% of Heads of schools perceive themselves as routine decision-makers, 27.28% as compromise decision-makers and 20.37% as heuristic decision-makers.

(iv) In the area of personnel problems, 53.70% of Heads perceive themselves as routine decision-makers, 25.93% as compromise and 20.37% as heuristic decision-makers. But in the whole sample, 53.70% of Heads of schools perceive themselves as routine, 25.93% as co.npromise and 20.37% as heuristic decision-makers.

From the table 5.9, the mean value of organisational health as a whole in routine style of decision-making was

468.38 and its standard deviation was 67.17. Similarly, mean in compromise style was 488.34 and standard deviation 70.09. In heuristic style, mean was 458.94 and standard deviation 84.49. The rest of the components of the organisational health in different types of decision-making styles of Heads of schools are presented in the table 5.9.

The table 5.10 results reveal that the mean value of organisational health as a whole in schools under Heads with initiating structure style of leadership was 472.08 and its standard deviation was 68.74. In consideration style the mean and standard deviation were 470.48 and 79.28 respectively. The details are presented in the table 5.10.

The table 5.11 results reveal that the mean value of organisational health in schools with male Heads was 478.44 and its standard deviation was 75.76. In schools with female Heads the mean and standard deviation were 456.82 and 58.89 respectively. The details are presented in the table 5.11.

The table 5.12 results reveal that the mean value of organisational health as a whole in schools with Heads with post-graduation as educational qualification was 460.73 and its standard deviation was 70.06. Heads of schools with graduation as a educational qualification the mean and standard deviation were 484.28 and 71.49 respectively. Other details are presented in the table 5.12.

From the table 5.13, the mean value of organisational health as a whole in schools with Heads belonging to 30-40 years age group was 481.83 and its standard deviation was 66.59. Similarly, mean in 40-50 years age group was 504.60 and standard deviation 58.28. In the age group 50-60 years, the mean was 455.25 and standard deviation was 73.79. The rest of the components of the organisational health in different age groups of Heads of schools are presented in the table 5.13.

From the table 5.14, the mean value of organisational health as a whole in schools with Heads belonging to below 15 years experience was 491.89 and its standard deviation was

Table 5.9: Mean and Standard Deviations of Organisational Health as a Whole and its Dimensions in Schools under Heads with Different Decision-Making Styles (Routine, Compromise and Heuristic)

Variables	*Summary*	*Routine*	*Compromise*	*Heuristic*	*Total*
n		*29*	*14*	*11*	*54*
Organisational Health as a whole	Mean	468.38	488.34	458.94	471.63
	Std. Dev.	67.17	70.09	84.49	71.05
Integrity	Mean	64.46	62.81	66.69	64.48
	Std. Dev.	7.55	8.59	4.49	7.33
Consideration	Mean	68.62	73.36	67.82	69.69
	Std. Dev.	14.48	15.48	18.29	15.41
Initiating Structure	Mean	67.76	75.07	64.55	69.00
	Std. Dev.	14.08	14.23	17.15	14.99
Resource Support	Mean	69.66	72.21	67.00	69.78
	Std. Dev.	15.21	14.59	17.87	15.42
Principal influence	Mean	70.03	75.36	70.64	71.54
	Std. Dev.	13.17	11.47	16.29	13.39
Morale	Mean	81.38	85.43	77.45	81.63
	Std. Dev.	9.51	11.30	14.82	11.32
Academic Emphasis	Mean	46.48	44.25	44.80	45.46
	Std. Dev.	5.58	6.72	8.67	6.54

Table 5.10: Mean and Standard Deviations of Organisational Health as a Whole and its Dimensions in the Different Leadership Styles (Initiating Structure, Consideration)

Variables	*Summary*	*Initiating Structure*	*Consideration*	*Total*
n		*39*	*15*	*54*
Organisational Health as a Whole	Mean	472.08	470.48	471.63
	Std. Dev.	68.74	79.28	71.05
Integrity	Mean	64.08	65.52	64.48
	Std. Dev.	7.70	6.41	7.33
Consideration	Mean	70.54	67.47	69.69
	Std. Dev.	15.04	16.68	15.41
Initiating Structure	Means	69.28	68.27	69.00
	Std. Dev.	15.23	14.83	14.99
Resource Support	Mean	69.15	71.40	69.78
	Std. Dev.	15.51	15.61	15.42
Principal Influence	Mean	72.13	70.00	71.54
	Std. Dev.	13.39	13.74	13.39
Morale	Mean	82.03	80.60	81.63
	Std. Dev.	10.77	12.98	11.32
Academic Emphasis	Mean	44.91	47.22	45.56
	Std. Dev.	6.10	7.52	6.54

Table 5.11: Mean and Standard Deviations of Organisational Health as a Whole and its Dimensions According to the Sex of Heads of Schools (Male and Female)

Variables	*Summary*	*Male*	*Female*	*Total*
n		*37*	*17*	*54*
Organisational Health as a Whole	Mean	478.44	456.82	471.63
	Std. Dev.	75.76	58.89	71.05
Integrity	Mean	64.69	64.03	64.48
	Std. Dev.	7.51	7.13	7.33
Consideration	Mean	71.35	66.06	69.69
	Std. Dev.	16.78	11.55	15.41
Initiating Structure	Mean	70.57	65.59	69.00
	Std. Dev.	16.21	11.60	14.99
Resource Support	Mean	71.00	67.12	69.78
	Std. Dev.	16.00	14.19	15.42
Principal Influence	Mean	72.22	70.06	74.54
	Std. Dev.	13.87	12.54	13.39
Morale	Mean	82.41	79.94	81.63
	Std. Dev.	12.34	8.79	11.32
Academic Emphasis	Mean	46.26	44.02	45.56
	Std. dev.	6.70	6.08	6.54

Table 5.12: Mean and Standard Deviations of Organisational Health as a Whole and its Dimensions According to the Educational Qualifications of Heads of Schools (UG & PG)

Variables	*Summary*	*Post-graduate*	*Graduate*	*Total*
n		29	25	54
Organisational Health as a whole	Mean	460.73	484.28	471.63
	Std. Dev.	70.06	71.49	71.05
Integrity	Mean	63.94	65.11	64.48
	Std. Dev.	7.36	7.40	7.33
Consideration	Mean	67.79	71.88	69.69
	Std. Dev.	15.09	15.80	15.41
Initiating Structure	Mean	66.55	71.84	69.00
	Std. Dev.	14.65	15.16	14.99
Resource Support	Mean	68.03	71.80	69.78
	Std. Dev.	15.36	15.56	15.42
Principal Influence	Mean	69.24	74.20	71.54
	Std. Dev.	14.14	12.20	13.39
Morale	Mean	80.79	82.60	81.63
	Std. Dev.	11.13	11.69	11.32
Academic Emphasis	Mean	44.44	46.84	45.56
	Std. Dev.	5.94	7.07	6.54

Table 5.13: Mean and Standard Deviation of Organisational Health as a Whole and its Dimensions According to Age of Heads of Schools (30-40, 41-50, 51-60 years)

Variables	*Summary*	*30-40*	*40-50*	*50-60*	*Total*
n		*11*	*12*	*31*	*54*
Organisational Health as a whole	Mean	481.83	504.60	455.25	471.63
	Std. Dev.	66.59	58.28	73.79	71.05
Integrity	Mean	65.97	67.74	62.70	64.48
	Std. Dev.	3.34	6.85	8.11	7.33
Consideration	Mean	73.55	74.83	66.32	69.69
	Std. Dev.	13.17	12.55	16.62	15.41
Initiating Structure	Mean	71.00	76.75	65.29	69.00
	Std. Dev.	14.44	11.14	15.55	14.99
Resource Support	Means	74.00	75.25	66.16	69.78
	Std. Dev.	15.59	14.27	15.25	15.42
Principal Influence	Mean	73.73	73.75	69.90	71.54
	Std. Dev.	14.72	12.86	13.32	13.39
Morale	Mean	79.55	86.42	80.52	81.63
	Std. Dev.	6.52	9.30	12.98	11.32
Academic Emphasis	Mean	44.04	49.86	44.43	45.56
	Std. Dev.	5.26	5.96	6.61	6.54

Table 5.14: Mean and Standard Deviations of Organisational Health as a Whole and its Dimensions According to Experience (Below 15, 15-25, and Above 25 years)

Variables	*Summary*	*Below 15*	*15-25*	*Above 25*	*Total*
n		*11*	*12*	*31*	*54*
Organisational Health as a whole	Mean	491.89	475.79	460.28	471.63
	Std. Dev.	61.79	77.95	72.57	71.05
Integrity	Mean	66.48	65.00	63.33	64.48
	Std. Dev.	4.14	9.06	7.81	7.33
Consideration	Mean	74.79	70.36	66.97	69.69
	Std. Dev.	12.16	17.57	15.81	15.41
Initiating Structure	Mean	73.07	71.64	66.03	69.00
	Std. Dev.	13.83	12.56	16.12	14.99
Resource Support	Mean	75.50	69.91	66.97	69.78
	Std. Dev.	14.01	16.71	15.33	15.42
Principal Influence	Mean	75.36	72.55	69.31	71.54
	Std. Dev.	13.44	13.90	13.18	13.39
Morale	Mean	81.50	80.27	82.21	81.63
	Std. Dev.	8.25	13.45	12.05	11.32
Academic Emphasis	Mean	45.20	46.06	45.54	45.56
	Std. Dev.	6.04	7.42	6.64	6.54

61.79, mean in 15-25 years group was 475.79 and standard deviation 77.95, and for above 25 years experience group the mean was 460.28 and standard deviation 72.57. The rest of the components of the organisational health in different types of teaching experience of Heads of schools are presented in the table 5.14.

From the table 5.15, the mean value of organisational health as a whole in schools belonging to government type of management was 474.53 and its standard deviation was 78.89, mean value in aided schools was 461.47 and standard deviation 72.60 and in unaided schools, the mean was 499.48 and standard deviation was 55.57. The rest of the components of the organisational health in different types of managements are presented in the table.

From the table 5.16, the mean value of teacher morale as a whole in schools with Heads belonging to routine type of decision-making style was 2123.50 and its standard deviation was 157.29. In schools with Heads belonging to compromise type of decision-making style the mean was 2161.96 and its standard deviation was 114.29 and in heuristic style mean and standard deviation were 2153.91 and 152.77 respectively. The details of the mean and standard deviations of components of teacher morale are presented according to three decision-making styles (Routine, Compromise, Heuristic) in the table 5.16.

The table 5.17 results reveal that the mean value of teacher morale as a whole in schools with Heads with initiating structure style of leadership was 2136.10 and its standard deviation was 130.98. In consideration type of leadership style the mean and standard deviation were 2148.94 and 181.07 respectively. The details of the mean and standard deviations for components of teacher morale are presented according to two types of leadership styles (initiating structure and consideration) in the same table.

The table 5.18 results reveal that the mean value of teacher morale as a whole in schools with male Heads was 2160.16 and its standard deviation was 138.93, whereas with

Table 5.15: Mean and Standard Deviations of Organisational Health as a Whole and its Dimensions Belonging to Different Types of Managements (Government, Aided and Un-aided)

Variables	*Summary*	*G*	*A*	*UA*	*Total*
n		*10*	*33*	*11*	*54*
Organisational Health as a whole	Mean	474.53	461.47	499.48	471.63
	Std. Dev.	78.89	72.60	55.57	71.05
Integrity	Mean	64.93	63.57	66.82	64.48
	Std. Dev.	4.03	8.90	2.79	7.33
Consideration	Mean	67.70	67.30	78.64	69.69
	Std. Dev.	17.86	15.19	11.09	15.41
Initiating Structure	Mean	70.30	66.79	74.45	69.00
	Std. Dev.	16.38	15.02	13.28	14.99
Resource Support	Mean	74.20	65.88	77.45	69.78
	Std. Dev.	15.48	15.09	13.50	15.42
Principal Influence	Mean	71.70	69.27	78.18	71.54
	Std. Dev.	17.59	12.21	11.36	13.39
Morale	Means	80.70	82.61	79.55	81.63
	Std. Dev.	7.85	13.50	5.65	11.32
Academic Emphasis	Mean	45.00	46.11	44.39	45.56
	Std. Dev.	6.39	7.23	4.41	6.54

Table 5.16: Mean and Standard Deviations of Teacher Morale as a Whole and its Dimensions According to Decision-Making Style of Heads of Schools (Routine, Compromise and Heuristic)

Variables	*Summary*	*Routine*	*Compromise*	*Heuristic*	*Total*
n		*29*	*14*	*11*	*54*
Teacher Morale as a whole	Mean	2123.50	2161.96	2153.91	2139.67
	Std. Dev.	157.29	114.29	152.77	144.89
Individual Characteristics	Mean	349.59	355.07	349.91	351.07
	Std. Dev.	22.19	17.93	25.87	21.70
Behavioural Characteristics	Mean	525.93	528.81	536.16	528.76
	Std. Dev.	34.32	22.20	21.48	29.08
Group Spirit	Mean	505.29	524.80	511.05	511.52
	Std Dev.	42.13	33.79	47.42	41.35
Attitude Towards the Job	Mean	490.39	501.17	497.96	494.73
	Std. Dev.	44.57	33.13	42.16	40.96
Community Involvement	Mean	252.31	252.11	258.82	253.58
	Std. Dev.	29.37	21.80	24.88	26.39

Table 5.17: Mean and Standard Deviations of Teacher Morale as a Whole and its Dimensions According to Leadership Behaviour Style of Heads of Schools (Initiating Structure, Consideration)

Variables	*Summary*	*Initiating Structure*	*Consideration*	*Total*
n		*39*	*15*	*54*
Teacher Morale as a whole	Mean	2136.10	2148.94	2139.67
	Std. Dev.	130.98	181.07	144.89
Individual Characteristics	Mean	350.08	353.67	351.07
	Std. Dev.	20.00	26.21	21.70
Behavioural Characteristics	Mean	525.96	536.04	528.76
	Std. Dev.	26.91	34.03	29.08
Group Spirit	Mean	512.61	508.69	511.52
	Std. Dev.	38.36	49.67	41.35
Attitude Towards the Job	Mean	493.84	497.04	494.73
	Std. Dev.	35.67	53.74	40.96
Community Involvement	Mean	253.62	253.50	253.58
	Std. Dev.	24.96	30.75	26.39

Table 5.18: Mean and Standard Deviations of Teacher Morale as a Whole and its Dimensions According to Sex of Heads of Schools (Male and Female)

Variables	*Summary*	*Male*	*Female*	*Total*
n		*37*	*17*	*54*
Teacher Morale as a whole	Mean	2160.16	2095.06	2139.67
	Std. Dev.	138.93	151.76	144.89
Individual Characteristics	Mean	352.59	347.76	351.07
	Std. Dev.	20.68	24.09	21.70
Behavioural Characteristics	Mean	532.70	520.20	528.76
	Std. Dev.	26.83	32.69	29.08
Group Spirit	Mean	516.14	501.48	511.52
	Std. Dev.	41.97	39.31	41.35
Attitude Towards the Job	Mean	501.10	480.85	494.73
	Std. Dev.	38.40	44.04	40.96
Community Involvement	Mean	257.64	244.76	253.58
	Std. Dev.	26.80	23.87	26.39

female school Heads, the mean and standard deviation were 2095.06 and 151.76 respectively. The details of the mean and standard deviations for components of teacher morale are presented according to sex (Male and Female) in the table 5.18.

The table 5.19 reveals that the mean value of teachers morale as a whole in schools with Heads of the schools with post graduation as educational qualification was 2114.20 and its standard deviation was 169.15. In schools with Heads with graduation as educational qualification, the mean and standard deviation were 2169.21 and 106.25 respectively. The details of the mean and standard deviations of components of teacher morale are presented according to educational qualification (UG, PG) of the Heads of schools in table 5.19.

From the table 5.20, the mean value of teacher morale as a whole in schools with Heads belonging to 30-40 years age group was 2128.18 and its standard deviation was 177.20. Similarly, mean in 40-50 years age group was 2193.26 and standard deviation was 146.15, and with Heads with age 50-60 years, the mean was 2123.00 and standard deviation was 131.55. The rest of the components of the teacher morale in different age groups of Heads of schools were presented in the table 5.20.

From the table 5.21, the mean value of organisational health as a whole in schools with Heads belonging to below 15 years teaching experience was 2164.14 and its standard deviation was 173.36; the mean in 15-25 years group was 2162.00 and standard deviation was 144.16 and for above 25 years experience, the mean was 2119.38 and standard deviation was 132.06. The details of the mean and standard deviations of components of teacher morale are presented according to experience (below 15, 15-25, above 25 years) of the Heads of schools in the table 5.21.

From the table 5.22 the mean value of organisational health as a whole in schools belonging to government type of management was 2179.15 and its standard deviation was

Table 5.19: Mean and Standard Deviations of Teacher Morale as a Whole and its Dimensions According to Educational Qualifications of Heads of Schools (Graduate and Post-graduate)

Variables	*Summary*	*PG*	*UG*	*Total*
n		*29*	*25*	*54*
Teacher Morale as a whole	Mean	2114.20	2169.21	2139.67
	Std. Dev.	169.15	106.25	144.89
Individual Characteristics	Mean	346.69	356.16	351.07
	Std. Dev.	26.35	13.40	21.70
Behavioural Characteristics	Mean	523.71	534.62	528.76
	Std. Dev.	34.82	19.68	29.08
Group Spirit	Mean	507.77	515.88	511.52
	Std. Dev.	47.75	32.85	41.35
Attitude Towards the Job	Mean	486.37	504.42	494.73
	Std. Dev.	45.20	33.73	40.96
Community Involvement	Mean	249.67	258.12	253.58
	Std. Dev.	29.61	21.80	26.39

Table 5.20: Mean and Standard Deviations of Teacher Morale as a Whole and its Dimensions According to Age of Heads of Schools (30-40, 41-50, 51-60 years)

Variables	*Summary*	*30-40*	*40-50*	*50-60*	*Total*
n		*11*	*12*	*31*	*54*
Teacher Morale as a whole	Mean	2128.18	2193.26	2123.00	2139.67
	Std. Dev.	177.20	146.15	131.55	144.89
Individual Characteristics	Mean	350.00	358.50	348.58	351.07
	Std. Dev.	26.80	17.06	21.37	21.70
Behavioural Characteristics	Mean	526.91	535.52	526.81	528.76
	Std. Dev.	35.26	28.30	27.62	29.08
Group Spirit	Mean	511.55	527.92	505.17	511.52
	Std. Dev.	47.54	36.86	40.25	41.35
Attitude Towards the Job	Mean	488.27	509.45	491.32	494.73
	Std. Dev.	49.09	46.77	35.27	40.96
Community Involvement	Mean	251.45	261.88	251.13	253.58
	Std. Dev.	25.30	27.57	26.51	26.39

Table 5.21: Mean and Standard Deviations of Teacher Morale as a Whole and its Dimensions According to Experience of Heads of Schools (Below 15, 15-25, Above 25 Years)

Variables	*Summary*	*Below 15*	*15-25*	*Above 25*	*Total*
n		*11*	*12*	*31*	*54*
Teacher Morale as a whole	Mean	2164.14	2162.00	2119.38	2139.67
	Std. Dev.	173.36	144.16	132.06	144.89
Individual Characteristics	Mean	353.64	354.82	348.41	351.07
	Std. Dev.	25.08	19.62	21.11	21.70
Behavioural Characteristics	Mean	530.96	535.87	525.01	528.76
	Std. dev.	33.03	30.49	26.94	29.08
Group Spirit	Mean	522.34	515.82	504.67	511.52
	Sted. Dev.	47.60	39.22	39.00	41.35
Attitude Towards the job	Mean	500.49	499.13	490.28	494.73
	Std. Dev.	49.60	44.34	35.86	40.96
Community Involvement	Mean	256.71	256.36	251.02	253.58
	Std. Dev.	24.87	23.42	28.64	26.39

Table 5.22: Mean and Standard Deviations of Teacher Morale as a Whole and its Dimensions According to Type of Management of Schools (Government, Aided and Unaided)

Variables	*Summary*	*Government*	*Aided*	*Unaided*	*Total*
n		*10*	*33*	*11*	*54*
Teacher Morale as a whole	Mean	2179.15	2122.03	2156.68	2139.67
	Std. dev.	112.35	146.86	167.29	144.89
Individual Characteristics	Mean	358.30	349.39	349.55	351.07
	Std. Dev.	16.86	21.57	26.22	21.70
Behavioural Characteristics	Mean	546.78	523.65	527.71	528.76
	Std. Dev.	25.19	27.69	32.35	29.08
Group Spirit	Mean	518.66	505.99	521.62	511.52
	Std. Dev.	29.84	44.00	42.45	41.35
Attitude Towards the Job	Mean	496.36	492.22	500.76	494.73
	Std. Dev.	39.87	40.13	47.36	40.96
Community Involvement	Mean	259.05	250.77	257.05	253.58
	Std. Dev.	19.09	29.08	24.22	26.39

112.35, mean in aided schools was 2122.03 and standard deviation was 146.86 and in unaided schools, the mean was 2156.68 and standard deviation was 167.29. The details of the mean and standard deviations for components of teacher morale are presented according to three types of managements (Govt., Aided, Unaided) in the table 5.22.

Differential Analysis

In this section the comparisons were made between different types of decision-making styles (Routine, Compromise and Heuristic) and leadership styles (Initiating Structure and Consideration) and organisational health as a whole and its components and teacher morale and in its components by applying 'ANOVA' or 'F' test and 'T'-test. The details are presented in this section.

1. **Major Hypothesis:** There is no significant difference between schools under Heads with different decision-making styles (Routine, Compromise and Heuristic), and organisational health as a whole.

To test this hypothesis, the ANOVA test was applied between styles (Routine, Compromise and Heuristic) and results are presented in table 5.23.

Table 5.23: Results of ANOVA Test for Organisational Health as a Whole and Decision-making Style of Heads of Schools

SV	*df*	*SS*	*MSS*	*F-value*	*p-value*	*Significance*
Between Styles	2	5985.3332	2992.666	0.5835	>.05	NS
Within Styles	51	261573.84	5128.898			
Total	53	267559.17	8121.56			

Here obtained value of F is 0.5835 as smaller than the theoretical value of 3.1504 under 2 and 51 df at 0.05 level. The null hypothesis is accepted. It means that, there is no significant difference observed between schools under Heads with different decision-making styles (Routine, Compromise and, Heuristic), in organisational health as a whole.

Sub-hypothesis: There is no significant difference between schools under Heads with different decision-making styles (Routine, Compromise and Heuristic), in integrity.

To test this hypothesis, the ANOVA test was applied between styles (Routine, Compromise and Heuristic) and results are presented in table 5.24.

Table 5.24: Results of ANOVA for Decision-making Style in the Dimension of Organisational Health—Integrity

SV	*df*	*SS*	*MSS*	*F-value*	*p-value*	*Significance*
Between styles	2	92.8821	46.4411			
Within styles	51	2756.5226	54.0495	0.8592	>0.05	NS
Total	53	2849.4048	100.4905			

From the table 5.24, we observed that, obtained value of F is 0.8592 and is smaller than the theoretical value of 3.1504 under df at 0.05 level. The null hypothesis is accepted. It means that, there is no significant difference between the schools under Heads with different decision-making styles (Routine, Compromise and Heuristic) in integrity.

Sub-hypothesis: There is no significant difference between schools under Heads with different decision-making styles (Routine, Compromise and Heuristic), in consideration.

To test this hypothesis, the ANOVA test was applied between styles (Routine, Compromise and Heuristic) and results are presented in table 5.25.

The obtained value of F is 0.5377 and is smaller than the theoretical value of 3.1504 under 2 and 51 df at 0.05 level. Therefore, the null hypothesis is accepted. It indicates that, there is no significant difference between Heads with different decision-making styles (Routine, Compromise and Heuristic), in consideration.

Table 5.25: Results of ANOVA for Decision-making Style in Organisational Health Dimension—Consideration

SV	*df*	*SS*	*MSS*	*F-value*	*p-value*	*Significance*
Between styles	2	259.9699	129.9850			
Within styles	51	12329.678	241.7584	0.5377	>0.05	NS
Total	53	12589.648	371.7434			

Sub-hypothesis: There is no significant difference between schools under Heads with different decision-making styles (Routine, Compromise and Heuristic), in initiating structure.

To test this hypothesis, the ANOVA test was applied between styles (Routine, Compromise and Heuristic), and results are presented in table 5.26.

Table 5.26: Results of ANOVA for Decision-making Styles in Organisational Health Dimension—Initiating Structure

SV	*df*	*SS*	*MSS*	*F-value*	*p-value*	*Significant*
Between styles	2	779.0338	389.5169			
Within styles	51	11122.966	218.0974	1.7860	>.05	NS
Total	53	11902.000	607.6143			

The table 5.26 result clearly indicates that, the obtained value of F 1.78 and is smaller than the theoretical value of 3.1504 (df = 2, 51) at 0.05 level. Therefore the null hypothesis is accepted. It indicates that, there is no significant difference between schools under Heads with different decision-making style (Routine, Compromise and Heuristic), in initiating structure.

Sub-hypothesis: There is no significant difference between schools under Heads with different decision-making styles (Routine, Compromise, Heuristic) in resource support.

To test this hypothesis, the ANOVA test was applied between styles (Routine, Compromise, Heuristic) and results are presented in the table.

Table 5.27: Results of ANOVA for Decision-making Styles in Organisational Health Dimension—Resource Support

SV	*df*	*SS*	*MSS*	*F-value*	*p-value*	*Significant*
Between styles	2	168.4245	84.2122			
Within styles	51	12440.908	243.9394	0.3452	>0.05	NS
Total	53	12609.333	328.1516			

The obtained value of F, 0.3452, is smaller than the theoretical value of 3.1504 at 0.05 level under 2 and 51 df. Therefore the null hypothesis is accepted. It indicates that, there is no significant difference between schools under Heads with different decision-making styles (Routine, Compromise and Heuristic), in resource support.

Sub-hypothesis: There is no significant difference between schools under Heads with different decision-making styles (Routine, Compromise and Heuristic), in principal influence.

To test this hypothesis, the ANOVA test was applied between styles (Routine, Compromise and Heuristic), and results are presented in table 5.28.

Table 5.28: Results of ANOVA for Decision Making Style in Organisational Health Dimension—Principal Influence

SV	*df*	*SS*	*MSS*	*F-value*	*p-value*	*Significance*
Between styles	2	278.7007	139.3503			
Within styles	51	9222.7253	180.8378	0.7706	>0.05	NS
Total	53	9501.4259	320.1881			

Obtained value of F 0.7706 is smaller than the theoretical value of 3.1504 at 0.05 level. Therefore the null hypothesis is accepted. It indicates that, there is no significant difference between the schools under Heads with different decision-making styles (Routine, Compromise and Heuristic), in principal influence.

Sub-hypothesis: There is no significant difference between schools under Heads of the schools with different decision-making styles (Routine, Compromise and Heuristic), in morale.

To test this hypothesis, the ANOVA test was applied between styles (Routine, Compromise and Heuristic), and results are presented in table 5.29.

Table 5.29: Results of ANOVA for Decision-making Styles in Organisational Health Dimension—Morale

SV	*df*	*SS*	*MSS*	*F-value*	*p-value*	*Significance*
Between styles	2	380.6250	190.3125			
Within styles	51	6330.4120	124.1257	1.5332	>0.05	NS
Total	53	6711.0370	314.4382			

Here obtained value of F 1.5332 is smaller than the theoretical value of 3.1504 at 0.05 level. Therefore the null hypothesis is accepted. It indicates that, there is no significant difference between schools under Heads with different decision-making style (Routine, Compromise and Heuristic), in morale.

> **Sub-hypothesis:** There is no significant difference between schools under Heads with different decision-making styles (Routine, Compromise and Heuristic), in academic emphasis.

To test this hypothesis, the ANOVA test was applied between styles (Routine, Compromise and Heuristic), and results are presented in table 5.30.

Table 5.30: Results of ANOVA for Decision-making Styles in Organisational Health Dimension—Academic Emphasis.

SV	*df*	*SS*	*MSS*	*F-value*	*p-value*	*Significance*
Between styles	2	54.8421	24.4211			
Within styles	51	2209.3554	43.3207	0.6330	>0.05	NS
Total	53	2264.1975	70.7418			

Here obtained value of F 0.6330 is small than the theoretical value of 3.1504 at 0.05 level. Therefore the null hypothesis is accepted. It indicates that, there is no significant difference between schools under Heads with different decision-making style (Routine, Compromise and Heuristic), in academic emphasis.

2. **Major Hypothesis:** There is no significant difference between schools under Heads with different leadership styles (Initiating Structure, Consideration) in organisational health as a whole.

To test this hypothesis, the t-test was applied between styles (Initiating Structure, Consideration) and results are presented in table 5.31

Table 5.31: Results of t-test for Leadership Style in Organisational Health as a Whole

Leadership Style	*Mean*	*Std. Dev.*	*t-value*	*p-value*	*Significant*
Initiating Structure	472.0757	68.7363			
Consideration	470.4794	79.2796	0.0733	>0.05	NS

The table results shows that, there is no significant difference between schools under different leadership styles (Initiating Structure and Consideration) of Heads in organisational health as a whole.

Sub-hypothesis: There is no significant difference between schools under Heads with different leadership styles (Initiating Structure, Consideration) in integrity.

To test this hypothesis, t-test was applied between styles (Initiating Structure, Consideration) and results are presented in table 5.32.

Table 5.32: Results of t-test for Leadership Style in Organisational Health Dimension—Integrity

Leadership Style	*Mean*	*Std. Dev.*	*t-value*	*p-value*	*Significance*
Initiating Structure	64.0842	7.6965	-0.6426	>0.05	NS
Consideration	65.5238	6.4142			

The table 5.32 results show that there is no significant difference between schools under Heads with different leadership styles (Initiating Structure, Consideration) in integrity. Hence the null hypothesis is accepted.

Sub-hypothesis: There is no significant difference between schools under Heads with different leadership styles (Initiating Structure, Consideration) in consideration.

To test this hypothesis, t-test was applied between styles (Initiating Structure, Consideration) and results are presented in table 5.33.

Table 5.33: Results of t-test Leadership Style in Organisational Health Dimension—Consideration

Leadership Style	*Mean*	*Std. Dev.*	*t-value*	*p-value*	*Significance*
Initiating Structure	70.5385	15.0365	0.6524	>0.05	NS
Consideration	67.4667	16.6813			

The table 5.33 results show that, there is no significant difference between schools under Heads with different leadership styles (Initiating Structure, Consideration) in consideration. Hence the null hypothesis is accepted.

Sub-hypothesis: There is no significant difference between schools under Heads with different leadership behaviour styles (Initiating Structure, Consideration) in initiating structure.

To test this hypothesis, t-test was applied between styles (Initiating Structure, Consideration) and results are presented in table 5.34.

Table 5.34: Results of t-test for Leadership Style in Organisational Health Dimension—Initiating Structure

Leadership Style	*Mean*	*Std. Dev.*	*t-value*	*p-value*	*Significance*
Initiating Structure	69.2821	15.2280	0.2210	>0.05	NS
Consideration	68.2667	14.8298			

The above table results show that, there is no significant difference between schools under Heads with different leadership styles (Initiating Structure, Consideration) in initiating structure. Hence the null hypothesis is accepted.

Sub-hypothesis: There is no significant difference between schools under Heads with different leadership styles (Initiating Structure, Consideration) in resource support.

To test this hypothesis, t-test was applied between styles (Initiating Structure, Consideration) and results are presented in table 5.35.

Table 5.35: Results of t-test for Leadership Style in Organisational Health Dimension—Resource Support

Leadership Style	*Mean*	*Std. Dev.*	*t-value*	*p-value*	*Significance*
Initiating Structure	69.1538	15.5132	-0.4758	>0.05	NS
Consideration	71.4000	15.6059			

The table 5.35 results show that, there is no significant difference between schools under Heads with different leadership behaviour styles (Initiating Structure, Consideration) in resource support. Hence the null hypothesis is accepted.

Sub-hypothesis: There is no significant difference between schools under Heads with different leadership styles (Initiating Structure, Consideration) in principal influence.

To test this hypothesis, t-test was applied (Initiating Structure, Consideration) and results are presented in the table 5.36.

Table 5.36: Results of t-test for Leadership Style in Organisational Health Dimension—Principal influence

Leadership Style	*Mean*	*Std. Dev.*	*t-value*	*p-value*	*Significance*
Initiating Structure	72.1282	13.3873			
Consideration	70.0000	13.7373	0.5195	>0.05	NS

The table results show that there is no significant difference between schools under Heads with different leadership styles (Initiating Structure and consideration) in principal influence. Hence the null hypothesis is accepted.

Sub-hypothesis: There is no significant difference between schools under Heads with different leadership styles (Initiating Structure, Consideration) in morale.

To test this hypothesis, t-test was applied between styles (Initiating Structure, Consideration) and results are presented in table 5.37.

Table 5.37: Results of t-test for Leadership Style in Organisational Health Dimension—Morale

Leadership Style	*Mean*	*Std. Dev.*	*t-value*	*p-value*	*Significance*
Initiating Structure	81.9744	10.6758			
Consideration	80.6000	12.9824	0.3988	>0.05	NS

The above table results show that there is no significant difference between schools under Heads with differing leadership styles (Initiating Structure and Consideration) in morale. Hence the null hypothesis is accepted.

Sub-hypothesis: There is no significant difference between schools under Heads with different leadership style (Initiating Structure, Consideration) in academic emphasis.

To test this hypothesis, t-test was applied (Initiating Structure, Consideration) and results are presented in table 5.38.

Table 5.38: Results of t-test for Leadership Style in Organisational Health Dimension—Academic Emphasis

Leadership Style	*Mean*	*Std. Dev.*	*t-value*	*p-value*	*Significance*
Initiating Structure	44.9145	6.0999			
Consideration	47.2222	7.5242	-1.660	>0.05	NS

The table above shows that there is no significant difference between schools under Heads with different leadership styles (Initiating Structure and Consideration) in academic emphasis. Hence the null hypothesis is accepted.

3. **Major Hypothesis:** There is no significant difference between schools with male and female Heads in organisational health as a whole.

To test this hypothesis, t-test was applied and results are presented in table 5.39.

Table 5.39: Results of t-test for Sex in Organisational Health as a Whole

Sex	*Mean*	*Std. Dev.*	*t-value*	*p-value*	*Significance*
Male	478.4389	75.7618			
Female	456.8179	58.8852	1.0393	>0.05	NS

Table 5.39 results show that there is no significant difference between schools with male and female Heads in organisational health scores as a whole. Hence the null hypothesis is accepted.

Sub-hypothesis: There is no significant difference between schools under male and female Heads in integrity.

To test this hypothesis, t-test was applied between sex (Male & Female) and results are presented in table 5.40.

Table 5.40: Results of t-test for Sex in Organisational Health Dimension—Integrity

Sex	*Mean*	*Std. Dev.*	*t-value*	*p-value*	*Significance*
Male	64.6911	7.5114			
Female	64.0336	7.1292	0.3034	>0.05	NS

The table 5.40 shows that there is no significant difference between schools under male and female Heads in integrity. Hence the null hypothesis is accepted.

Sub hypothesis: There is no significant difference between schools under male and female Heads in consideration.

To test this hypothesis, t-test was applied and results are presented in table 5.41.

Table 5.41: Results of t-test for Sex in Organisational Health Dimension—Consideration

Sex	*Mean*	*Std. Dev.*	*t-value*	*p-value*	*Significance*
Male	71.3514	16.7750			
Female	66.0588	11.5459	1.1762	>0.05	NS

The above table results shows that there is no significant difference between schools under male and female Heads in consideration. Hence the null hypothesis is accepted.

Sub-hypothesis: There is no significant difference between schools under male and female Heads in initiating structure.

To test this hypothesis, the t-test was applied and results are presented in the table 5.42.

Table 5.42: Results of t-test for Sex in Organisational Health Dimension—Initiating Structure

Sex	*Mean*	*Std. Dev.*	*t-value*	*p-value*	*Significance*
Male	70.5676	16.2096			
Female	65.5882	11.6031	1.1372	>0.05	NS

The above table results show that there is no significant difference between schools under male and female Heads in initiating structure. Hence the null hypothesis is accepted.

Sub-hypothesis: There is no significant difference between schools under male and female Heads in resource support.

To test this hypothesis, the t-test was applied and results are presented in table 5.43.

Table 5.43: Results of t-test for Sex in Organisational Health Dimension—Resource Support

Sex	*Mean*	*Std. Dev.*	*t-value*	*p-value*	*Significance*
Male	71.0000	15.9983			
Female	67.1176	14.1857	0.8569	>0.05	NS

The table 5.43 shows that there is no significant difference between schools under male and female Heads in resource support. Hence the null hypothesis is accepted.

Sub-hypothesis: There is no significant difference between schools under male and female Heads in principal influence.

To test this hypothesis, the t-test was applied and results are presented in table 5.44.

Table 5.44: Results of t-test for Sex in Organisational Health Dimension—Principal Influence

Sex	*Mean*	*Std. Dev.*	*t-value*	*p-value*	*Significance*
Male	72.2162	13.8747			
Female	70.0588	12.5423	0.5463	>0.05	NS

The above table results shows that there is no significant difference between schools under male and female Heads in principal influence. Hence the null hypothesis is accepted.

Sub-hypothesis: There is no significant difference between schools under male and female Heads in morale.

To test this hypothesis, the t-test was applied and results and presented in table 5.45.

Table 5.45: Results of t-test for Sex in Organisational Health Dimension—Morale

Sex	*Mean*	*Std. Dev.*	*t-value*	*p-value*	*Significance*
Male	82.3514	12.2547			
Female	79.9412	8.7925	0.7278	>0.05	NS

The table 5.45 shows that there is no significant difference between schools under male and female Heads in morale. Hence the null hypothesis is accepted.

Sub-hypothesis: There is no significant difference between schools under male and female Heads in academic emphasis.

To test this hypothesis, the t-test was applied and results are presented in table 5.46.

Table 5.46: Results of t-test for Sex in Organisational Health Dimension—Academic Emphasis

Sex	*Mean*	*Std. Dev.*	*t-value*	*p-value*	*Significance*
Male	46.2613	6.6970			
Female	44.0196	6.0780	1.1747	>0.05	NS

The above table result shows that there is no significant difference between schools under male and female Heads in academic emphasis. Hence the null hypothesis is accepted.

4. **Major Hypothesis:** There is no significant difference between schools under Heads with varying experience (below 15, 15-25, above 25 years) in organisational health as a whole.

To test this hypothesis, the ANOVA test was applied and results are presented in table 5.47.

Table 5.47: Results of ANOVA for Experience (Below 15, 15-25, Above 25 years) in Organisational Health as a Whole

SV	*df*	*SS*	*MSS*	*F-value*	*p-value*	*Significance*
Between exp.	2	9676.9504	4838.475			
Within exp.	51	257882.22	5056.514	0.9569	>0.05	NS
Total	53	267559.17	9894.989			

Here obtained value of F is 0.9569 which is smaller than the theoretical value of 3.1504 under 2 and 51 df at 0.05 level. The null hypothesis is accepted. It means that, there is no significant difference observed between schools under Heads with varying experience (below 15, 15-25, above 25 years) in organisational health as a whole.

Sub-hypothesis: There is no significant difference between schools under Heads with varying experience (below 15, 15-25 above 25 years) in integrity.

To test this hypothesis, the ANOVA test was applied and results are presented in table 5.48.

Table 5.48: Results of ANOVA for Experience (Below 15, 15-25, Above 25 years) in Organisational Health Dimension—Integrity

SV	*df*	*SS*	*MSS*	*F-value*	*p-value*	*Significance*
Between	2	97.6291	48.8146			
Within	51	2751.7757	53.9564	0.9047	>0.05	NS
Total	53	2849.4048	102.7709			

The table 5.48 reveals that, obtained value of F is 0.9047 is smaller than the theoretical value of 3.1504 under same df at 0.05 level. The null hypothesis is accepted. It means that, there is no significant difference between schools under Heads with varying experience (below 15, 15-25, above 25 years) in integrity. In other words, schools under Heads with different experience do not differ in integrity.

Sub-hypothesis: There is no significant difference between schools under Heads with varying experience (below 15, 15-25, above 25 years) in consideration.

To test this hypothesis, the ANOVA test was applied between experience (below 15, 15-25, above 25 years) and results are presented in table 5-49.

Table 5.49: Results of ANOVA for Experience (Below 15, 15-25, above 25 years) in Organisational Health Dimension—Consideration

SV	*df*	*SS*	*MSS*	*F-value*	*p-value*	*Significance*
Between	2	583.7800	291.8900			
Within	51	12005.868	235.4092	1.2399	>0.05	NS
Total	53	12589.648	527.2992			

The obtained value of F is 1.2399, which is smaller than the theoretical value of 3.1504 under 2 and 51 df at 0.05 level. Therefore, the null hypothesis is accepted. It indicates that, there is no significant difference between schools under Heads with varying experience (below 15, 15-25, above 25 years) in consideration. In other words, schools under Heads with different experience do not differ in consideration.

Sub-hypothesis: There is no significant difference between schools under Heads with varying experience (below 15, 15-25, above 25 years) in initiating structure.

To test this hypothesis, the ANOVA test was applied between experience (below 15, 15-25, above 25 years) and results are presented in table 5.50.

Table 5.50: Results of ANOVA for Experience (below 15, 15-25, Above 25 years) in Organisational Health Dimension—Initiating Structure

SV	*df*	*SS*	*MSS*	*F-value*	*p-value*	*Significance*
Between	2	563.5605	281.7802			
Within	51	11338.439	222.3223	1.2674	>0.05	NS
Total	53	11902.000	504.1026			

The table 5.50 results clearly indicate that, the obtained value of F, which is 1.2674, is smaller than the theoretical value of 3.1504 (df = 2, 51) at 0.05 level. Therefore the null hypothesis is accepted. It indicates that, there is no significant difference between schools under Heads of schools with varying experience (below 15, 15-25, above 25 years) in initiating structure. In other words, schools under Heads with different experience do not differ in initiating structure.

Sub-hypothesis: There is no significant difference between schools under Heads with varying experience (below 15, 15-25, above 25 years) in resource support.

To test this hypothesis, the ANOVA test was applied between experience (below 15, 15-25, above 25 years) and results are presented in table 5.51.

Table 5.51: Results of ANOVA for experience (below 15, 15-25, above 25 years) in Organisational Health Dimension—Resource Support

SV	*df*	*SS*	*MSS*	*F-value*	*p-value*	*Significance*
Between	2	687.9587	343.9794			
Within	51	11921.374	233.7524	1.4716	>0.05	NS
Total	53	12609.333	577.7318			

The obtained value of F is 1.4716 is smaller than the theoretical value of 3.1504 at 0.05 level under 2, and 51 df.

Therefore the null hypothesis is accepted. It indicates that there is no significant difference between schools under Heads with varying experience (below 15, 15-25, above 25 years) in resource support. In other words, schools under Heads with different experience do not differ in resource support.

Sub-hypothesis: There is no significant difference between schools under Heads with varying experience (below 15, 15-25, above 25 years) in principal influence.

To test this hypothesis, the ANOVA test was applied between experience (below 15, 15-25, above 25 years) and results are presented in table 5.52.

Table 5.52: Results of ANOVA for Experience (Below 15, 15-25, Above 25 years) in Organisational Health Dimension—Principal Influence

SV	*df*	*SS*	*MSS*	*F-value*	*p-value*	*Significance*
Between	2	359.2775	179.6387			
Within	51	9142.1485	179.2578	1.0021	>0.05	NS
Total	53	9501.4259	358.8965			

Obtained value of F is 1.0021 is smaller than the theoretical value of 3.1504 at 0.05 level. Therefore the null hypothesis is accepted. It indicates that, there is no significant difference between schools under Heads with varying experience (below 15, 15-25, above 25 years) in principal influence. Schools under Heads with different experience do not differ in principal influence.

Sub-hypothesis: There is no significant difference between schools under Heads with varying experience (below 15, 15-25, above 25 years) in morale.

To test this hypothesis, the ANOVA test was applied between experience (below 15, 15-25, above 25 years) and results are presented in table 5.53.

Table 5.53: Results of ANOVA for Experience (Below 15, 15-25, Above 25 years) in Organisational Health Dimension—Morale

SV	*df*	*SS*	*MSS*	*F-value*	*p-value*	*Significance*
Between	2	27.9069	13.9535			
Within	51	6683.1301	131.0418	0.1065	>0.05	NS
Total	53	6711.0370	144.9952			

Here obtained value of F as 1.1065, which is smaller than the theoretical value of 3.1504 at 0.05 level. Therefore the null hypothesis is accepted. It indicates that, there is no significant difference between schools under Heads with varying experience (below 15, 15-25, above 25 years) in morale. In other words schools under Heads with different experience do not differ in morale.

Sub-hypothesis: There is no significant difference between schools under Heads with varying experience (below 15, 15-25, above 25 years) in academic emphasis.

To test this hypothesis, the ANOVA test was applied between experience (below 15, 15-25, above 25 years) and results are presented in table 5.54.

Table 5.54: Results of ANOVA for Experience (Below 15, 15-25, Above 25 years) in Organisational Health Dimension—Academic Emphasis

SV	*df*	*SS*	*MSS*	*F-value*	*p-value*	*Significance*
Between	2	4.6022	2.3011			
Within	51	2259.5953	44.3058	0.0519	>0.05	NS
Total	53	2264.1975	46.6069			

Here obtained value of F as 0.0519 is smaller than the theoretical value of 3.1504 at 0.05 level. Therefore the null hypothesis is accepted. It indicates that, there is no significant difference between schools under Heads with varying experience (below 15, 15-25, above 25 years) in academic emphasis. In other words, schools under Heads with different experience do not differ in academic emphasis.

5. **Major Hypothesis:** There is no significant difference between schools under Heads with different decision-making styles (Routine, Compromise, Heuristic) in teacher morale as a whole.

To test this hypothesis, the ANOVA test was applied and results are presented in table 5.55.

Table 5.55: Results of ANOVA test for Teacher Morale as a Whole and Decision-making Style of Heads of Schools

SV	*df*	*SS*	*MSS*	*F-value*	*p-value*	*Significance*
Between	2	16768.13	8384.06			
Within	51	1095917.8	21488.58	0.3902	>0.05	NS
Total	53	1112685.9	29872.65			

The value of F obtained is 0.3902, which is smaller than the theoretical value of 3.1504 under 2 and 51 df at 0.05 level. The null hypothesis is accepted. It means that there is no significant difference observed between schools under Heads with different decision-making styles in teacher morale as a whole.

Sub-hypothesis: There is no significant difference between schools under Heads with different decision-making styles (Routine, Compromise, Heuristic) in individual characteristics.

To test this hypothesis, the ANOVA test was applied and results are presented in table 5.56.

Table 5.56: Results of ANOVA for Teacher Morale Component— Individual Characteristics and Decision-making Styles of Heads of Schools

SV	*df*	*SS*	*MSS*	*F-value*	*p-value*	*Significant*
Between	2	302.83	151.42			
Within	51	24654.87	483.43	0.3132	>0.05	NS
Total	53	24957.70	634.84			

From the above table it is observed that, obtained value of F 0.3132 is smaller than the theoretical value of 3.1504 under same df at 0.05 level. The null hypothesis is accepted. It means there is no significant difference between the schools under Heads with different decision-making styles in individual characteristics.

Sub-hypothesis: There is no significant difference between schools under Heads with different decision-making styles (Routine, Compromise, Heuristic) in behavioural characteristics.

To test this hypothesis, the ANOVA test was applied and results are presented in table 5.57.

Table 5.57: Results of ANOVA for Teacher Morale Component—Behavioural Characteristics and Decision-making Styles

SV	*df*	*SS*	*MSS*	*F-value*	*p-value*	*Significance*
Between	2	835.08	417.54			
Within	51	43996.12	862.67	0.4840	>0.05	NS
Total	53	44831.21	1280.21			

From the table 5.57, it is observed that, obtained value of F 0.4840 is smaller than the theoretical value of 3.1504 under same df at 0.05 level. The null hypothesis is accepted. It means that, there is no significant difference between schools under Heads with different decision-making styles in behavioural characteristics. In other words, schools under Heads with different decision-making styles do not differ on behavioural characteristics.

Sub-hypothesis: There is no significant difference between schools under Heads with different decision-making styles (Routine, Compromise, Heuristic) in group spirit.

To test this hypothesis, the ANOVA test was applied and the results are presented in table 5.58.

Table 5.58: Results of ANOVA for Teacher Morale Component—Group Spirit and Decision-making Style

SV	*df*	*SS*	*MSS*	*F-value*	*p-value*	*Significance*
Between	2	3597.10	1798.55			
Within	51	87035.97	1706.59	1.0539	>0.05	NS
Total	53	90633.07	3505.14			

From the table 5.58, we observe that, the value of F 1.0539 is smaller than the theoretical value of 3.1504 under same df at 0.05 level. The null hypothesis is accepted. It means there is no significant difference between schools under Heads with different in decision-making style in group spirit. In other words, schools under Heads with different decision-making styles do not differ in group spirit.

Sub-hypothesis: There is no significant difference between schools under Heads with different decision-making styles (Routine, Compromise, Heuristic) in attitude towards job.

To test this hypothesis, the ANOVA test was and the results are presented in table 5.59.

Table 5.59: Results of ANOVA for Attitude Towards Job and Decision-making Style

SV	*df*	*SS*	*MSS*	*F-value*	*p-value*	*Significance*
Between	2	1243.10	621.55			
Within	51	87657.89	1718.78	0.3616	>0.05	NS
Total	53	88900.98	2340.33			

From the table 5.59, we observe that, the value of F 0.3616 is smaller than the theoretical value of 3.1504 under df at 0.05 level. The null hypothesis is accepted. It means that, there is no significant difference between schools under Heads with different decision-making styles in attitude towards job. In other words, schools under Heads with different decision-making styles do not differ in attitude towards job.

Sub-hypothesis: There is no significant difference between schools under Heads with different decision-making styles (Routine, Compromise, Heuristic) in community involvement.

To test this hypothesis, the ANOVA test was applied and the results are presented in table 5.60.

Table 5.60: Results of ANOVA for Teacher Morale Component Community Involvement and Decision-making Style

SV	*df*	*SS*	*MSS*	*F-value*	*p-value*	*Significant*
Between	2	378.94	189.47			
Within	51	36522.93	716.14	0.2646	>0.05	NS
Total	53	36901.88	905.61			

From the above table we observe that, obtained value of F 0.2646 is smaller than the theoretical value of 3.1504 under same df at 0.05 level. The null hypothesis is accepted. It means there is no significant difference between schools under Heads with different decision-making styles in community involvement. In other words, schools under Heads with different decision-making styles do not differ in community involvement.

6. **Major Hypothesis:** There is no significant difference between schools under Heads with different leadership styles (Initiating Structure and Consideration) in teacher morale as a whole.

To test this hypothesis, the t-test was applied and the results are presented in table 5.61.

Table 5.61: Results of t-test for Teacher Morale as a Whole and Leadership Style

Leadership Style	*Mean*	*SD*	*t-value*	*p-value*	*Significance*
Initiating structure	2136.1026	130.9796			
Consideration	2148.9400	181.0654	0.2891	>0.05	NS

The table 5.61 results show that there is no significant difference between schools under Heads with (Initiating Structure and Consideration) different leadership style in teacher morale as a whole. Hence the null hypothesis is accepted.

Sub-hypothesis: There is no significant difference between schools under Heads of schools with different leadership style (Initiating Structure, Consideration) in individual characteristics.

To test this hypothesis, the student's t-test was applied and the results are presented in table 5.62.

Table 5.62: Results of t-test for Teaching Morale Component—Individual Characteristics and Leadership Style

Leadership Style	*Mean*	*SD*	*t-value*	*p-value*	*Significance*
Initiating structure	350.0769	19.9992	0.5408	>0.05	NS
Consideration	353.6667	26.2125			

The table 5.62 results show that, there is no significant difference between schools under Heads with different leadership styles (Initiating Structure and Consideration) in individual characteristics. Hence the null hypothesis is accepted.

Sub-hypothesis: There is no significant difference between schools under Heads with different leadership styles (Initiating Structure and Consideration) in behavioural characteristics.

To test this hypothesis, t-test test was applied and the results are presented in table 5.63.

Table 5.63: Results of t-test for Teacher Morale Component—Behavioural Characteristics and Leadership Style

Leadership Style	*Mean*	*SD*	*t-value*	*p-value*	*Significance*
Initiating structure	525.9641	26.9119	1.1436	>0.05	NS
Consideration	536.0400	34.0271			

The table 5.63 results show that there is no significant difference between schools under Heads with different leadership styles (Initiating Structure and Consideration) in behavioural characteristics. Hence the null hypothesis is accepted.

Sub-hypothesis: There is no significant difference between schools under Heads with different leadership styles (Initiating Structure and Consideration) in group Spirit.

To test this hypothesis, the t-test test was applied and the results are presented in table 5.64.

Table 5.64: Results of t-test for Teacher Morale Component—Group Spirit and Leadership Style

Leadership Style	*Mean*	*SD*	*t-value*	*p-value*	*Significance*
Initiating structure	512.6103	38.3649	0.3091	>0.05	NS
Consideration	508.6933	49.6674			

The table 5.64 results show that there is no significant difference between Heads of schools with differing leadership styles (Initiating Structure and Consideration) in group spirit. Hence the null hypothesis is accepted.

Sub-hypothesis: There is no significant difference between schools under Heads with different leadership styles (Initiating Structure and Consideration) in attitude towards the job.

To test this hypothesis, the t-test test was applied and the results are presented in table 5.65.

Table 5.65: Results of t-test for Teacher Morale Component—Attitude Towards Job and Leadership Style

Leadership Style	*Mean*	*SD*	*t-value*	*p-value*	*Significance*
Initiating structure	493.8359	35.6740			
Consideration	497.0400	53.7385	0.2552	>0.05	NS

The table 5.65 results show that there is no significant difference between schools under Heads with different leadership styles (Initiating Structure and Consideration) in attitude towards job. Hence the null hypothesis is accepted.

Sub-hypothesis: There is no significant difference between schools under Heads with different leadership styles (Initiating Structure and Consideration) in community involvement.

To test this hypothesis, the t-test test was applied and the results are presented in table 5.66.

Table 5.66: Results of t-test for Teacher Morale Component—Community Involvement and Leadership Style

Leadership Style	*Mean*	*SD*	*t-value*	*p-value*	*Significance*
Initiating structure	253.6154	24.9564	0.0143	>0.05	NS
Consideration	253.5000	30.7461			

The table 5.66 results show that there is no significant difference between schools under Heads with different leadership styles (Initiating Structure and Consideration) in community involvement. Hence the null hypothesis is accepted.

7. **Major Hypothesis**: There is no significant difference between schools under male and female Heads in teacher morale as a whole.

To test this hypothesis, the t-test test was applied and the results are presented in table 5.67.

Table 5.67: Results of t-test for Teacher Morale as a whole and Sex of Heads of Schools

Sex	*Mean*	*SD*	*t-value*	*p-value*	*Significance*
Male	2160.1649	138.9272			
Female	2095.0588	151.7573	1.5539	>0.05	NS

The table 5.67 results show that there is no significant difference between schools under male and female Heads in teacher morale as a whole. Hence the null hypothesis is accepted.

Sub-hypothesis: There is no significant difference between schools under male and female Heads in individual characteristics.

To test this hypothesis, the t-test test was applied and the results are presented in table 5.68.

Table 5.68: Results of t-test for Teacher Morale Component—Individual Characteristics and Sex of Heads of Schools

Sex	*Mean*	*SD*	*t-value*	*p-value*	*Significance*
Male	352.5946	20.6834			
Female	347.7647	24.0898	0.7566	>0.05	NS

The table 5.68 results show that there is no significant difference between schools under male and female Heads in individual characteristics. Hence the null hypothesis is accepted.

Sub-hypothesis: There is no significant difference between schools under male and female Heads in behavioural characteristics.

To test this hypothesis, the t-test test was applied and the results are presented in table 5.69.

Table 5.69: Results of t-test for Teacher Morale Component—Behavioural Characteristics and Sex of Heads of Schools

Sex	*Mean*	*SD*	*t-value*	*p-value*	*Significance*
Male	532.6973	26.8289			
Female	520.2000	32.6912	1.4830	>0.05	NS

The table 5.69 results show that there is no significant difference between schools under male and female Heads in behavioural characteristics. Hence the null hypothesis is accepted.

Sub-hypothesis: There is no significant difference between schools under male and female Heads in group spirit.

To test this hypothesis, the t-test test was applied and the results are presented in table 5.70.

Table 5.70: Results of t-test for Teacher Morale Component—Group Spirit and Sex of Heads of Schools

Sex	*Mean*	*SD*	*t-value*	*p-value*	*Significance*
Male	516.1351	41.9678			
Female	501.4824	39.3109	1.2147	>0.05	NS

The table 5.70 results show that there is no significant difference between schools under male and female Heads in group spirit. Hence the null hypothesis is accepted.

Sub-hypothesis: There is no significant difference between schools under male and female Heads in attitude towards job.

To test this hypothesis, the t-test test was applied the and results are presented in table 5.71.

Table 5.71: Results of t-test for Teacher Morale Component—Attitude Towards Job and Sex of Heads of Schools

Sex	*Mean*	*SD*	*t-value*	*p-value*	*Significance*
Male	501.1027	38.4004			
Female	480.8471	44.0430	1.7188	>0.05	NS

The table 5.71 results show that there is no significant difference between schools under male and female Heads in attitude towards job. Hence the null hypothesis is accepted.

Sub-hypothesis: There is no significant difference between schools under male and female Heads in community involvement.

To test this hypothesis, the t-test test was applied and the results are presented in table 5.72.

Table 5.72: Results of t-test for Teacher Morale Component—Community Involvement and Sex of Heads of Schools

Sex	*Mean*	*SD*	*t-value*	*p-value*	*Significance*
Male	257.6351	26.8011	1.6938	>0.05	NS
Female	244.7647	23.8662			

The above table results show that there is no significant difference between schools under male and female Heads in community involvement. Hence the null hypothesis is accepted.

8. **Major Hypothesis:** There is no significant difference between schools under Heads with varying experience (below 15, 15-25, above 25 years) in teacher morale as a whole.

To test this hypothesis, the ANOVA test was applied and the results are presented in table 5.73.

Table 5.73: Results of ANOVA test for Teacher Morale as a Whole and Experience of Heads of Schools

SV	*df*	*SS*	*MSS*	*F-value*	*p-value*	*Significance*
Between	2	25805.40	12902.70			
Within	51	1086880.5	21311.38	0.6054	>0.05	NS
Total	53	1112685.9	34214.08			

Here obtained value of F 0.6054 is smaller than the theoretical value of 3.1504 under 2 and 51 df at 0.05 level. The null hypothesis is accepted. It means there is no significant difference observed between schools under Heads with varying experience in teacher morale as a whole.

Sub-hypothesis: There is no significant difference between schools under heads with varying experience (below 15, 15-25, above 25 years) in individual characteristics.

To test this hypothesis, the ANOVA test was applied and the results are presented in table 5.74.

Table 5.74: Results of ANOVA Test for Teacher Morale Component—Individual Characteristics and Experience of Heads of Schools

SV	*df*	*SS*	*MSS*	*F-value*	*p-value*	*Significance*
Between	2	451.82	225.91			
Within	51	24505.89	480.51	0.4701	>0.05	NS
Total	53	24957.70	706.42			

From the table 5.74, we observe that, obtained value of F 0.4701 is smaller than the theoretical value of 3.1504 under df at 0.05 level. The null hypothesis is accepted. It means there is no significant difference between the schools under Heads with varying experience in individual characteristics.

Sub-hypothesis: There is no significant difference between schools under Heads with varying experience (below 15, 15-25, above 25 years) in behavioural characteristics.

To test this hypothesis, the ANOVA test was applied and the results are presented in table 5.75.

Table 5.75: Results of ANOVA Test for Teacher Morale Component—Behavioural Characteristics and Experience of Heads of Schools

SV	*df*	*SS*	*MSS*	*F-value*	*p-value*	*Significance*
Between	2	1032.57	516.29			
Within	51	43798.63	858.80	0.6012	>0.05	NS
Total	53	44831.21	1375.08			

From the above table we observe that, obtained value of F 0.4840 is smaller than the theoretical value of 3.1504 under same df at 0.05 level. The null hypothesis is accepted. It means that, there is no significant difference between the schools under Heads with varying experience in behavioural characteristics.

Sub-hypothesis: There is no significant difference between schools under Heads with varying experience (below 15, 15-25, above 25 years) in group spirit.

To test this hypothesis, the ANOVA test was applied and the results are presented in table 5.76.

Table 5.76: Results of ANOVA Test for Teacher Morale Component—Group Spirit and Experience of Heads of Schools

SV	*df*	*SS*	*MSS*	*F-value*	*p-value*	*Significance*
Between	2	3204.26	1602.13			
Within	51	87428.81	1714.29	0.9346	>0.05	NS
Total	53	90633.07	3316.42			

From the above table we observe that, obtained value of F 1.0539 is smaller than the theoretical value of 3.1504 under df at 0.05 level. The null hypothesis is accepted. It means there is no significant difference between schools under Heads with varying experience in group spirit.

Sub-hypothesis: There is no significant difference between schools under Heads with varying experience (below 15, 15-25, above 25 years) in attitude towards job.

To test this hypothesis, the ANOVA test was applied and the results are presented in table 5.77.

Table 5.77: Results of ANOVA Test for Teacher Morale Component—Attitude Towards Job and Experience of Heads of Schools

SV	*df*	*SS*	*MSS*	*F-value*	*p-value*	*Significance*
Between	2	1251.83	625.92			
Within	51	87649.15	1718.61	0.3642	>0.05	NS
Total	53	88900.98	2344.53			

From the above table we observe that, obtained value of F 0.3616 is smaller than the theoretical value of 3.1504 under df at 0.05 level. The null hypothesis is accepted. It means there is no significant difference between schools under Heads with varying experience in attitude towards job.

Sub-hypothesis: There is no significant difference between schools under Heads with varying experience (below 15, 15-25, above 25 years) in community involvement.

To test this hypothesis, the ANOVA test was applied and the results are presented in table 5.78.

Table 5.78: Results of ANOVA Test for Teacher Morale Component—Community Involvement and Experience of Heads of Schools

SV	*df*	*SS*	*MSS*	*F-value*	*p-value*	*Significance*
Between	2	413.23	206.62			
Within	51	36488.64	715.46	0.2888	>0.05	NS
Total	53	36901.88	922.08			

From the above table we observe that, obtained value of F 0.2646 is smaller than the theoretical value of 3.1504 under df at 0.05 level. The null hypothesis is accepted. It means there is no significant difference between the schools under Heads with varying experience in community involvement.

9. **Major Hypothesis:** There is no interaction effect of Heads decision-making styles (Routine, Compromise, Heuristic) and leadership styles (Initiating Structure and Consideration) on organisational health.

To achieve this, the two-way ANOVA with interaction statistical tool was applied between two factors, decision-making styles (Routine, Compromise and Heuristic), and leadership styles (Initiating Structure and Consideration), on organisational health as a whole. The results are presented in table 5.79.

Table 5.79: ANOVA for Interaction Between Decision-making Styles and Leadership Styles on Organisational Health as a Whole

SV	*df*	*SS*	*MSS*	*F-value*	*p-value*	*Significance*
Main effects						
Decision-making styles	2	4136.38	2068.19	0.3816	>0.05	NS
Leadership Styles	1	269.57	269.57	0.0497	>0.05	NS
Interaction						
Decision-making Styles and Leadership Styles	2	712.17	356.08	0.0657	>0.05	NS
Error	48	260149.01				
Total	53	265267.13	5419.77			

The above table result reveals that:

(i) There is no significant difference between Heads with three different decision-making styles (Routine, Compromise and Heuristic), in organisational health.

(ii) There is no significant difference between Heads with different leadership styles (Initiating Structure and Consideration) in organisational health at 0.05 level.

(iii) The interaction effects of decision-making styles (Routine, Compromise and Heuristic), and leadership styles (Initiating Structure and Consideration) on organisational health scores of teache as a whole are not significant at 0.05 level.

10. **Major Hypothesis:** There is no interaction effect of decision-making styles (Routine, Compromise and

Heuristic), and leadership styles (Initiating Structure and Consideration) on teacher morale.

To achieve this, the two-way ANOVA with interaction statistical tool was applied between two factors—decision-making styles (Routine, Compromise and Heuristic), and leadership styles (Initiating Structure and Consideration)—on teacher morale as a whole. The results are presented in table 5.80.

Table 5.80: ANOVA with Interaction Between Decision-making Styles and Leadership Styles on Teacher Morale as a Whole

SV	*df*	*SS*	*MSS*	*F-value*	*p-value*	*Significance*
Main effects						
Decision-making Styles	2	28481	14241	0.6414	>0.05	NS
Leadership Styles	1	6795	6795	0.3061	>0.05	NS
Interaction						
Decision-making Styles and Leadership Styles	2	20097	10048	0.4526	>0.05	NS
Error	48	1065770	22204			
Total	53	1121143				

The above table result reveals that:

(i) There is no significant difference between different decision-making styles (Routine, Compromise and Heuristic), of Heads of schools at 0.05 level.

(ii) There is no significant difference between leadership styles (Initiating Structure and Consideration) of Heads of schools at 0.05 level.

(iii) The interaction effects of decision-making styles (Routine, Compromise and Heuristic), and

leadership styles (Initiating Structure and Consideration), on teacher morale scores as a whole are not significant at 0.05 level.

Correlation Analysis

In case of bi-variate analyses, one has to face questions such as (i) Does there exist an association between the two variables? If so, to what extent? (ii) Is there any cause and effect relationship between two variables? If one increases or decreases, does it affect the other? If yes, to what extent and in which direction. The first question is answered by the use of correlation technique. But the correlation coefficient 'r' usually estimates the degree of closeness of linear relationship between two variables (Y and X). Many apparently unrelated variables rise or fall together. Therefore, it does not answer the second question dealing with cause and effect relationship. How much does it change for a given change in X? What is the shape of the curve connecting Y and X? How accurately can 'Y' be predicted from X? These questions are handled by the regression technique.

In the present study correlation analysis was done using the measures of two variables, say (X_1 = Organisational Health, X_2 = Teachers Morale) and their respective dimensions.

The 54 Heads of schools formed the sample for the present study. The Karl Pearson's correlation coefficient test was applied. Bi-variate correlations between the variables studied are worked out and the chi-square test was applied to assess the significant association between two qualitative variables or two attributes. The details are furnished in this section.

11. **Major Hypothesis:** There is no association between decision-making styles (Routine, Compromise and Heuristic), and leadership styles (Initiating Structure, Consideration) of Heads of schools.

To achieve this hypothesis, the chi-square test was applied and results are presented in table 5.81.

Table 5.81: Results of Chi-square Test Between Decision-making Styles (Routine, Heuristic) and Leadership Styles (Initiating Structure, Consideration)

Decision-making Styles	*Leadership Styles*		*Total*
	Initiating Structure	*Consideration*	
Routine	17 58.62%	12 41.38%	29
Heuristic	8 72.73%	3 27.27%	11
Total	25	15	40
Chi-square = .54 (P > .05) (<0.05)			

The above table results reveal that there is no significant association between decision-making styles (Routine, Heuristic) and leadership styles (Initiating Structure, Consideration) at 0.05 level (chi-square = .54). Hence the null hypothesis is accepted. It means there is no association between decision-making style and leadership style of Heads of Schools.

12. **Major Hypothesis:** There is no association between decision-making styles (Routine, Compromise, Heuristic) and organisational health (High, Average, Low).

To test this hypothesis, the chi-square test was applied and results are presented in table 5.82.

Table 5.82: Results of Chi-square Test Between Decision-making Styles (Routine, Compromise, Heuristic) and Organisational Health (High, Average, Low)

Decision-making Styles	*Organisational Health*			*Row Total*
	H	*A*	*L*	
Routine	7 24.14%	15 51.72%	7 24.14%	29
Compromise	3 21.43%	8 57.14%	3 21.43%	14
Heuristic	3 27.27%	4 36.36%	4 36.36%	11
Total	13	27	14	54
Chi-square = 1.2639, >0.05, NS				

There is no significant association between decision-making styles (Routine, Compromise, Heuristic) of Heads of Schools and organisational health (High, Average, Low) at 0.05 level (chi-square = 1.2639). Hence the null hypothesis is accepted. It means that decision-making styles (Routine, Compromise, Heuristic) of Heads of schools is independent of organisational health (High, Average, Low).

13. **Major Hypothesis:** There is no association between decision-making style of Heads of Schools (Routine, Compromise, Heuristic) and teacher morale (High, Average, Low).

To test this hypothesis, the chi-square test was applied and results are presented in table 5.83.

Table 5.83: Results of Chi-square Test Between Decision-making Styles of Heads of Schools (Routine, Compromise, Heuristic) and Teacher Moralc (High, Average, Low)

Decision-making	*Teacher Morale*			*Row*
Styles	*H*	*A*	*L*	*Total*
Routine	5 17.24%	18 62.07%	6 20.69%	29
Compromise	3 21.43%	9 64.29%	2 14.29%	14
Heuristic	4 36.36%	5 45.45%	2 18.18%	11
Total	12	32	10	54
Chi-square = 1.9796, >0.05, NS				

There is no significant association between decision-making styles (Routine, Compromise, Heuristic) of Heads of schools and teacher morale (High, Average, Low) at 0.05 level (Chi-square = 1.9796). Hence the null hypothesis is accepted. It means decision-making styles (Routine, Compromise, Heuristic) of Heads of schools is independent of teacher morale (High, Average, Low).

14. Major Hypothesis: There is no association between decision-making style (Routine, Compromise, Heuristic) and sex (Male, Female) of Heads of schools.

To test this hypothesis, the chi-square test was applied and results are presented in table 5.84.

Table 5.84: Results of Chi-square Test Between Decision-making Styles (Routine, Compromise, Heuristic) and Sex (Male, Female)

Decision-making Styles	*Sex*		*Total*
	Male	*Female*	
Routine	16 55.17%	13 44.83%	29
Compromise	11 78.57%	3 21.43%	14
Heuristic	10 90.91%	1 9.09%	11
Total	37	17	54
Chi-square = 6.1312, <0.05, S			

The above table results reveal that there is a significant association between decision-making style (Routine, Compromise, Heuristic) and sex (male and female) at 0.05 level (chi-square = 6.1312, <0.05). Hence the null hypothesis is rejected. Compromise and Heuristic style go more with male than with female Heads of schools.

15. Major Hypothesis: There is no association between decision-making style (Routine, Compromise, Heuristic) and teaching experience (below 15, 15-25, above 25 years) of Heads of schools.

To test this hypothesis, the chi-square test was applied and results are presented in table 5.85.

There is no significant association between decision-making style (Routine, Compromise, Heuristic) and teaching experience (below 15, 15-25, above 25 years) of Heads at 0.05

Table 5.85: Results of Chi-square Test Between Decision-Making Styles (Routine, Compromise, Heuristic) and Experience

Decision-making	*Teaching experience (in Years)*			
Styles	*Below 15*	*15-25*	*Above 25*	*Total*
Routine	6 20.69%	6 20.69%	17 58.62%	29
Compromise	4 28.57%	2 14.29%	8 57.14%	14
Heuristic	4 36.36%	3 27.27%	4 36.36%	11
Total	14	11	29	54
Chi-square = 2.0971, >0.05, NS				

level (chi-square = 2.0971). Hence the null hypothesis is accepted. It means that decision-making style (Routine, Compromise, Heuristic) is independent of experience (below 15, 15-25, above 25 years) of Heads of schools.

16. **Major Hypothesis:** There is no association between decision-making style of Heads of schools (Routine, Compromise, Heuristic) and type of management (Govt. aided, unaided) of schools.

To test this hypothesis, the chi-square test was applied and results are presented in table 5.86.

Table 5.86: Results of Chi-square Test Between Decision-making Styles (Routine, Compromise, Heuristic) and Type of Management (Aided, Unaided)

Decision-making	*Type of Management*		
Styles	*Aided*	*Unaided*	*Total*
Routine	18 15.75%	3 5.25%	21
Compromise	9 10.5%	5 3.5%	14
Heuristid	6 6.75%	3 2.25%	9
Total	33	11	44
Chi-square = 9.2921, <0.05, S			

There is no significant association between decision-making style (Routine, Compromise, Heuristic) and type of management (aided, unaided) at 0.05 level (chi-square = 2.46). Hence the null hypothesis is accepted. It means that decision-making style (Routine, Compromise, Heuristic) of Heads of schools is independent of type of management (Aided, Unaided).

17. **Major Hypothesis:** There is no association between leadership style of Heads of schools and organisational health (High, Average, Low).

To test this hypothesis, the chi-square test was applied and results are presented in table 5.87.

Table 5.87: Results of Chi-square Test Between Leadership Style (Initiating Structure and Consideration) and Organisational health (High, Average, Low)

Leadership Styles	*Organisational Health*			
	High	*Average*	*Low*	*Total*
Initiating Structure	7 17.95%	23 58.97%	9 23.08%	39
Consideration	6 40.00%	4 26.67%	5 33.33%	15
Total	13	27	14	54
Chi-square = 4.8892, >0.05, NS				

There is no significant association between leadership style and organisational health (High, Average, Low) at 0.05 level, (chi-square = 4.8892). Hence the null hypothesis is accepted at 0.05 level. It means that leadership style (Initiating Structure and Consideration) of Heads of schools is independent of organisational health (High, Average, Low).

18. **Major Hypothesis:** There is no association between leadership style of Heads of schools (Initiating Structure and Consideration) and teacher morale (High, Average, Low).

To test this hypothesis, the chi-square test was applied and results are presented in table 5.88:

Table 5.88: Results of Chi-square Test Between Leadership Style of Heads of Schools and Teacher Morale (High, Average, Low)

Leadership Styles	*Teacher Morale* High	Average	Low	*Total*
Initiating Structure	7 17.95%	25 64.10%	7 17.95%	39
Consideration	5 33.33%	7 46.67%	3 20.00%	15
Total	12	32	10	54

Chi-square = 1.7342, >0.05, NS

There is no significant association between leadership style and teacher morale (High, Average, Low) at 0.05 level. Hence the null hypothesis is accepted at 0.05 level (Chi-square = 1.7342). It means that leadership style (Initiating Structure and Consideration) of Heads of schools is independent of teacher morale (High, Average, Low).

19. Major Hypothesis: There is no association between leadership style and sex (Male, Female) of Heads of schools.

To test this hypothesis, the chi-square test was applied and results are presented in table 5.89.

Table 5.89: Results of Chi-square Test Between Leadership Style (Initiating Structure and Consideration) and Sex of Heads of Schools

Leadership Styles	*Sex* Male	Female	*Total*
Initiating Structure	28 71.79%	11 28.21%	39
Consideration	9 60.00%	6 40.00%	15
Total	37	17	54

Chi-square = 0.6986, >0.05, NS

There is no significant association between leadership style and sex at 0.05 level. Hence the null hypothesis is accepted at 0.05 level (chi-square = 0.6986). It means that leadership styles (Initiating Structure and Consideration) of Heads of schools is independent of sex (Male, Female).

20. Major Hypothesis: There is no association between leadership style and experience of Heads of schools.

To test this hypothesis, the chi-square test was applied and results are presented in table 5.90.

Table 5.90: Results of Chi-square Test Between Leadership Style (Initiating Structure and Consideration) of Heads of Schools and Experience (Below 15, 15-25, Above 25 years)

Leadership	*Teaching experience (in years)*			
Styles	*Below 15*	*15-25*	*Above 25*	*Total*
Initiating Structure	9 23.08%	7 17.95%	23 58.97%	39
Consideration	5 33.33%	4 26.67%	6 40.00%	15
Total	14	11	29	54
Chi-square = 1.5700, > 0.05, NS				

There is no significant association between leadership style and experience of Heads of schools (below 15, 15-25 above 25 years) at 0.05 level. Hence the null hypothesis is accepted at 0.05 level (chi-square = 1.5700). It means that leadership style is independent of experience (below 15, 15-25, above 25 years) of Heads of schools.

21. Major Hypothesis: There is no association between leadership style of Heads of schools and type of management (Govt. aided, unaided) of schools.

To test this hypothesis, the chi-square test was applied and results are presented in table 5.91.

Table 5.91: Results of Chi-square Test Between Leadership Style (Initiating Structure and Consideration) and Type of Management (Govt. Aided, Unaided) of Schools

Leadership Styles	*Type of Management*			
	Govt.	*Aided*	*Unaided*	*Total*
Initiating Structure	4 10.26% 7.2	25 64.10% 23.8	10 25.64% 7.9	39
Consideration	6 40.00% 2.8	8 53.33% 9.2	1 6.67% 3.1	15
Total	10	33	11	54
	Chi-square = 7.2957, >0.05, S			

There is significant association between leadership style (Initiating Structure and Consideration) and type of management (Govt. aided, unaided) at 0.05 level. Hence the null hypothesis is rejected at 0.05 level (chi-square = 7.2957). It means that leadership style (Initiating Structure, Consideration) of Heads of schools is dependent on type of management (Govt. aided, unaided).

The Heads of aided schools are high on leadership style initiating structure.

22. Major Hypothesis: There is no significant relationship between organisational health and teacher morale in high schools.

To prove the above statement, the Karl Pearson's correlation coefficient test with t-test was applied and results are presented in table 5.92.

Table 5.92: Results of Correlation Co-efficient Test Between Organisational Health as a Whole and Teacher Morale as a Whole

Variable	*Teacher Morale*
Organisational Health	0.6439 p = <0.01, S

The above table results reveal that significant positive relationship was observed between organisational health as a whole and teacher morale as a whole at 0.05 level ($r = 0.6439$, $p < 0.01$). Hence the null hypothesis is rejected. In other words, the organisational health scores as a whole are increasing with increase in teacher morale scores as a whole. When teacher morale in schools is high organisational health of the schools is also high.

23. Major Hypothesis: There is no significant relationship between dimensions of organisational health and components of teacher morale.

To test the above statement, the Karl Pearson's correlation coefficient test was applied and results are presented in table 5.93.

From table 5.93 we see the following:

(i) The component of organisational health integrity has significant positive correlation with components of teacher morale, i.e., behavioural characteristics ($r = 0.3200$, <0.05), group spirit ($r = 0.4002$, $p < 0.01$), attitude towards the job ($r = 0.2796$, $P < 0.01$) and community involvement ($r = 0.4005$, $P < 0.01$).

(ii) The component of organisational health consideration has significant positive correlation with components of teacher morale, i.e., individual characteristics ($r = 0.4737$, $p < 0.01$), behavioural characteristics ($r = 0.4303$, $p < 0.01$), group spirit ($r = 0.5830$, $p < 0.01$), attitude towards the job ($r = 0.6528$, $p < 0.01$) and community involvement ($r = 0.5804$, $P < 0.01$).

(iii) The component of organisational health initiating structure has significant positive correlation with components of teacher morale, i.e., individual characteristics ($r = 0.5232$, $p < 0.01$), behavioural characteristics ($r = 0.4046$,

Table 5.93: Results of Correlation Coefficient Test Between Dimensions of Organisational Health and Dimensions of Teacher Morale

Dimensions	*Individual Characteristics*	*Behavioural Characteristics*	*Group Spirit*	*Attitude Towards the job*	*Community Involvement*
Integrity	0.2316 >0.05, NS	0.3022 <0.05, S	0.4002 <0.01, S	0.2786 <0.05, S	0.4005 <0.01, S
Consideration	0.4737 <0.01, S	0.4303 <0.01, S	0.583 <0.01, S	0.6528 <0.01, S	0.5834 <0.01, S
Initiating Structure	0.5232 <0.01, S	0.4046 <0.01, S	0.5039 <0.01, S	0.5842 <0.01, S	0.5075 <0.01, S
Resource Support	0.5551 <0.01, S	0.5496 <0.01, S	0.6381 <0.01, S	0.6679 <0.01, S	0.6171 <0.01, S
Principal Influence	0.5831 <0.01, S	0.5342 <0.01, S	0.5743 <0.01, S	0.6629 <0.01, S	0.5931 <0.01 S
Moral	0.3996 <0.01, S	0.3076 <0.01, S	0.507 <0.01, S	0.4552 <0.01, S	0.4036 <0.01 S
Academic Emphasis	0.3624 <0.01, S	0.2843 <0.05, S	0.3847 <0.01, S	0.4626 <0.01, S	0.3581 <0.01, S

$p < 0.01$), group spirit ($r = 0.5039$, $p < 0.01$), attitude towards the job ($r = 0.5842$, $p < 0.01$) and community involvement ($r = 0.5075$, $P < 0.01$).

(iv) The component of organisational health resource support has significant positive correlation with components of teacher morale, i.e., individual characteristics ($r = 0.5551$, $p < 0.01$), behavioural characteristics ($r = 0.5498$, $p < 0.01$), group spirit ($r = 0.6391$, $p < 0.01$), attitude towards the job ($r = 0.6679$, $p < 0.01$) and community involvement ($r = 0.6171$, $p < 0.01$).

(v) The component of organisational health principal influence has significant positive correlation with components of teacher morale, i.e., individual characteristics ($r = 0.5831$, $p < 0.01$), behavioural characteristics ($r = 0.5342$, $p < 0.01$), group spirit ($r = 0.5743$, $p < 0.01$), attitude towards the job ($r = 0.6629$, $p < 0.01$) and community involvement ($r = 0.5931$, $p < 0.01$).

(vi) The component of organisational health morale has significant positive correlation with components of teacher morale, i.e., individual characteristics ($r = 0.3996$, $p < 0.01$), behavioural characteristics ($r = 0.3076$, $p < 0.01$), group spirit ($r = 0.5070$, $p < 0.01$), attitude towards the job ($r = 0.4552$, $p < 0.01$) and community involvement ($r = 0.4036$, $p < 0.01$).

(vii) The component of organisational health academic emphasis has significant positive correlation with components of teacher morale, i.e., individual characteristics ($r = 0.3624$, $p < 0.01$), behavioural characteristics ($r = 0.2843$, $p < 0.05$), group spirit ($r = 0.3847$, $p < 0.01$), attitude towards the job ($r = 0.4626$, $P < 0.01$) and community involvement ($r = 0.3581$, $p < 0.01$).

24. Major Hypothesis: There is no significant relationship between dimensions of organisational health.

To test above statement, the Karl Pearson's correlation coefficient test was applied and results are presented in table 5.94.

The table 5.94 results show that, the component integrity has significant positive correlation with components consideration, initiating structure, resource support, morale, and academic emphasis at 0.05 level respectively.

(i) The component consideration has significant positive correlation with components initiating structure, resource support, principal influence, morale, academic emphasis at 0.01 level.

(ii) The component initiating structure has significant positive correlation with components resource support, principal influence, morale, and academic emphasis at 0.01 level.

(iii) The component resource support has significant positive correlation with components principal influence, morale, and academic emphasis at 0.01 level.

(iv) The component principal influence has significant positive correlation with components morale and academic emphasis at 0.01 level.

(v) The component morale has significant positive correlation with component academic emphasis at 0.01 level.

The details of the individual characteristics are presented in table 5.94.

25. Major Hypothesis: There is no significant relationship between dimensions of teacher morale.

Table 5.94: Results of Correlation Coefficient Test Between Dimensions of Organisational Health

Dimensions	*Integrity*	*Consider-ation*	*Initiating Structure*	*Resource Support*	*Principal Influence*	*Morale*	*Academic Emphasis*
Integrity	1.0000 p = —						
Consideration	0.3430 < 0.05, S	1.0000 p = —					
Initiating Structure	0.2870 <0.05, S	0.9090 <0.01, S	1.0000 p = —				
Resource Support	0.3830 <0.01, S	0.8710 <0.01, S	0.8570 <0.01, S	1.0000 p =—			
Principal Influence	0.2430 >0.05, NS	0.8780 <0.01, S	0.8480 <0.01, S	0.8380 <0.01, S	1.0000 P = —		
Morale	0.4080 <0.01, S	0.5690 <0.01, S	0.5810 <0.01 S	0.6210 <0.01, S	0.4920 <0.01, S	1.0000 p = —	
Academic Emphasis	0.3350 <0.05, S	0.5700 <0.01, S	0.5610 <0.01, S	0.5950 <0.01, S	0.5090 <0.01, S	0.6920 <0.01, S	1.0000 p=—

To prove the above statement, the Karl Pearson's coefficient test was applied and results are presented in table 5.95.

Table 5.95: Results of Correlation Coefficient Test Between Dimensions of Teacher Morale

Components	*Individual Characteristics*	*Behavioural Characteristics*	*Group Spirit*	*Attitude Towards the Job*	*Community Involvement*
Individual Characteristics	1.0000 p = —				
Behavioural Characteristics	0.7832 < 0.01, S	1.0000 p = —			
Group Spirit	0.7135 < 0.01, S	0.7743 < 0.01, S	1.0000 p = —		
Attitude Towards the Job	0.7240 <0.01, S	0.7863 <0.01, S	0.8527 <0.01, S	1.0000 p = —	
Community Involvement	0.6558 <0.01, S	0.7646 <0.01, S	0.7692 <0.01, S	0.8375 <0.01, S	1.0000 p = —

The above table results show that:

(i) The component individual characteristics has significant positive correlation with components behavioural characteristics, group spirit, attitude towards the job and community involvement at 0.01 level.

(ii) The component behavioural characteristics has significant positive correlation with components group spirit, attitude towards the job and community involvement at 0.01 level.

(iii) The component group spirit has significant positive correlation with components attitude towards the job and community involvement at 0.01 level.

(iv) The component attitude towards the job has significant positive correlation with component community involvement at 0.01 level.

Regression Analysis

Regression is a statistical tool with the help of which one can predict the unknown values of one variable from known values of other variables. Regression analysis is concerned with the derivation of an appropriate mathematical expression of the functional relationship between variables. This expression is derived for the purpose of predicting values of a dependent variable on the basis of independent variables. Regression analysis is thus designed to examine the relationship of a variable 'Y' to a set of other variables X_1, X_2, ...X_k.

The relationship between dependent variable (Y) and the independent variables (X) can be studied through mathematical formulas. The most commonly used linear equation is:

$$Y = b_1X_1 + b_2X_2.......b_kX_k + b_o$$

Here 'Y' the dependent variable is to be predicted, X_1, X_2, ...X_k are the known variables with which prediction is to be made and b_1, b_2 .... b_k are the coefficients of X_1, X_2, ...X_k variables that are determined from the observed data and b_o is the constant (Y intercept).

The present study considers the organisational health and teacher morale as a whole as the dependent variables and decision-making style, leadership style, teacher morale, sex, experience and type of management are considered as independent variables.

Multiple Regressions

The present study considers decision-making style, leadership style, teacher morale, sex, experience and type of management as independent variables. Multiple regression analysis was done taking organisational health and teacher morale as a whole as the dependent variables and other

Table 5.96: Multiple Regression Summaries for Dependent Variable: Organisational Health

	Variable	*β-Coefficient*	*Reg. Coeff.*	*SE of B*	*r*	*% of contrn*	*t-value*	*p-level*
	Intercept		81.6311	52.1790			1.5644	>0.05, NS
X_1	Teacher Morale	0.0952	0.1019	0.1491	0.1330	1.2661	0.6839	>0.05, NS
X_2	Decision-making Style	0.1958	0.1143	0.1578	0.1159	2.2694	0.7242	>0.05, NS
X_3	Leadership Style	0.1983	0.3708	0.1542	0.2277	4.5147	2.4051	<0.05, S
X_4	Sex	-0.2764	-0.2378	0.1599	-0.0908	2.5103	-1.4870	<0.10, S
X_5	Experience	0.1106	0.0112	0.1489	0.2186	2.4171	0.0750	>0.05, NS
X_6	Type of Management	-0.1998	-0.2685	0.1081	-0.2398	4.7922	-2.4830	<0.05, S
						17.770		

R = 0.3332, F = 4.35687, < 0.05, S, SE = 0.8434

Table 5.97: Multiple Regression Summaries for Dependent Variable: Teacher Morale

	Variable	*β-Coefficient*	*Reg. Coeff.*	*SE of B*	*r*	*% of contrn*	*t-value*	*p-level*
	Intercept		84.5788	31.6319			2.6738	<0.05, S
X_1	Organisational Health	0.2235	0.2966	0.1413	0.1330	2.9718	2.0990	<0.05, S
X_2	Decision-making Style	0.1257	0.1237	0.0545	-0.2310	-2.9037	2.2697	<0.05, S
X_3	Leadership Style	0.2937	0.1636	0.2903	0.1116	3.2772	0.5636	>0.05, NS
X_4	Sex	0.1105	0.2176	0.0538	-0.1038	-1.1464	4.0436	<0.05, S
X_5	Experience	-0.2347	-0.2835	0.1445	-0.1696	3.9818	-1.9627	>0.05, NS
X_6	Type of Management	-0.0463	-0.0582	0.2060	-0.1985	0.9198	-0.2822	>0.05, NS
						7.1005		

R = 0.2839, F = 3.3325, <0.05, S, SE = 0.8241

variables studied as independent variables, namely decision-making style, leadership style, teacher morale, sex, experience and type of management are considered as independent variables. The regression equations were computed for the whole sample.

26. **Major Hypothesis:** There is no significant influence of leadership style (Initiating Structure), decision-making style (Routine, Compromise, Heuristic.), teacher morale, sex, experience and type of management on organisational health.

Table 5.96 shows that the organisational health is taken as dependent variable, which regresses on selected independent variables. This linear multiple regression model was significant at 0.05 level which explains a proportion of variance R = 0.3332. In the model, leadership style of Heads of schools is significantly positively influencing, but sex and type of management are significantly negatively influencing. Organisational health leadership style of Heads of schools has significant positive influence on organisational health. And sex and type of management have significant negative influence on organisational health.

27. **Major Hypothesis:** There is no significant influence of leadership style (Initiating Structure and Consideration), decision-making style (Routine, Compromise, Heuristic.), organisational health, sex, experience and type of management on teacher morale.

Table 5.97 shows that teacher morale is taken as dependent variable, which regresses on selected independent variables. This linear multiple regression model was also significant at 0.05 level which explains a proportion of variance R = 0.2839. In the model, organisational health, decision-making style and sex of the Heads of schools are significantly positively influencing teacher morale. Teacher Morale is influenced by organisational health, decision-making style and sex of Heads of schools.

Conclusion

Details of data analyses using appropriate statistics are given in this chapter. A summary of findings and implications of the findings for the secondary schools are presented in the next chapter.

6

Retrospects and Prospects

INTRODUCTION

The Head of the school is the chief executive and acts as the link between the management and the routine administration of the high school. In a private high school the Head is usually a member of the governing council. But the precise scope of his rights and duties vis-à-vis the governing council may vary a great deal from society to society and within the same society from time to time depending on the degree of confidence of the governing council he enjoys.

Other high school officials such as the Vice Headmaster, and the heads of the departments, both academic and non-academic, too form part of the administration.

The different management functions are sponsoring a high school, staffing it, making policy decisions, controlling finances etc. The management literature distinguishes between six major management or administrative functions, which are present in a high school. They are: planning, organising, staffing, directing, controlling, and communicating.

'Planning' involves the formulation of objectives and goals. In order to achieve objectives strategies have to be worked out, policies formulated, programmes to be arranged and procedures developed. Planning includes of course decision–making. The following statement strengthens the view that high school administration in general is in doldrums. The administration of school education is not founded on sound principals but on the idiosyncrasies of the administrators.

If the high school is to measure up to the tremendous tasks before it, the right type of persons must man it. The Head happens to be the catalytic agent in shaping, supporting, operating and controlling the educational programmes.

Educational administration by its very nature is generally tradition based, for one of the important functions of education is preservation of tradition. As a result high schools manifest themselves prominently in to what is popularly called 'maintenance administration' which believes in keeping the routine going. This pattern worked satisfactorily when educational systems were rather static in character and limited in size. But now the very size and viability of educational establishments bring forth demands for a sound educational management as a necessary ingredient of the legitimacy of the prevailing arrangement. While education has become a vast undertaking, administrative bodies and methods remain as they were in the beginning of the century.

Now the range of education has been extended but the administrative structures have not been reorganised correspondingly. The existing system of high school administration handed down from the political past, is essentially concerned with controlling, its purpose being to make certain that everything slow, lethargic, uninspiring and time-consuming. So, if the plans of educational development are to be implemented successfully the traditional administrative set-up must be thoroughly overhauled. For this the Head of the school must be aware of the innovative techniques of educational administration.

Moreover, as a result of the development of the organisation theory and the science of operations research the traditional concept of educational administration has been undergoing a change. A comprehensive research is needed in the area of educational administration. Above all the new administrative and budgetary techniques collectively known as 'modern management techniques' embody the spirit of effective planning and implementation. They provide powerful tools in comparison with more traditional techniques, which can help administration to be more efficient.

Mathematical techniques and systems analysis have been successfully applied to complex scientific, economic and industrial problems. The executive has a very powerful and versatile tool in his hand as a provider of information for effective decision-making, planning and control. One of the planning techniques which has received wide acceptance and has demonstrated its effectiveness in terms of savings on cost and time is PERT (Programme Evaluation Review Technique) and CPM (Critical Path Method). Similarly O and M (Organisation and Management), simplifying office procedures, reducing waste and promoting organisational efficiency is universally recognised.

Management science has made rapid advances in recent years and these techniques are playing significant roles in business and industry and they prove to be fruitful to a large extent. So the occasion demands that these techniques have to be implemented and the educationists should find out to what extent the modern management techniques can be adopted in educational administration. Taking this into consideration, the study was undertaken.

But before any of these can be utilised for educational administration, their relevance, suitability, and practicability have to be ascertained in the light of specific objectives and targets of educational efforts.

But owing to non-availability of trained personnel, persons who learn by their own experience the hard way carry on educational administration.

In educational administration the problems are more future-oriented and more human-oriented than in business management. Educational administration involves long-range objectives.

From the foregoing consideration, it is clear that there is a need for systematic research to assess the applicability of these techniques to educational administration.

In short, democratic pressures, rising expectation and need for equality of educational opportunity, student unrest, demand for student participation in administration, political interference in education demand a systematic study in educational management.

School education having rapid horizontal and vertical growth in recent years and labour intensive activities rapidly expanding, there is a strong and inevitable need for scientific development of educational administration. In the words of Coombs (1969) "unless educational systems are well equipped with appropriately trained modern managers who in turn are well equipped with good information flows, modern tools of analysis, research and evaluation and are supported by well trained teams of specialists—the transition of education from its semi handicraft state to a modern condition is not likely to happen." Instead educational crisis will grow steadily from bad to worse. In seeking to modernise its management system, education can find many useful clauses in the practices, including the concepts and the methodologies of system analysis and of integrated long range planning.

In educational administration, management skills and educational experience interlock at every point. A high school administrator who has no insight of education is likely to prove a poor administrator however accomplished he may be in terms of management skills.

So the secret of good administration lies not in the administrator's vast and exact knowledge but in his skill at navigating in areas of ignorance. Administration is an unmodified art. Therefore the only sure way to learn administration is to administer.

So, if all any advancement is to be made in the field of higher education, it is necessary that such administrative practices be evolved that were suitable for the growth of these new programmes and projects. In the lines of 'green revolution' and 'white revolution' an administrative revolution is also imperative.

Blocker et al. (1965) opine that 'Administration is creative; it provides both structure and functions necessary for the systematic operation of an organisation. Furthermore it maintains equilibrium and stability within the organisation, hopefully without satisfying the creativity of individuals and the necessary trend towards gradual change and improvement."

Administration should be effervescent enough to stimulate organisational change and modification and adaptation to changing needs. So if innovations and modifications are to be done in any organisation, the concept of decisions making should be decision-making in the process of educational administration. Griffths(1969) states as follows: "Central function of administration is directing and controlling the decision-making process." McCamy (1947) lends support to this idea when he remarks, "the making of decisions is at the very center of administration."

Since decision-making is at the very core of the process of administration, it becomes the pivotal task of any Head of the school. Livingston (1953) emphasises the place of decision-making in educational administration ".... this is a continuing dynamic process rather than an occasional event, then decisioning means something quite different and becomes the basis of all managerial action."

THE PROBLEM

The Head of the school is the kingpin of the school. It is said that as is the Head, so is the school. The Planning, Organising, Stafling, Directing, Co-ordinating, Reporting and Budgeting (POSDCORB) functions of the Head of the school are dependent on his decision-making style. The quality and style of decision-making influences the rank and file of the school towards quality, excellence and productivity. The style of decision-making makes or mars the quality of the school system. The style of decision-making brings in change-proneness and a climate for experimenting innovations and bringing positive ripple effects in the school. The style of decision-making is dependent on various factors operating within and outside the school system.

Various variables such as climate, change-proneness, school organisation health, teacher morale, teacher involvement, teachers value system, teacher commitment, leadership behaviour of Head of the school shape the decision-making style of the Head of the school. In Indian context research studies relating these variables are very few. Hence, the present study attempts to fill this gap.

The present study is entitled as "A Study of Decision-making Style and Leadership Behaviour of Heads of Schools in Relation to Teacher Morale and Organisational Health in Secondary Schools".

OBJECTIVES OF THE STUDY

1. To study the relationship between schools under Heads with different decision-making styles (Routine, Compromise and Heuristic) and organisational health as a whole.

2. To study the relationship between schools under Heads with different decision-making styles (Routine, Compromise and Heuristic) and the following dimensions of organisational health.

   (i) Integrity

   (ii) Consideration

   (iii) Initiating Structure

   (iv) Resource Support

   (v) Principal Influence

   (vi) Morale

   (vii) Academic Emphasis

3. To study the relationship between schools under Heads with different leadership styles (Initiating Structure and Consideration) and organisational health as a whole.

4. To study the relationship between schools under Heads with different leadership styles and the following dimensions of organisational health.

    (i) Integrity

    (ii) Consideration

    (iii) Initiating Structure

    (iv) Resource Support

    (v) Principal Influence

    (vi) Morale

    (vii) Academic Emphasis

5. To study the relationship between schools under male and female Heads and organisational health as a whole.

6. To study the relationship between schools under male and female Heads and the following dimensions of organisational health.

    (i) Integrity

    (ii) Consideration

    (iii) Initiating Structure

    (iv) Resource Support

    (v) Principal Influence

    (vi) Morale

    (vii) Academic Emphasis

7. To study the relationship between schools under Heads with varying experience (Below 15, 15-25, Above 25) and organisational health as a whole.

8. To study the relationship between schools under Heads with varying experience (Below 15,15-25, Above 25) and the following dimensions of organisational health.

   (i) Integrity

   (ii) Consideration

   (iii) Initiating Structure

   (iv) Resource Support

   (v) Principal Influence

   (vi) Morale

   (vii) Academic Emphasis

9. To study the relationship between schools under Heads with different decision-making styles (Routine, Compromise and Heuristic) and teacher morale as a whole.

10. To study the relationship between schools under Heads with different decision-making styles (Routine, Compromise and Heuristic) and the following components of teacher morale.

    (i) Individual characteristics

    (ii) Behavioural characteristics

    (iii) Group spirit

    (iv) Attitude towards the job

    (v) Community involvement

11. To study the relationship between schools under Heads with different leadership style (Initiating Structure, Consideration) and teacher morale as a whole.

12. To study the relationship between schools under Heads with different leadership styles (Initiating Structure, Consideration) and the following components of teacher morale.

(i) Individual characteristics

(ii) Behavioural characteristics

(iii) Group spirit

(iv) Attitude towards the job

(v) Community involvement

13. To study the relationship between schools under male and female Heads and teacher morale as a whole.

14. To study the relationship between schools under male and female Heads and the following components of teacher morale.

 (i) Individual characteristics

 (ii) Behavioural characteristics

 (iii) Group spirit

 (iv) Attitude towards the job

 (v) Community involvement

15. To study the relationship between schools under Heads with varying experience (Below 15, 15-25, Above 25) and teacher morale as a whole.

16. To study the relationship between schools under Heads with varying experience (Below 15, 15-25, Above 25) and the following components of teacher morale.

 (i) Individual characteristics

 (ii) Behavioural characteristics

 (iii) Group spirit

 (iv) Attitude towards the job

 (v) Community involvement

17. To study the association between decision-making style (Routing, Compromise, Heuristic) and leadership style (Initiating Structure, Consideration) of Heads of Schools.

18. To study the association between decision-making style (Routine, Compromise, Heuristic) and sex (Male and Female) of Heads of Schools.
19. To study the association between decision-making style (Routine, Compromise, Heuristic) and experience (Below 15,15-25, Above 25) of Heads of Schools.
20. To study the association between decision-making style (Routine, Compromise, Heuristic) of Heads of Schools and type of management (Government, Aided, Unaided).
21. To study the association between leadership style (Initiating Structure, Consideration) and sex (Male and Female) of Heads of Schools.
22. To study the association between leadership style (Initiating Structure, Consideration) and experience (Below 15, 15-25, Above 25) of Heads of Schools.
23. To study the association between leadership style (Initiating Structure, Consideration) of Heads of Schools and type of management (Government, Aided, Unaided).
24. To study the relationship between organisational health and teacher morale.
25. To study the relationship between dimensions of organisational health and components of teacher morale.
26. To study the relationship between dimensions of organisational health.
27. To study the relationship between components of teacher morale.
28. To study the significant influence of leadership styles (Initiating Structure and Consideration), decision-making styles (Routine, Compromise, Heuristic), teacher morale, sex, experience and type of management on organisational health.

29. To study the significant influence of leadership styles (Initiating Structure and Consideration), decision-making styles (Routine, Compromise, Heuristic), organisational health, sex, experience, and type of management on teacher morale.
30. To study the interactive effect of Heads of schools decision-making styles (Routine, Compromise, Heuristic) and leadership styles (Initiating Structure and Consideration) on organisational health.
31. To study the interactive effect of Heads of schools decision-making styles (Routine, Compromise, Heuristic) and leadership styles (Initiating Structure and Consideration) on teacher morale

HYPOTHESES

1. **Major Hypothesis:** There is no significant difference between schools under Heads with different decision-making styles (Routine, Compromise, Heuristic) and organisational health as a whole.

   Sub-hypothesis: There is no significant difference between schools under Heads with different decision-making style (Routine, Compromise, Heuristic) in integrity.

   Sub-hypothesis: There is no significant difference between schools under Heads with different decision-making styles (Routine, Compromise, Heuristic) in consideration.

   Sub-hypothesis: There is no significant difference between schools under Heads with different decision-making styles (Routine, Compromise, Heuristic) in initiating structure.

   Sub-hypothesis: There is no significant difference between schools under Heads with different decision-making styles (Routine, Compromise, Heuristic) in resource support.

Sub-hypothesis: There is no significant difference between schools under Heads with different decision-making styles (Routine, Compromise, Heuristic) in principal influence.

Sub-hypothesis: There is no significant difference between schools under Heads of the schools with different decision-making styles (Routine, Compromise, Heuristic) in morale

Sub-hypothesis: There is no significant difference between schools under Heads with different decision-making styles (Routine, Compromise, Heuristic) in academic emphasis.

2. **Major Hypothesis:** There is no significant difference between schools under Heads with different leadership styles (Initiating Structure, Consideration) in organisational health as a whole.

   Sub-hypothesis: There is no significant difference between schools under Heads with different leadership styles (Initiating Structure, Consideration) in integrity.

   Sub-hypothesis: There is no significant difference between schools under Heads with different leadership styles (Initiating Structure, Consideration) in consideration.

   Sub-hypothesis: There is no significant difference between schools under Heads with different leadership behaviour styles (Initiating Structure, Consideration) in initiating structure.

   Sub-hypothesis: There is no significant difference between schools under Heads with different leadership styles (Initiating Structure, Consideration) in resource support.

   Sub-hypothesis: There is no significant difference between schools under Heads with different leadership styles (Initiating Structure, Consideration) in principal influence.

Sub-hypothesis: There is no significant difference between schools under Heads with different leadership styles (Initiating Structure, Consideration) in morale.

Sub-hypothesis: There is no significant difference between schools under Heads with different leadership styles (Initiating Structure, Consideration) in academic emphasis.

3. **Major Hypothesis:** There is no significant difference between schools with male and female Heads in organisational health as a whole.

   Sub-hypothesis: There is no significant difference between schools under male and female Heads in integrity.

   Sub-hypothesis: There is no significant difference between schools under male and female Heads in consideration.

   Sub-hypothesis: There is no significant difference between schools under male and female Heads in initiating structure.

   Sub-hypothesis: There is no significant difference between schools under male and female Heads in resource support.

   Sub-hypothesis: There is no significant difference between schools under male and female Heads in principal influence.

   Sub-hypothesis: There is no significant difference between schools under male and female Heads in morale.

   Sub-hypothesis: There is no significant difference between schools under male and female Heads in academic emphasis.

4. **Major Hypothesis:** There is no significant difference between schools under Heads with varying experience (below 15, 15-25, above 25 years) in organisational health as a whole.

Sub-hypothesis: There is no significant difference between schools under Heads with varying experience (below 15, 15-25, above 25 years) in integrity.

Sub-hypothesis: There is no significant difference between schools under Heads with varying experience (below 15, 15-25, above 25 years) in consideration.

Sub-hypothesis: There is no significant difference between schools under Heads with varying experience (below 15, 15-25, above 25 years) in initiating structure.

Sub-hypothesis: There is no significant difference between schools under Heads with varying experience (below 15, 15-25, above 25 years) in resource support.

Sub-hypothesis: There is no significant difference between schools under Heads with varying experience (below 15, 15-25, above 25 years) in principal influence.

Sub-hypothesis: There is no significant difference between schools under Heads with varying experience (below 15, 15-25, above 25 years) in morale.

Sub-hypothesis: There is no significant difference between schools under Heads with varying experience (below 15, 15-25, above 25 years) in academic emphasis.

5. **Major Hypothesis:** There is no significant difference between schools under Heads with different decision-making styles (Routine, Compromise, Heuristic) in teacher morale as a whole.

Sub-hypothesis: There is no significant difference between schools under Heads with different decision-making styles (Routine, Compromise, Heuristic) in individual characteristics.

Sub-hypothesis: There is no significant difference between schools under Heads with different decision-making styles (Routine, Compromise, Heuristic) in behavioural characteristics.

Sub-hypothesis: There is no significant difference between schools under Heads with different decision-making styles (Routine, Compromise, Heuristic) in group spirit.

Sub-hypothesis: There is no significant difference between schools under Heads with different decision-making styles (Routine, Compromise, Heuristic) in attitude towards job.

Sub-hypothesis: There is no significant difference between schools under Heads with different decision-making styles (Routine, Compromise, Heuristic) in community involvement.

6. **Major Hypothesis:** There is no significant difference between schools under Heads with different leadership styles (Initiating Structure and Consideration) in teacher morale as a whole.

Sub-hypothesis: There is no significant difference between schools under Heads with different leadership styles (Initiating Structure, Consideration) in individual characteristics.

Sub-hypothesis: There is no significant difference between schools under Heads with different leadership styles (Initiating Structure and Consideration) in behavioural characteristics.

Sub-hypothesis: There is no significant difference between schools under Heads with different leadership styles (Initiating Structure and Consideration) in group spirit.

Sub-hypothesis: There is no significant difference between schools under Heads with different leadership styles (Initiating Structure and Consideration) in attitude towards the job.

Sub-hypothesis: There is no significant difference between schools under Heads with different leadership styles (Initiating Structure and Consideration) in community involvement.

7. **Major Hypothesis:** There is no significant difference between schools under male and female Heads in teacher morale as a whole.

   Sub-hypothesis: There is no significant difference between schools under male and female Heads in individual characteristics.

   Sub-hypothesis: There is no significant difference between schools under male and female Heads in behavioural characteristics.

   Sub-hypothesis: There is no significant difference between schools under male and female Heads in group spirit.

   Sub-hypothesis: There is no significant difference between schools under male and female Heads in attitude towards job.

   Sub-hypothesis: There is no significant difference between schools under male and female Heads in community involvement.

8. **Major Hypothesis:** There is no significant difference between schools under Heads with varying experience (below 15, 15-25, above 25 years) in teacher morale as a whole.

   Sub-hypothesis: There is no significant difference between schools under Heads with varying experience (below 15, 15-25, above 25 years) in individual characteristics.

   Sub-hypothesis: There is no significant difference between schools under Heads with varying experience (below 15, 15-25, above 25 years) in behavioural characteristics.

Sub-hypothesis: There is no significant difference between schools under Heads with varying experience (below 15, 15-25, above 25 years) in group spirit.

Sub-hypothesis: There is no significant difference between schools under Heads with varying experience (below 15, 15-25, above 25 years) in attitude towards job.

Sub-hypothesis: There is no significant difference between schools under Heads with varying experience (below 15, 15-25, above 25 years) in community involvement.

9. **Major Hypothesis:** There is no interaction effect of Heads' decision-making styles (Routine, Compromise, Heuristic) and leadership styles (Initiating Structure and Consideration) on organisational health.

10. **Major Hypothesis:** There is no interaction effect of decision-making styles (Routine, Compromise, Heuristic) and leadership styles (Initiating Structure and Consideration) on teacher morale.

11. **Major Hypothesis:** There is no association between decision-making styles (Routine, Compromise, Heuristic) and leadership styles (Initiating Structure, Consideration) of Heads of schools.

12. **Major Hypothesis:** There is no association between decision-making styles (Routine, Compromise, Heuristic) and organisational health (High, Average, Low).

13. **Major Hypothesis:** There is no association between decision-making styles of Heads of Schools (Routine, Compromise, Heuristic) and teacher morale (High, Average, Low)

14. **Major Hypothesis:** There is no association between decision-making styles (Routine, Compromise, Heuristic) and sex (Male, Female) of Heads of schools.

15. **Major Hypothesis:** There is no association between decision-making style (Routine, Compromise, Heuristic) and teaching experience (below 15, 15-25, above 25 years) of Heads of schools.

16. **Major Hypothesis:** There is no association between decision-making style of Heads of schools (Routine, Compromise, Heuristic) and type of management (Govt. aided, unaided) of schools.

17. **Major Hypothesis:** There is no association between leadership style of Heads of schools and organisational health (High, Average, Low)

18. **Major Hypothesis:** There is no association between leadership style of Heads of schools (Initiating Structure and Consideration) and teacher morale (High, Average, Low).

19. **Major Hypothesis:** There is no association between leadership style and sex (Male, Female) of Heads of schools.

20. **Major Hypothesis:** There is no association between leadership style and experience of Heads of schools.

21. **Major Hypothesis:** There is no association between leadership style of Heads of schools and type of management (Govt. aided, unaided) of schools.

22. **Major Hypothesis:** There is no significant relationship between organisational health and teacher morale in high schools.

23. **Major Hypothesis:** There is no significant relationship between dimensions of organisational health and components of teacher morale.

24. **Major Hypothesis:** There is no significant relationship between dimensions of organisational health.

25. **Major Hypothesis:** There is no significant relationship between dimensions of teacher morale.

26. Major Hypothesis: There is no significant influence of leadership style (Initiating Structure), decision-making style (Routine, Compromise, Heuristic), Teacher morale, sex, experience and type of management on organisational health.

27. Major Hypothesis: There is no significant influence of leadership style (Initiating Structure and Consideration), decision-making style (Routine, Compromise, Heuristic), organisational health, sex, experience, type of management on teacher morale.

METHOD OF THE STUDY

The present study involved a descriptive survey (expost facto) method of research.

Population and Sample of the Study

The data required for the present study is collected from the Heads and assistant teachers of secondary schools working in Dharwad Taluka.

Karnataka State has 27 districts. Out of these 27 districts Dharwad district is known for academic activities and educational institutions. Dharwad district has 5 talukas, from among these taluks Dharwad taluka was selected as the locale of the study. Finally the data was collected from 54 Heads of schools and 270 assistant teachers. From each school five teachers were selected. All the Heads of 54 schools were involved in the study.

Tools

For collection of the data required for the present study the following tools were used:

(i) Decision-making Style Questionnaire (DMSQ)

(ii) Teacher Morale Inventory (TMI)

(iii) Organisational Health Inventory(OHI)

(iv) Leadership Behaviour Description Questionnaire (LBDQ)

Data Collection

The investigator personally collected the data from 54 Heads of secondary schools and 270 assistant teachers of Dharwad Taluka. Heads of schools and assistant teachers were personally administered the tools. Clear-cut instructions were given to fill up the responses to the items in the tools. The filled in performas and tools were collected. The Heads of schools and assistant teachers were informed the purpose of the study. The Decision-making Style Questionnaire was administered to the Heads of schools. The Teacher Morale Inventory, Organisational Health Inventory and Leadership Behaviour Description Questionnaire were administered to the assistant teachers. The confidentiality of the responses was assured. The collected data was systematically pooled for analyses.

Data Analysis

For the purpose of analysis of the empirical data, the following statistical techniques were used:

(i) Descriptive statistics

(ii) Differential statistics

(iii) Correlational analysis

(iv) Regression analysis

Major Findings of the Study

Findings of Descriptive Analysis

1. 53.70% of the Heads of schools perceive themselves to be routine decision-makers. That means, they see themselves as adapting programmed type of decisions. Their schools are usually hierarchically structured. The functioning of the schools and the relationship among the people are more formal and they are following a rigid routine. 25.92% of the Heads perceived themselves to be compromise decision-makers, that: they see their role as negotiatiors. They are concerned with a strategy

for dealing with conflicts that may occur because of difference among school personnel. They serve as the impartial mediators in the decision-making process. Only 20.38% of the Heads perceive themselves to be heuristic, that is creative in decision-making. It implies that there is not a rigid hierarchical structure in their schools. It means there is freedom for the faculty and there is an emotional and social tone in their role as negotiators.

2. Out of 54 school Heads 72.00% have initiating structure leadership style and 28.00% have consideration leadership style.

3. Out of 54 Heads of schools, 68.52% are male and only 31.48% are female.

4. In the present study 53.70% of the school Heads have graduate degree compared to 46.30% of the Heads of schools who have a post-graduate degree. But in general nearly equal percentage of Heads have graduate and postgraduate educational qualification.

5. 57.41% of Heads of schools are in the age category of 51-60 years, 22.22% in 41-50 years and 20.37% of Heads of schools in the lower age category, i.e. 30-40 years.

6. In the present study, 53.70% of the Heads of schools have more than 25 years teaching experience, 25.93% with below 15 years teaching experience and 20.37% with 15-25 years teaching experience.

7. The mean value of organisational health as a whole in routine style of decision-making was 468.38 and its standard deviation was 67.17. Similarly, mean in compromise style was 488.34 and standard deviation was 70.09. In heuristic style, mean was 458.94 and standard deviation was 84.49.

8. The mean value of organisational health as a whole in schools under Heads with initiating structure style of leadership was 472.08 and its standard deviation was

68.74. In consideration style the mean and standard deviation were 470.48 and 79.28 respectively.

9. The mean value of organisational health in schools with male Heads was 478.44 and its standard deviation was 75.76. In schools with female Heads the mean and standard deviation were 456.82 and 58.89 respectively.

10. The mean value of organisational health as a whole in schools with Heads with postgraduation as educational qualification was 460.73 and its standard deviation was 70.06.With Heads of schools with graduation as an educational qualification the mean and standard deviation were 484.28 and 71.49 respectively.

11. The mean value of organisational health as a whole in schools with Heads belonging to 30-40 years age group was 481.83 and its standard deviation was 66.59. Similarly, mean in 40-50 years age group was 504.60 and standard deviation was 58.28. In the age group 50-60 years, the mean was 455.25 and standard deviation was 73.79.

12. The mean value of organisational health as a whole in schools with Heads belonging to below 15 years experience was 491.89 and its standard deviation was 61.79, mean in 15-25 years group was 475.79 and standard deviation was 77.95 and for above 25 years experience, the mean was 460.28 and standard deviation was 72.57.

13. The mean value of organisational health as a whole in schools belonging to government type of management was 474.53 and its standard deviation was 78.89, mean in aided schools was 461.47 and standard deviation was 72.60 and in unaided schools, the mean was 499.48 and standard deviation was 55.57.

14. The mean value of organisational health as a whole in schools belonging to government type of management was 474.53 and its standard deviation was 78.89, mean

in aided schools was 461.47 and standard deviation was 72.60 and in unaided schools, the mean was 499.48 and standard deviation was 55.57.

15. The mean value of teacher morale as a whole in schools with Heads belonging to routine type of decision-making style was 2123.50 and its standard deviation was 157.29. In schools with Heads belonging to compromise type of decision-making style the mean was 2161.96 an its standard deviation was 114.29 an in heuristic style mean and standard deviation were 2153.91 nad 152.77 respectively.

16. The mean value of teacher morale as a whole in schools with Heads with initiating structure style of leadership was 2136.10 and its standard deviation was 130.98. In consideration type of leadership style the mean and standard deviation were 2148.94 and 181.07 respectively.

17. The mean value of teacher morale as a whole in schools with male Heads was 2160.16 and its standard deviation was 138.93, when compared to female school Heads, the mean and standard deviation were 2095.06 and 151.76 respectively.

18. The mean value of teacher morale as a whole in schools with Heads with postgraduation as an educational qualification was 2114.20 and its standard deviation was 169.15. In schools with Heads of schools with graduation as an educational qualification, the mean and standard deviation were 2169.21 and 106.25 respectively.

19. The mean value of teacher morale as a whole in schools with Heads belonging to 30-40 years age group was 2128.18 and its standard deviation was 177.20. Similarly, mean in 40-50 years age group was 2193.26 and standard deviation was 146.15, and with Heads with age 50-60 years, the mean was 2123.00 and standard deviation was 131.55

20. The mean value of organisational health as a whole in schools with Heads belonging to below 15 years teaching experience was 2164.14 and its standard deviation was 173.36, the mean in 15-25 years group was 2162.00 and standard deviation was 144.16 and for above 25 years experience the mean was 2119.38 and standard deviation was 132.06.

21. The mean value of organisational health as a whole in schools belonging to government type of management was 2179.15 and its standard deviation was 112.35, means in aided schools was 2122.03 and standard deviation was 146.86 and in unaided schools, the mean was 2156.68 and standard deviation was 167.29.

Findings of Differential Analysis

22. There is no significant difference observed between schools under Heads with different decision-making styles (Routine, Compromise, Heuristic) in organisational health as a whole.

23. There is no significant difference between the schools under Heads with different decision-making styles (Routine, Compromise and Heuristic) in integrity.

24. There is no significant difference between Heads with different decision-making styles (Routine, Compromise and Heuristic) in consideration.

25. There is no significant difference between schools under Heads with different decision-making styles (Routine, Compromise, Heuristic) in initiating structure.

26. There is no significant difference between the schools under Heads with different decision-making style (Routine, Compromise, Heuristic) in resource support.

27. There is no significant difference between schools under Heads with different decision-making styles (Routine, Compromise, Heuristic) in principal influence.

28. There is no significant difference between schools under Heads with different decision-making styles (Routine, Compromise, Heuristic) in morale.

29. There is no significant difference between schools under Heads with different decision-making styles (Routine, Compromise, Heuristic) in academic emphasis.
30. There is no significant difference between schools under different leadership styles (Initiating Structure and Consideration) of Heads in organisational health as a whole.
31. There is no significant difference between schools under Heads with different leadership styles (Initiating Structure, Consideration) in integrity.
32. There is no significant difference between schools under Heads with different leadership styles (Initiating Structure, Consideration) in consideration.
33. There is no significant difference between schools under Heads with different leadership styles (Initiating Structure, Consideration) in initiating structure.
34. There is no significant difference between schools under Heads with different leadership behaviour styles (Initiating Structure, Consideration) in resource support.
35. There is no significant difference between schools under Heads with different leadership styles (Initiating Structure and Consideration) in principal influence.
36. There is no significant difference between schools under Heads with different leadership styles (Initiating Structure and Consideration) in morale
37. There is no significant difference between schools under Heads with different leadership styles (Initiating Structure and Consideration) in academic emphasis.
38. There is no significant difference between schools with male and female Heads in organisational health as a whole.
39. There is no significant difference between schools under male and female Heads in integrity.

40. There is no significant difference between schools under male and female Heads in consideration.

41. There is no significant difference between schools under male and female Heads in initiating structure.

42. There is no significant difference between schools under male and female Heads in resource support.

43. There is no significant difference between schools under male and female Heads in principal influence.

44. There is no significant difference between schools under male and female Heads in morale.

45. There is no significant difference between schools under male and female Heads in academic emphasis.

46. There is no significant difference observed between schools under Heads of schools with varying experience (below 15, 15-25, above 25 years) in organisational health as a whole.

47. There is no significant difference between schools under Heads with varying experience (below 15, 15-25, above 25 years) in integrity. In other words, schools under Heads with different experience do not differ in integrity.

48. There is no significant difference between schools under Heads with varying experience (below 15, 15-25, above 25 years) in consideration. In other words, schools under Heads with different experience do not differ in consideration.

49. There is no significant difference between schools under Heads of schools with varying experience (below 15, 15-25, above 25 years) in initiating structure. In other words, schools under Heads with different experience do not differ in initiating structure.

50. There is no significant difference between schools under Heads with varying experience (below 15, 15-25, above

25 years) in resource support. In other words, schools under Heads with different experience do not differ in resource support.

51. There is no significant difference between schools under Heads with varying experience (below 15, 15-25, above 25 years) in principal influence. Schools under Heads with different experience do not differ in principal influence.

52. There is no significant difference between schools under Heads with varying experience (below 15, 15-25, above 25 years) in morale. In other words, schools under Heads with different experience do not differ in morale.

53. There is no significant difference between schools under Heads with varying experience (below 15, 15-25 above 25 years) in academic emphasis. In other words, schools under Heads with different experience do not differ in academic emphasis.

54. There is no significant difference observed between schools under Heads with different decision-making styles in teacher morale as a whole.

55. There is no significant difference between schools under Heads with different decision-making styles in individual characteristics.

56. There is no significant difference between schools under Heads with different decision-making styles in behavioural characteristics. In other words, schools under Heads with different decision-making styles do not differ on behavioural characteristics.

57. There is no significant difference between schools under Heads with different decision-making styles in group spirit. In other words, schools under Heads with different decision-making styles do not differ in group spirit.

58. There is no significant difference between schools under Heads with different decision-making styles in attitude

towards job. In other words, schools under Heads with different decision-making styles do not differ in attitude towards job.

59. There is no significant difference between schools under Heads with different decision-making styles in community involvement. In other words, schools under Heads with different decision-making styles do not differ in community involvement.
60. There is no significant difference between schools under Heads with different leadership styles (Initiating Structure and Consideration) in teacher morale as a whole.
61. There is no significant difference between schools under Heads with different leadership styles (Initiating Structure and Consideration) in individual characteristics.
62. There is no significant difference between schools under Heads with different leadership styles (Initiating Structure and Consideration) in behavioural characteristics.
63. There is no significant difference between Heads of schools with differing leadership styles (Initiating Structure and Consideration) in group spirit.
64. There is no significant difference between schools under Heads with different leadership styles (Initiating Structure and Consideration) in attitude towards job.
65. There is no significant difference between schools under Heads with different leadership styles (Initiating Structure and Consideration) in community involvement.
66. There is no significant difference between schools under male and female Heads in teacher morale as a whole.
67. There is no significant difference between schools under male and female Heads in individual characteristics.

68. There is no significant difference between schools under male and female Heads in behavioural characteristics.

69. There is no significant difference between schools under male and female Heads in group spirit.

70. There is no significant difference between schools under male and female Heads in attitude towards job.

71. There is no significant difference between schools under male and female Heads in community involvement.

72. There is no significant difference observed between schools under Heads with varying experience in teacher morale as a whole.

73. There is no significant difference between schools under Heads with varying experience in individual characteristics.

74. There is no significant difference between schools under Heads with varying experience in behavioural characteristics.

75. There is no significant difference between schools under Heads with varying experience in group spirit.

76. There is no significant difference between schools under Heads with varying experience in attitude towards job.

77. There is no significant difference between schools under Heads with varying experience in community involvement.

78. There is no significant difference between Heads with three different decision-making styles (Routine, Compromise, Heuristic) in organisational health.

79. There is no significant difference between Heads with different leadership styles (Initiating Structure and Consideration) in organisational health.

80. The interaction effect of decision-making styles (Routine, Compromise, Heuristic) and leadership styles (Initiating

Structure and Consideration) on organisational health as a whole is not significant.

81. There is no significant difference between different decision-making styles (Routine, Compromise, Heuristic) of Heads of schools.

82. There is no significant difference between leadership styles (Initiating Structure, Consideration) of Heads of schools teachers

83. The interaction effect of decision-making styles (Routine, Compromise, Heuristic) and leadership styles (Initiating Structure and Consideration) on teacher morale scores as a whole is not significant.

Findings of Correlation Analysis

84. There is no significant association between decision-making style (Routine, Compromise, Heuristic) and leadership style (Initiating Structure, Consideration). It means that, there is no association between decision-making style and leadership style of Heads of Schools.

85. There is no significant association between decision-making style (Routine, Compromise, Heuristic) of Heads of schools and organisational health (High, Average, Low). It means that decision-making style (Routine, Compromise, Heuristic) of Heads of schools is independent of organisational health (High, Average, Low).

86. There is no significant association between decision-making style (Routine, Compromise, Heuristic) of Heads of schools and teacher morale (High, Average, Low). It means that decision-making style (Routine, Compromise, Heuristic) of Heads of schools is independent of teacher morale (High, Average, Low).

87. There is a significant association between decision-making style (Routine, Compromise, Heuristic) and sex (male and female). Compromise and Heuristic style go more with male than with female Heads of schools.

88. There is no significant association between decision-making style (Routine, Compromise, Heuristic) and teaching experience (below 15, 15-25, above 25 years) of Heads. It means that decision-making style (Routine, Compromise, Heuristic) is independent of experience (below 15, 15-25, above 25 years) of Heads of schools.

89. There is no significant association between decision-making style (Routine, Compromise, Heuristic) and type of management (aided, unaided). It means that decision-making style (Routine, Compromise, Heuristic) of Heads of schools is independent of type of management (Aided, Unaided).

90. There is no significant association between leadership style and organisational health (High, Average, Low). It means that leadership style (initiating Structure and Consideration) of Heads of schools is independent of organisational health (High, Average, Low).

91. There is no significant association between leadership style and teacher morale (High, Average, Low). It means that leadership style (Initiating Structure and Consideration) of Heads of schools is independent of teacher morale (High, Average, Low)

92. There is no significant association between leadership style and sex. It means that leadership style (Initiating Structure and Consideration) of Heads of schools is independent of sex (Male, Female).

93. There is no significant association between leadership style and experience of Heads of schools (below 15, 15-25, above 25 years). It means that leadership style is independent of experience (below 15, 15-25, above 25 years) of Heads of schools.

94. There is no significant association between leadership style (Initiating Structure and Consideration) and type of management (Govt. aided, unaided).It means that leadership style (Initiating Structure, Consideration) of

Heads of schools is dependent on type of management (Govt. aided, unaided).

95. Significant positive relationship was observed between organisational health as a whole and teacher morale as a whole. In other words, the organisational health scores as a whole increase with increase in teacher morale as a whole. When teacher morale in schools is high, organisational health of schools is also high.

96. The dimension of organisational health integrity has significant positive correlation with components of teacher morale, i.e. behavioural characteristics (discipline, effect, good personal adjustment, rationality, efficiency, willingness), group spirit (pride in group, cohesiveness, climate, feelings about institutional roles, individual ambition towards accomplishment of goals, leadership behaviour), attitude towards the job (to stick to job, job satisfaction, satisfaction with salary, attitude towards environment, workload curriculum) and community involvement (community support, community pressure). When integrity is high, behavioural characteristics, group spirit, attitude towards the job and community involvement are also high.

97. The dimension of organisational health consideration has significant positive correlation with components of teacher morale, i.e. individual characteristics (confidence, zeal, cheerfulness, hope), behavioural characteristics (discipline, effect, good personal adjustment, rationality, efficiency, willingness), group spirit (pride in group, cohesiveness, climate, feelings about institutional roles, individual ambition towards accomplishment of goals, leadership behaviour), attitude towards the job (to stick to job, job satisfaction, satisfaction with salary, attitude towards environment, workload, curriculum) and community involvement (community support, community pressure). When consideration is high, individual characteristics, behavioural characteristics group spirit, attitude towards the job and community involvement are also high.

98. The dimension of organisational health initiating structure has significant positive correlation with components of teacher morale, i.e. individual characteristics (confidence, zeal, cheerfulness, hope), behavioural characteristics (discipline, effect, good personal adjustment, rationality, efficiency, willingness), group spirit (pride in group, cohesiveness, climate, feelings about institutional roles, individual ambition towards accomplishment of goals, leadership behaviour), attitude towards the job (to stick to job, job satisfaction, satisfaction with salary, attitude towards environment, workload, curriculum) and community involvement (community support, community pressure). When initiating structure is high, individual characteristics, behavioural characteristics, group spirit, attitude towards the job and community involvement are also high.

99. The dimension of organisational health resource support has significant positive correlation with components of teacher morale, i.e. individual characteristics (confidence, zeal, cheerfulness, hope), behavioural characteristics (discipline, effect, good personal adjustment, rationality, efficiency, willingness), group spirit (pride in group, cohesiveness, climate, feelings about institutional roles, individual ambition towards accomplishment of goals, leadership behaviour), attitude towards the job (to stick to job, job satisfaction, satisfaction with salary, attitude towards environment, workload, curriculum) and community involvement (community support, community pressure). When resource support is high, individual characteristics, behavioural characteristics, group spirit, attitude towards the job and community involvement are also high.

100. The dimension of organisational health principal influence has significant positive correlation with dimensions of teacher morale, i.e. individual characteristics (confidence, zeal, cheerfulness, hope), behavioural characteristics (discipline, effect, good

personal adjustment, rationality, efficiency, willingness), group spirit (pride in group, cohesiveness, climate, feelings about institutional roles, individual ambition towards accomplishment of goals, leadership behaviour), attitude towards the job (to stick to job, job satisfaction, satisfaction with salary, attitude towards environment, workload, curriculum) and community involvement (community support, community pressure). When principal influence is high, individual characteristics, behavioural characteristics, group spirit, attitude towards the job and community involvement are also high.

101. The dimension of organisational health morale has significant positive correlation with components of teacher morale, i.e. individual characteristics (confidence, zeal, cheerfulness, hope), behavioural characteristics (discipline, effect, good personal adjustment, rationality, efficiency, willingness), group spirit (pride in group, cohesiveness, climate, feelings about institutional roles, individual ambition towards accomplishment of goals, leadership behaviour), attitude towards the job (to stick to job, job satisfaction, satisfaction with salary, attitude towards environment, workload, curriculum) and community involvement (community support, community pressure). When morale is high, individual characteristics, behavioural characteristics, group spirit, attitude towards the job and community involvement are also high.

102. The dimension of organisational health academic emphasis has significant positive correlation with components of teacher morale, i.e. individual characteristics (confidence, zeal, cheerfulness, hope), behavioural characteristics (discipline, effect, good personal adjustment, rationality, efficiency, willingness), group spirit (pride in group, cohesiveness, climate, feelings about institutional roles, individual ambition towards accomplishment of goals, leadership behaviour), attitude towards the job (to stick to job, job satisfaction, satisfaction

with salary attitude towards environment, workload, curriculum) and community involvement (community support, community pressure). When academic emphasis is high, individual characteristics, behavioural characteristics, group spirit, attitude towards the job and community involvement are also high.

103. The dimension integrity of organisational health has significant positive correlation with dimension consideration, initiating structure, resource support, morale, academic emphasis of organisational health. When integrity is high in schools, consideration, initiating structure, resource support and morale are also high.

104. The dimension consideration of organisational health has significant positive correlation with dimensions initiating structure, resource support, principal influence, morale and academic emphasis. When consideration is high in schools, initiating structure, resource support, principal influence, academic emphasis and morale are also high.

105. The dimension initiating structure of organisational health has significant positive correlation with dimensions resource support, principal influence, morale and academic emphasis of organisational health. When initiating structure is high in schools, resource support, principal influence, academic emphasis and morale are also high.

106. The dimension resource support of organisational health has significant positive correlation with dimensions principal influence, morale and academic emphasis. When resource support is high in schools, principal influence, academic emphasis and morale are also high.

107. The dimension principal influence of organisational health has significant positive correlation with dimensions morale and academic emphasis of organisational health. When principal influence is high in schools, academic emphasis and morale are also high.

108. The dimension morale of organisational health has significant positive correlation with dimension academic emphasis of organisational health. When morale is high, academic emphasis is also high.

109. The component individual characteristics of teacher morale has significant positive correlation with components behavioural characteristics, group spirit, attitude towards the job and community involvement of teacher morale. When individual characteristics are high, behavioural characteristics, group spirit, attitude towards the job and community involvement are also high.

110. The component behavioural characteristics of teacher morale has significant positive correlation with components group spirit, attitude towards the job and community involvement of teacher morale. When behavioural characteristics are high, group spirit, attitude towards the job and community involvement are also high.

111. The component group spirit of teacher morale has significant positive correlation with components attitude towards the job and community involvement of teacher morale. When group spirit is high, attitude towards the job and community involvement are also high.

112. The component attitude towards the job of teacher morale has significant positive correlation between with component community involvement of teacher morale. When attitude towards the job is high community involvement is also high.

Findings of Regression Analysis

113. Here organisational health is taken as dependent variable, which regresses on selected independent variables. In the model, leadership style of the Heads of schools is significantly positively influencing, but sex and type of management are significantly negatively

influencing organisational health. Leadership style of Heads of schools has significant positive influence on organisational health. And sex and type of management have significant negative influence on organisational health.

114. Here teacher morale is taken as dependent variable, which regresses on selected independent variables. In the model, organisational health, decision-making style and sex of the Heads of schools are significantly positively influencing teacher morale. Teacher morale is influenced by organisational health, decision-making style and sex of Heads of schools.

Educational Implications of the Study

The results of differential analysis have clearly revealed that there are significant differences between groups in various variables of the study. However, the correlation analysis has revealed the significant association between certain variables of the study. These findings of the study have significant implications on the functioning of secondary schools, the note of which needs to be taken by Government, educational administration, managements of private schools, Heads of schools, and assistant teachers and public at large. The educational implications of the present study are:

1. There is a positive correlation between teacher morale and organisational health. This is the single most important outcome of the present study. In order to improve the organisational health of schools all the agencies and individuals should focus their effort on promoting the morale of the teachers.

2. Male Heads of schools of secondary schools are high on routine, compromise and heuristic styles of decision-making when compared to female Heads of schools. This reveals that male Heads are flexible in their style of decision-making and hence this should be kept in mind in the appointment of Heads of schools.

3. The Heads of private aided schools are high on routine, compromise and heuristic style of decision-making, when compared to Government and unaided schools. This reveals that under existing conditions private aided school. Heads follow all the three styles of decision-making (routine, compromise, heuristic), when compared to Government and un-aided schools. This speaks of the climate existing in private aided schools when compared to Government and unaided schools.

4. The Heads of aided schools are high on leadership styles initiating structure and consideration, when compared to Heads of Government and unaided schools. This reveals that under existing conditions private aided school Heads are good in initiating structure and consideration style of leadership. They follow a situational approach to leadership style, i.e. shifting from initiating structure to consideration style. This 'situation' warrants changing the climate in Government and unaided schools, so as to make them on par with aided schools.

5. The decision-making style of Heads and their leadership style are associated. The routine, compromise and heuristic style decision-makers are high on initiating structure leadership style.

6. The components of teacher morale, viz., individual characteristics (confidence, zeal, cheerfulness, hope), behavioural characteristics (discipline, effect, good personal adjustment, rationality, efficiency, willingness), group spirit (pride in group, cohesiveness, climate, feelings about institutional roles, individual ambition towards accomplishment of goals, leadership behaviour), attitude towards the job (to stick to job, job satisfaction, satisfaction with salary, attitude towards environment, workload, curriculum) and community involvement (community support, community pressure) are positively) correlated with organisational health dimensions integrity, initiating structure, consideration,

resource support, principal influence, morale and academic emphasis of secondary schools. These findings deserve the attention of Government and private managements to boost these dimensions of teacher morale where by the teachers will be motivated to contribute their best for making schools more effective and productive.

7. The dimensions of organisational health are found significantly Inter-correlated. The study of organisational health is important to know the dimension, which are to be manipulated to improve the morale of the teachers. Hence to realise the chief objective of institutional effectiveness it is imperative that the organisational health of the institution should be improved. In the era of competition and demand for better schools, the authorities should pay due consideration to improving the health of their schools and the morale of the teachers. Hence the present study is timely and of significant importance. The findings of the study may help the authorities concerned to concentrate on the dimensions of organisational health in which improvement is needed.

8. The components of teacher morale are found significantly correlated. The dimensions individual characteristics, behavioural characteristics, group spirit, attitude towards the job, community involvement should be promoted in order to boost the morale of the teachers by school authorities.

9. The regression analysis revealed that leadership style of Heads of schools has significant positive influence on organisational health. The leader should help improve the organisational health of the schools. The Heads of schools should be high both on initiating structure and consideration leadership styles in order to promote healthy organisations.

10. The regression analysis also revealed that organisational health, decision-making styles and sex of Heads of

schools are significantly positively influencing teacher morale. If the schools are healthy, teacher morale in the schools will also be high. So efforts have to be made by school authorities to build healthy organisation, which in turn will influence teacher morale and help the schools to be productive. Decision-making as a phenomenon is so complex and so critical to the development of school life that it constitutes a major challenge to even the most able Heads of schools. Effective decision-making is possible only through an analysis of the situational elements in a particular school system. A decision-making style that is most effective differs in many respects from one situation to another. Decision-making styles of Heads of schools are related to teacher morale. The Heads of schools should not overlook these human factors while taking decisions.

Conclusion

Decision-making is the pivotal aspect in the process of educational management. Heads of schools can be effective when learned behaviour and knowledge of modern management techniques, especially decision-making, are used along with intuitive insight in sensing needs of teachers and taking right type of decisions in the appropriate situations. Decision-making as a phenomenon is so complex and constitutes a major challenge to even the most able Heads of schools.

Effective decision is possible only through an analysis of the situational elements in a particular school system. There is no single decision-making style which can be followed to assure effective headship. A decision-making style that is most effective in one situation may not be effective in a different situation.

The study implies that Heads of schools must maintain good relationship evincing interest in the welfare of the teachers, sharing their joys, grievances and helping them find in their job a source of fulfilment, whatever be the Heads decision-making style—be it routine, compromise or heuristic.

The study categorically reveals that any decision-making style and leadership style of a Head of school will affect any member of a school in one way or other; only the degree of influence differs.

The significant relationship between decision-making style and morale in this study demands that the Heads of schools and the teachers should have a mutual agreement. Timely decision benefit the teachers. Once the decisions are accepted and implemented, teachers performance improve, which signifies high morale and benefits the Heads of schools.

From the significant findings of the study it is inferred that in order to boost up morale among the teachers suggestions can be given to the Heads of schools to adopt heuristic decision-making style depending on the situation. The teachers working with Heads of schools who are heuristic decision-makers perceive that their Heads have positive dimensions such as speedy and objective decisions, look for evidences while making decisions, have time horizons for decisions and are anxious to know the consequences of the decision. So in order to maintain high morale among the teachers, the Heads of schools can be encouraged to settle the issues promptly, to be more objective in decisions, to find solutions on the basis of more factual evidences, to be conscious with the time of decisions and to be more anxious about the consequences of their decisions.

Teacher morale is without doubt the most studied of all teacher attitudes. Educators seem to be enthralled with morale. Its most typical conception is as an effective response to work on job or components of a job. In order to boost up morale among the teachers, suggestions can be given to the Heads of schools to adopt leadership style depending on the situation.

This study leads to the conclusion that, the prevalent system of making selection of Heads of schools needs change. Now the time is ripe for a switch over from old system promoting on the basis of seniority to a well-planned new system.

Today we are in a competitive world. The competitive spirit is felt everywhere and anywhere. This type of situation compels the present teachers to work more enthusiastically and also efficiently. To make this possible the organisation should be healthy. It is said, the healthier the organisational dynamics of an institution, the greater the degree of teachers trust in the Heads, trust in the colleagues and trust in the organisation itself (Tarter and Hoy 1988). Indeed, trust has been identified as a basic characteristic of effective organisational culture (Ouchi 1981: Peters and Waterman 1982). Ouchi noted productivity and trust go hand in hand.

In the light of the present study, the researcher desires that Heads of schools through their strategic decision-making style and leadership style boost the teacher morale and improve the organisational health.

Suggestions for Further Study

1. The present study may be conducted on the following samples.

   (a) College principals

   (b) Chairpersons of University Departments

2. The present study may be conducted on educational administrators, in relation to the following factors:

   (a) Personality factors,

   (b) Creativity,

   (c) Attitude,

   (d) Achievement motivation, and

   (e) Managerial skill.

Bibliography

Abendroth, W.W. (1956). The Research and Decision-making Process. In Jesse Shera et al., (Eds) *Documentation in Action*, New York: Reinhold.

Adelson, Marvin (1961). Human Decisions in Command Control Centres. *Annals of the New York Academic of Science.* 89, pp. 726-731.

Anastasi, (1965) Psychological Testing. New York: The Macmillan Company, Argyris, (1962). *Interpersonal Competence and Organisational Effectiveness*, Illinois: Inwin.

Arrow, K.J.(1957). Decision Theory and Operations Research. *Operations Research*, 5, pp. 765-774.

Ary et al., (1972) *Introduction to Research in Education.* New York: Holt Rinehart and Winston, Inc.

Atkinson, J.W.(1957). Motivational Determinants of Risk Taking Behaviour. *Psychological Review*. 64, pp. 359-372.

Back, K.W. (1961). Decisions Under Uncertainty: Rational, Irrational and Non-rational, *American Behavioural Scientist.* 4, pp. 14-19.

Baker, C.H. (1957). The Objective Study of Judgement and Decision-making. *Occupational Psychology*, 31, pp. 225-233.

Bass, B.M. (1960). *Leadership Psychology and Organisational Behaviour*. New York: Harper and Row.

Bassett, G.N. Cfol (1967). *Headmaster for Better School.* Queenland: University of Queenland Press.

Basu, K.S. (1979). *New Dimensions in Personal Management.* Mac Millan Company of India Ltd.

Baterman, (2000). Relationships Among Empowerment, Organisational Health and Principals Effectiveness. *Dissertation Abstracts International,* 60 (09) March, pp. 3232.

Benson, W.W. (1970). A Study of Personal Professional Factors Constellations as Revolted by the Administrative Decision of Secondary School Principals. *Dissertation Abstracts International*, 70, p. 255.

Best, J.N. (1970). *Research in Education*. New Delhi: Prentice Hall of India Pvt. Ltd.

Bocker, E.C. et al. (1965). *The Two-Year College:* A Social Synthesis. New Jersey: Prentice Hall Inc.

Bradshaw, L.J. (1971). *The Relationship of Administration and Special Education Training and Experience to Decision-making in Special Educational Administration*. Columbia: University of Missouri.

Buzzell, D. and Slater C.C. (1962). Decision Theory and Marketing Management, *Journal of Marketing*, 26, pp. 7-16.

Calkins, R.D. (1959). The Decision Process in Administration. *Business Horizons*, 2 (3), pp. 19-25.

Campbell, R.J. (1961). Team Composition and Group Decision-making in Collective Bargaining Situation. *Dissertation Abstracts International*. 21, p. 3539.

Carol, N.W., Joseph, Wyeth, A. (1992). Trouble in Paradise: Teacher Conflicts in Shared Decision-making: *Educational Administration Quarterly*, 28, pp. 315-367.

Casello, D.A. (2001). A Study of Site based Decision-making Based on the Perspective of the Participants. *Dissertation Abstracts International*, 62 (08), November, p. 1646A.

Chalbra, R.K. (1982). Decision-making and Faculty Participation, *Journal of Higher Education*, 7 (3), pp. 266-271.

Chernoff, and Moses, L.E. (1959). *Elementary Decision Theory*. New York: Wiley and Sons.

Churchman, C.W. (1961) Prediction and Optimal Decision: *Philosophical Issues of a Science of Values*, New Jersey: Prentice Hall.

Connor, W.A. (1972). The Pennsylvania Community College President as a Decision-maker. *Dissertation Abstracts International*. 72, p. 193.

Conty, J.M. (1959). *Psychological de la Decision*. Paris: Les Editions Organisation.

Cornell, J.P. (1972). Relationship between Negotiation Function and Leadership Behaviour of Superintendents of School Districts in the State of New Jersey. *Dissertation Abstracts International*, 73 (1499), pp. 3182-A.

Culbertson, A.J. et al. (1961). *Administrative Relationships—A Case Book*. New Jersey: Prentice Hall.

Culbertson, A.J. et al. (1960) *Administrative Relationships: A Case Book*. New Jersey: Prentice Hall.

Dahl, R.A. (1961). *Who Governs? Democracy and Power in an American City*. Connecticut: Tale University Press.

Daniel, E.G. (1959) *Administrative Theory*. New York: Appleton.

Darji, D.R. (1975). A Study of Leadership Behaviour and its Correlates in the Secondary Schools of Panchmahals District. In *Second Survey of Research in Education*, M.B. Buch (Ed). NCERT, New Delhi: pp. 466-467.

Darji, D.R., (1975). A Study of Leadership Behaviour and its Correlates in the Secondary Schools of Panchmahal District. *Unpublished Ph.D. Thesis*, Baroda: M.S. University of Baroda.

Darji, D.R. and Dongre, P.K. (1982). A Study of School Renewal with Respect to Organisational Health, In *Third Survey of Research in Education*, M.B. Buch (Ed), NCERT, New Delhi, p. 880.

Dean, B.V. (1958). Application of Operations Research to Managerial Decision-making. *Administrative Science Quarterly*, 3, pp. 412-428.

Dekhtawala, P.B. (1977). Study of Teacher Morale in Secondary Schools of Gujarat. *Unpublished Ph.D.* Thesis, Baroda: M.S. University, Baroda

Dekhtawala, P.B. (1977). Teacher Morale in Secondary Schools of Gujarat. *Second Survey of Research in Education*. M.B. Buch (Ed). NCERT, New Delhi; p. 467.

Delahanty, J.P. (1972). Decision-making of the Diocesan Level for Catholic Schools—Two Case Studies, *Dissertation Abstracts International*. 72, p. 375.

Dolan, J.P. (2000). Decision of the Commissioner of Education of New York State on Residency: 1958 to 1997. *Dissertation Abstracts International*, 62 (08) February, p. 2639A.

Drucker, F.P. *Management: Tasks, Responsibilities and Practices*. New Delhi: Allied Publishers Pvt. Ltd.

Drucker, P.F. (1964). *Managing for Results.* New York: Harper and Row.

Dufty, N.F. and Taylor, P.M. (1962). The Implementation of a Decision, *Administrative Science Quarterly*, 7, pp. 110-119.

Duncan, A.R.C. (1965). Techniques of Decision-making. In *Readings in Management* (Ed). Ernest Dale New York: *McGraw Hill Inc.*

Duncan, J.W. (1973). *Decision-making and Social Issues.* A Guide to Administrative Action in an Environment Context, Illinois: The Dryden Press.

Dykman, J.W. (1961). Planning and Decision Theory. *American Institute Planning Journal*. 27, pp. 335-345.

Ebert, J.R. and Mitchell, T. (1975). *Organisational Decision Process, Decision Analysis*, New York: Grane, Russak and Co. Inc.

Enthoven, A.C., (1963). Systems Analysis and Decision-making. *Military Review.* 43, pp. 7-17.

Eric, H.R., Agnes, M. (1986). *The Management of School.* London: Kogan Page.

Everard K.B. (1986). *Developing Management in School.* England: Sasil Blackwell Ltd.

Finkelastein, (1999). The Effects of Organisational Health and Pupil Control Ideology on the Achievement and Alienation of High School Students. *Dissertation Abstracts International*, 59 (11) May, p. 4018.

Freishman, E.A. (1973). *Current Development in the Study of Leadership Carbondale*. Southern Illinois: University Press.

Folsom, M.B. (1962). *Executive Decision-making;* Observations and Experience in Business and Government. New York: McGraw Hill.

Frueauff, (1998). Organisational Health and Influences that Enable and Constrain the Development of Healthy Schools. *Dissertation Abstracts International*, 59(02) August, p. 382.

Gabriele, (1987). Values and Decision-making in Educational Administration. *Educational Administration Quarterly*, 23, pp. 72-82.

Ganapathy, K.S. (1982). A Study of Decision-making Process in Relation to Innovation and Change in Schools. In *Third Survey of Research in Education*, Buch, M.B. (Ed.) NCERT, New Delhi: pp. 887-888.

Garrett, H.E. (1976). Statistical Methods in Psychology and Education. New York: David Mckay Co.

Gatza, J.M., and Boseman. (1979): *Decision-making in Administration*. London: W.B. Saunders Company.

Geraghty, E.T. (1998). Site-based Decision-making in the Realm of Middle School Reform, *Dissertation Abstracts International*, 58 (11) May, p. 4138A.

Gerald, J.K. and Norma G.K. (1968). *Operating Guidance Service for the Modern School*. New York: Holt Rinehart and Winston Inc.

Goel, S.L. (1987). *Modern Management Techniques*. New Delhi: Deep and Deep Publication.

Gore, W.J. (1964). Administrative Decision-making: *A Heuristic Model*. New York: Wiley.

Gorton, R.W.(1976). *School Administration: Challenge and Opportunity for Leadership*. Iowa: C. Brown Company Publishers.

Graves, B.C. (1960). Interrelationships Between Some Personality and Decision-making Variables. *Dissertation Abstracts International*, 20, p. 4729.

Grifflhs, E.D. (1969). *Administration as Decision-making in the Book Administrative Theory in Education*. London: The Macmillan Co.

Grifflhs, E.D.N. (1959). *Administrative Theory*. New York: Appleton Century Crofts.

Guest, R.H. (1962) Organisational Change: *The Effect of Successful Leadership*. Illinois: Dorsey Press.

Guilford, J.F. (1956). *Fundamental Statistics in Psychology and Education*, New York: McGraw Hill Book Company, Inc.

Gupta, G.P. (1978). Leadership Behaviour of Secondary School Headmasters in Relation to their Personality and the Climate of their Schools. In *Second Survey of Research in Education*. M.B. Buch (Ed) NCERT, New Delhi: pp. 472-473.

Halpin, W.A. (Ed.) (1969). *Administrative Theory in Education*. London: The Macmillan Company.

Hennessey, B.K. (2000). In Analysis of Leadership Decision in Implementing Middle School Standards Based Foreign Language Programmes. *Dissertation Abstracts International*, 61 (2), August, pp. 439-A.

Herbert, A.S. (1993). Decision-making Rational, Non-Rational and Irrational. *Educational Administration Quarterly*, 29, pp. 393-413.

Holt, K.E. (2000). Relationship Between the Organisational Health of Selected Public School in Texas and Strategies for Communicating with the Public. *Dissertation Abstracts International*, 60 (07), January. p. 2306.

Hopkin, M.C. (1999). Group Decision Support Systems; An Investigation of Communication Technology Applied to the Term Planning Process for Technology Investigation in a Private Saudi Arabian School, *Dissertation Abstracts International*, 60 (2), August, p. 295A.

Howertion, E.B.(1971). Frameworks for School Board Decision-making. An Analysis of the Process. *Dissertation Abstracts International*, 72, p. 154.

James, D. (1973) *A Dictionary of Psychology*. Revised by Harvey Wallerstein. Maryland: Penguin Books.

James, J.J., Jackson C.S. and Ralpn, L.S. (1969). *Secondary School Administration*. New York: McGraw Hill Book Company.

Jarvis, T.O. (1971). *Cases in Elementary School Administration*. Iowa: Brown Company Publishers.

Jaswant, S. (1964) *The Successful Headmaster*. New Delhi: University Publishers.

Jennings, M.K. (1963). Public Administrators and Community Decision-making, *Administrative Science Quarterly*, 8, pp. 18-43.

John, D. Roan, S.R. (1971). Decision-making as Perceived by Appointed and Elected School Superintendents in Florida. *Dissertation Abstracts International*, 71 (28), p. 2363A.

Johnson, D.C. (1972). Decision-making Characteristics of Administrators in Predominantly Black Institutions of Higher Education. *Dissertation Abstracts International*, 73, p. 122.

Johnson, S.D. (1962). Issues, Perception and Decision-making Among Religious Leaders. *Dissertation Abstracts International*, 22, pp. 4109-4110.

Jones, M.H. (1957). *Executive Decision-making*. Illinois: Home Wood.

Jones, W.D. (1964). *On Decision-making in Large Organisations*. California. RAND Corp.

Jones, W.T. and Jones B.J. (1978). The Use of Discrete Digital Simulation for Assessing for Administrative Performance. *Behavioural Science*, 23 (1), pp. 45-48.

Kapur, J.N. (1975). *Current Issues in Higher Education in India*. New Delhi, S. Chand and Co. Pvt. Ltd.

Katz D. and Kahn, L.R. (1970). *The Social Psychology of Organisations*. New Delhi: Wiley Eastern Private Ltd.

Katz, L.R. (1955) Skills of an Effective Administrator. *Harvard Business Review*. 33, February, pp. 33-42.

Kiefer, R.A. (2000). Visible Control: The Art of District Dicision-making. Dissertation *Abstracts International*, 61(3), pp. 834A.

Kildow, M.A. (2000). A Case Study of Decision Made by a School Management Team in the Initial Phase of Whole School Reform. *Dissertation Abstracts International*, 61 (6) December, pp. 2125 A.

Killian, A.R. (1979). *Managers Must Lead*. New York: AMACOM.

Klapp, O.E. and Padgett, L.V. (1960) Power Structure and Decision-making in a Mexican Border City. *American Journal Sociology*, 65, pp. 400-406.

Klein, B. and Meckling, W. (1958). Application of Operations Research to Development Decisions. *Operations Research*, 6, pp. 358-363.

Krishnaraj, R. (1987). Organisation Structure Leadership Behaviour and Decision-making in Autonomous and Affiliated Colleges. In *Fourth Survey of Research in Education*, Buch, M.B. (Ed.), NCERT, New Delhi: 1983-1988, p. 213.

Krishnaraj, R. (1987). Organisation Structure Leadership Behaviour and Decision-making in Autonomous and Affiliated Colleges. In *Fourth Survey of Research in Education*, M.B Buch (Ed.) NCERT, New Delhi.

Lee, K.A. (1992). Principal Leadership Behaviour and Teacher Morale in the Most Effective Private Academic High Schools and in the Least Effective Academic High Schools in Seoul, Korea. *Dissertation Abstracts International*, 52, (09), March, p. 3144-A.

Lin, H.C. (2000). A Study of Principal's Leadership Style and School Effectiveness in Selected Public Secondary School in New Jersey, *Dissertation Abstract International*, 60 (10) April, 3582-A.

Lindsay, F.A. (1958). *New Techniques for Management Decision-making.* New York: McGraw Hill.

Lipham, J.M. (1974). Making Effective Decisions, In Jack A. Culbertson, Curtis Henson and Ruel Morrison, (Eds), *Performance Objectives for School Headmasters*. Berkeley: California, Mc Cutchan.

Lipham, M.J. and Hoeh, A.J. (1974). *The Principalship: Foundations and Functions.* New York: Harper and Row.

Lopez, F.L. (1977). *The Making of a Manager*. Mumbai: Taraporevala.

Luthans, F. (1985). *Organisational Behaviour*. New York: McGraw Hill Book Company.

Machol R.E. (Ed.) (1960). *Information and Decision Processes*. New York: McGraw Hill.

Mahatma, C.M.(1980). Classroom Ethos and their Relation with Teacher Behaviour Characteristics and Teacher Morale. In *Third Survey of Research in Education*, M.B. Buch (Ed.) NCERT, New Delhi; pp. 766, 767.

Maheswari, B.L. (1980). *Decision Styles and Organisational Effectiveness*. New Delhi: Vikas Publishing House Pvt. Ltd.

Mair, N.F. (1963). *Problem Solving Discussions and Conferences*. New York: McGraw and Sons.

Mair, N.R.F. and Hayes, J.J. (1962). *Creative Management*. New York: Wiley and Sons.

McCamny, L.J. (1947). *Analysis of the Process of Decision-making*, Public Administrative Review. III. (1), p. 41.

Meghee, P.R. (1971). An Investigation of the Relationship Between Principals, Decision-making Attitudes, Leader Behaviour and Teacher Grievances in Public Schools, *Dissertation Abstracts International*, 72, p. 146.

Melman, S. (1958). *Decision-making and Productivity*. New York: Wiley and Sons.

Mickerson, C.A. and Mickerson I.A. (1978). *Statistical Analysis for Decision-making*, New York: Petrocelli Books Inc.

Miller, D.C. (1958). Decision-making Cliques in Community Power Structures: A Comparative Study of an American and English City. *American Journal of Sociology*, 64, pp. 299-310

Miller, D.W. and Start, M.K. (1960). *Executive Decisions and Operations Research*. New Jersey: Prentice Hall.

Mohanty, J. (1990). *Educational Administration, Supervision and School Management*. New Delhi: Deep and Deep Publications.

Mohiyuddin, M.S. (1943). *School Organisation and Management*. Bombay: Universal Book Corporation.

Moore, J.B. (1970). A Study of the Local School Superintendents Political Role in State-level Educational Decision-making. *Dissertation Abstracts International*, 71, p. 141.

Moore, W.M. (1978). *The Professions: Roles and Rules*, New York: Basic Books.

Morrison, D.C. (1999). An Investigation of Leadership Practices Demonstrated by Two Women Principals Identified by their Supervisors as Risk-takers in one North Carolina Country. *Dissertation Abstracts International*, 60 (6), December, pp. 1854-A.

Naik, D.G. (1982). An Inquiry into Relationship Between Leadership Behaviour of Secondary School Headmasters and Teacher Morale. In *Third Survey of Research in Education,* M.B. Buch (Ed.) New Delhi: NCERT, pp. 916-917.

Narula, R.K. (1986). Analysis of Common Factors of Teacher Morale. In *Fourth Survey of Research in Education*. M.B. Buch (Ed.) NCERT, New Delhi, p. 1101.

Newton, L.B. (1972). The Relationships Among Teachers' Perceptions of their Participation in Decision-making, Openers of Organisational Climate and Organisational Output in a Sample of Non-Secondary Public School. *Dissertation Abstracts International*,72 (28), pp. 2004-2005.

O'prey, S.J. (2000). A Study of Selected Middle School Assistant Principals as Instructional leaders. *Dissertation Abstracts International*, 60 (7), p. 2314A.

Oxenfeldt, R.A. (1979). Cost Benefit Analysis for Executive Decision-making. New York: AMACON.

Pandey, S. (1985). A Study of Leadership Behaviour of the Principal Organisational Climate and Teacher Morale of the Secondary

School, In *Fourth Survey of Research in Education*, M.B. Buch (Ed.) NCERT, New Delhi; p. 1106.

Patel, R.M. (1983). A Study of the Leadership Behaviour of Principals of Higher Secondary Schools of Gujarat State. *In Fourth Survey of Research in Education*, M.B. Buch (Ed.) NCERT, New Delhi. p. 1107.

Paul, R.M. (1971). An Investigation of the Relationship Between Principals Decision-making Attitudes Leaders Behaviour and Teacher Grievances in Public Schools. *Dissertation Abstracts International*, 72 (601), pp. 4294-4295A.

Perrone, S.M. (1972). *Understanding the Decision Process in Administrative Management*. Paul E. Torgerson and Irwin T. Weinstok (Eds.) Eaglewood Cliffs: Prentice Hall, Inc.

Peternick, L.E. (2000). Site-based Decision-making in Fortworth Texas: Analysis of Variability Within a Single District. *Dissertation Abstracts International*, 60 (7), January, p. 2314A.

Peters, F.J. (1999) Site-based Decision-making, The Perceptions of Teachers and Administrators in Oakland Country. *Dissertation Abstracts International*, 60(6), December, p. 1857A.

Pillai, J.K. (1974). Organisational Climate, Teacher Morale and School Quality. In *Second Survey of Research in Education*. M.B. Buch (Ed.) NCERT, New Delhi: p. 486.

Pillai, J.K. (1979). Management Techniques in Education, *New Frontiers in Education*, IX. (2).

Pirtle, R.W. (1971). Integrative Complexity, Administrative Judgement and Mental Ability as Correlates of Administrative Decision-making Styles. *Dissertation Abstracts International*, 71, p. 212.

Pranklin, L. (1975). A Study of Organisational Climate and Teacher Morale in College of Education in Gujarat, In *Second Survey of Research in Education*, M.B. Buch (Ed.) NCERT, New Delhi: p. 468.

Pruitt, D.G. (1961). Informal Requirements in Making Decisions *American Journal of Psychology*. 74, pp. 433-439.

Ranschburg, H.J. (1961). The Role of a Civic Agency in the Decision-making Process at the Local Government Level. *Dissertation Abstracts International*, 22, p. 458.

Rarelas, Ales. (1960). Leadership: Man and Function. *Administrative Science Quarterly*, 4, pp. 491-498.

Redeefer, F.L. (1959). *Factors that Affect Teacher Morale*. Nations Schools, 63.

Retzlaff, P.S. (1998). The Perceptions of Leadership in Shared Decision-making Schools. *Dissertation Abstracts International*, 58 (08), February, p. 2945.

Reynolds, D. (1982). The Search for Effective Schools. *School Organisation*, 2 (3), pp. 215-37.

Reynoldson, R.L. (1970). The Interrelationship Between the Decision-making Process and the Innovativeness of Public Schools. *Dissertation Abstracts International*, 71, p. 72.

Richfield, J. and Copi, I.M. (1961). Discussion: Deciding and Predicting. *Philosophy of Science*, 28, pp. 47-51.

Roan, J.D. (1971). Decision-making as Perceived by Appointed and Elected School Superintendents in Florida. *Dissertation Abstracts International*, 71, p. 148.

Robert, C.W. (1971). A Study of Relationships Among Faculty Morale Philosophies of Human Nature of High School, Principals and Teachers Perceived Participations in Educational Decision-making, *Dissertation Abstracts International*, 71 (26), p. 1823A.

Robinson, J.S. (1970). An Analysis of the Role of the Principal in Decision-making, *Dissertation Abstracts International*, 71, p. 147.

Rord, C.H. (1973) Structuring the Organisation for Fast Decision-making. *Human Resource Management*, 12 (2), Summer, pp. 2-14.

Roscoe, C.M. et al. (1961) *Decision in Syracuse,* Indiana; Indiana University Press.

Ross, C and Stanley, J. (1955). *Measurement in Today's Schools*. New York: Prentice Hall, Inc.

Samuel, B.B., Peter, B., Sharon C., Conley, S.B. (1990). The Dimensionality of Decision Participation in Educational Organisations: The Value of a Multi-Domain Evaluative Approach. *Educational Administrative Quarterly*, 26, pp. 127-167.

Schlotterer, J.H. (1971). Identification of Influentials in Decision-making Within the Superintendents Cabinet. *Dissertation Abstracts International*, 72, p. 188.

Sen, S.N. (1949). *Educational Reforms of Sir Asutosh Mukherjee*. Baroda; Govt. Press.

Sexena, S.C. (1972). *Organisation and Management*. Agra: Sahitya Bhavan.

Sharma, D.K. (1982). A Study of Management of Education Systems with Special Reference to Decision-making and Organisational Health. In *Third Survey of Research in Education*, Buch, M.B. (Ed.), NCERT, New Delhi: p. 957.

Shelat, N.A. (1975). A Study of Organisational Climate, Teacher Morale and Pupil Motivation towards Institution in Secondary School of Baroda District. In *Second Survey of Research in Education*, M.B. Buch (Ed.) NCERT, New Delhi: pp. 493-494.

Shubik, M. (1958). Studies and Theories of Decision-making *Administrative Science Quarterly*, 3, pp. 289-306.

Shull, F.A. Delbecq, A.L. and Larry, L.C. (1980). *Organisational Decision-making*, New York: McGraw-Hill.

Sid J.D. (1973). *Political Decision-making Process*. NewYork: Elsevier Scientific Publishing Co.

Singh, H.M. (1978). A Study of Leadership Behaviour of Heads of Secondary Schools in Haryana and its Correlates. In *Second Survey of Research in Education*, M.B. Buch (Ed.), NCERT, New Delhi pp. 494-495.

Singh, N. (1998). Decision-making. *University News*. XXVI (32) August, 8, pp. 9-14.

Sinha, (1967). College Administration and Academic Freedom. In *The Higher Education in India,* A.B. Shah. Bombay. Lalvani Publishing House.

Snider, J.A. (2001). The Organisational Health of High School Departments and its Relationship to Department Effectiveness. *Dissertation Abstracts International*, 61 (9), March, p. 3430A.

Somnurs, L.N. (1969). *Factors Influencing Teacher Morale in Selected Secondary Schools*. Nent State University.

Srivastava, R.C. (1980). College Administration (The study of Faculty and Student Participation in College Administration).New Delhi Metropolitan Book Co. Pvt. Ltd.

Stern, R.I. (1972). The Influential and their Involvement in the Decision-making Process in a Selected School District *Dissertation Abstracts International*, 72, p. 221.

Stogdill, R.M. (1948). Personal Factors Associated with Leadership. *A Survey of the Literature Journal of Psychology*, 25, pp. 35-71.

Stoner, J.A.F. and Charts W. (1987). *Third Education Management*. New Delhi: Prentice Hall of India Private Ltd.

Stoner, J.A.F. and Nankel, C. (1987). *Management (Third Edition)*, New Delhi: Prentice Hall of India Pvt. Ltd.

Stravas, G. and Sayles, L.R. (1985). *The Human Problem of Management*. New Delhi: Prentice Hall of India Pvt. Ltd.

Stringham, O.W. (2000). A Study of Leadership Style of Principals and the Organisational Climate in Successful Public Secondary Schools in New Jersey. *Dissertation Abstracts International*, 61 (2) August, p. 453A.

Suppes P. (1961) The Philosophical Relevance of Decision Theory. *Journal of Philosophy*, 58, pp. 605-614.

Thompson, J.D. and Tuden, A. (1959). *Strategies, Structures and Processes of Organisational Decisions*. Administrative Science Centre, and Comparative Studies in Administration.

Tripathi, P.C. and Reddy, P.N. (1995). *Principals of Management*. New Delhi: Tata McGraw-Hill Publishing Company Ltd.

Truman, M.P. and Edward, C.M. and Rulph, B.K. (1955). *Community Leadership for Public Education*, New York: Hall Inc.

Vyas, V.C. (1980) Factors Affecting Teacher Morale. In *Third Survey of Research in Education*. M.B. Buch (Ed.), NCERT, New Delhi: p. 987.

Watts, L..K. (1997). The Relationship of School Organisational Health and Teacher Commitment to Student Achievement in Selected West Virginia Elementary Schools. *Dissertation Abstracts International*, 58 (03), September, p. 691.

William, P.A. (1981). *Management Competencies and Incompetencies*. Addison-Wesley Publishing Company, Inc.

Wilson, C.Z. and Alexis, M (1962). Basic Frameworks for Decisions. *Journal of the Academy of Management*. 5, pp. 150-164.

Worral, Norman (1980). *People and Decisions*. London: Longman Group Ltd.

Index

V

W

Y